# My View of the Bright Moon

D1520654

## Cathy Kern

ISBN: 979-8-86239-179-4

*To*

*… all those who seek healing*

*…. all who have been healed*

*… all who heal.*

*And*

*To the horses.*

*"My storehouse having been burnt down, nothing obstructs my view of the bright moon."*

Masahide, Zen poet

# Chapter One

## June 25th

Kyle's body wrenched free of the motorcycle as he skidded along the base of the roughhewn fence, and his world distilled to senses. The brain-rattling scrape and thud of his head within the grip of his helmet. The vibrating blur of weathered wood and searing blue sky seen through his face shield. Popping sounds as the plastic shield tore away. He squeezed his eyes tight against the sharp peppering of flying dirt and the sensation of heat as asphalt shaved skin off his bare arms and legs onto the shoulder of Jebavy Road.

A single, cold thought formed, and he fought to remember: *Is there a tree ahead of me?*

Patches of scrubby grass, made rough with clots of drying mud slowed then stopped his slide. He coiled into a partial crouch, backside high, his head—helmet still on and intact—resting on a mound of sunburnt grass. Trying to crawl forward a couple feet, he gave up and collapsed. The dirt in his mouth tasted gritty and warm; he chewed at it, biting and spitting, scrubbing his chin against the earth as his body protested the abuse he'd inflicted on it. Shoulders, arms, legs. Hands.

A sudden, visceral need gripped him. He clawed at his helmet, desperate to get it off. His blood-slick palms slipped and smeared over its glossy roundness. Flinching, he gave up to squint at his hands, but couldn't find the reason he'd ridden without gloves. In shorts, yeah, he'd taken that risk all summer, every summer. Gloves and a helmet though? Every ride. No exception. Despite Michigan law allowing him to ride without a helmet, he valued his brain too much to go without. As for gloves, he'd never jeopardize his ability to paint. So, what had possessed him today?

*I'm sorry and I don't want to explain. I just can't do this anymore. We're done, Kyle.*

*Shit.* Kyle tried to turn off the memory, to just be there in the dirt, inches from the empty road, bloody and quiet, baking in the evening sun. To focus on how much everything hurt. How hot his head felt inside the helmet. To see where the bike had ended up.

There. The bike's front tire broke the far horizon of his boot-level view. Protruding above the ditch like an aneurysm in the pavement's edge, it spun ever slower, then stilled as he watched.

He rested the front of his helmet against a clump of grass, and the thin blades, crisp from the sun, pricked into his face. He moved his eyes, searching for somewhere more comfortable to lay his head. *More comfortable.* He heard a single, low bark—his own laugh—and mumbled against the dirt, "Make yourself more comfortable. Shithead."

Then he heard other noises coming from deep inside his throat and the hot stream of tears started.

***

Taking Gillian's curve at speed, Joe tested the cornering abilities of his latest find. He'd always rated the street racers and this little classic, a '69 model Camaro, oozed with looks and promise. With the final notes of "Little Deuce Coupe" coursing through him, he yelled once for pure joy, then yelled again in surprise and stomped the brake. As he flicked off the radio, the outraged howl that had overlapped the song's end rose again, higher now and barely human.

With the car barely out of gear, he flung open the door and left it running, skewed across the center line. The animal sounds came from a contorted figure at the road's edge. Goosebumps sprouted along Joe's arms and neck as he took in the familiar shape of the lean torso and muscled legs—too like his own. *Kyle?* He crossed the pavement at a run and squatted close to the man's head. The howl started shuddering down, stair-stepping into hard sobs.

Taking care not to bump the writhing body and trying to force soothing sounds through his constricted throat, Joe leaned low to peer inside the helmet then dropped even lower.

"Oh Jesus, Kyle! It *is* you! What the hell have you done?" His voice cracked but seemed to clip Kyle in mid-roar.

The silence, underscored by the thrum of the Camaro, felt elongated and surreal. Holding his breath, Joe stared into the cave of the helmet as it turned, rolling against the dead grass, bringing his brother's face into full view: patterned cheek to chin with smears and streaks, reddened eyelids squeezed closed, and flecks of dirt layered like thick mascara on wet lashes. One eye, blue-gray and full of tears, opened, then winked.

Joe exhaled in a gush that morphed into a shaky laugh. "Looking good, dude."

Squelching a sudden sob of his own, he knelt closer and ordered, "Gimme a paw. I'll help you out of the dirt," then recoiled at the sight of Kyle's hand. "Whoa. Maybe not that paw. Or that one—it's even worse. Heck, Kyle! You rode without your gloves? What gives, man—you giving up painting? Okay, just take it slow, try to keep your hands clear and see what you can and can't move."

"I can move it all. Get this helmet off me."

Joe felt a knot of fear loosen in his chest; despite being raspy and thick, Kyle's voice carried a subtle note of impatience.

"You *know* if you're breathing okay, it stays on till the *medics* take it off. Cardinal rule!" Joe yanked his cell phone from his shirt pocket, ignoring Kyle's growl. "Is your breath—?"

"Yeah, yeah. Go check my bike."

"Sure, after I call 91—"

"Check the bike, dammit! I don't need an ambulance!"

Grinning, Joe saluted, pushed up from the dirt, and loped across the hot, empty road. The Suzuki had left very little debris as it skated over the asphalt, and what he could see of Kyle's blood had already baked and darkened, just another skid mark on the mud-crusted tarmac. Gaping into the ditch, Joe sent a long whistle back to Kyle then stepped down closer to the motorcycle.

"Pretty messed up," he shouted over his shoulder. "But how 'bout I bring you the mirror? You always like having a mirror handy." Brandishing one of the Suzuki's side mirrors like a wand he returned to present it to Kyle. "And it's not even broken. Your luck's going to hold."

"Luck? Fuck."

Joe shook his head and the knot in him loosened further. Under the flayed outer layer, Kyle sounded like his usual self.

Hobbling and swearing together, Joe helped him fold into the Camaro's front passenger seat, positioning Kyle's bloody legs as straight as the space allowed, then paused a second to scan the visible injuries.

It looked as if Kyle's left hip and the heel of his left hand had borne the brunt of his slide, but also as if – were they to look - they'd find more than a little skin from his left shoulder, and from both palms, thighs, and forearms, drying into Jebavy Road.

"Man, we really should get an ambulance."

"Why? You're here. You drive faster. Get in."

Swallowing hard, Joe leapt into the driver's seat. "Pretty decent road rash."

"Road rash. Two little words that pack a punch." Kyle's voice sounded strained.

"Understatement of the year." Joe stomped the gas pedal, heading back to Ludington and the hospital.

A strangled yelp erupted from beside him. Glancing sideways, he cringed and eased off the accelerator. Not quite able to sit upright, Kyle tried to brace through the U-turn, the battered helmet still in place and rubbing against the low interior roof.

"God, sorry!" Joe grimaced. "I couldn't get that seat to go back. This is one of my new ones; haven't started any work on her, yet."

His eyes flicked between the road and his passenger. Kyle glared at the sun-soaked landscape. Silent. What Joe could see of his face shone pale and pinched within the helmet's padding.

"So?" Joe reached over and swatted the passenger's sun visor down. He waited, then tried again, "What gives?"

Still staring as if early June apple orchards were actually interesting, Kyle answered, tight-lipped, "Maria dumped me."

Joe's foot flew to the brake then hovered there; he resisted stomping it again. "*No. Way.*" He tried to catch Kyle's eye, show the giant "*sorry*" caught in his chest.

"Way."

"Shit, dude." Shaking his head, Joe gave up on eye contact and upped his speed a little.

He tried to concentrate on just driving but, *Jesus!* Seeing Kyle so messed up, knowing how bad it *could* have been, and Maria gone? He gripped the steering wheel and swallowed hard. *That howling at the roadside was about more than grated skin. What the hell?*

They didn't speak again for the five minutes it took to reach the hospital. At the emergency entrance, Joe stuck his head into the foyer and yelled for help, wondering if Kyle heard the little choke in his voice.

Two ER attendants appeared at a run pushing a gurney between them. The world sped up and he became a bystander, trying to answer terse questions, trying to help, then trying to stay out of the way.

The attendants, efficient and calm, loaded Kyle up and wheeled him past. Joe craned to see around their blue-shirted backs, wanting to make eye contact, wanting to joke about how ridiculous Kyle looked with his bloody, dirt-streaked helmet resting against the white sheet of the gurney, his filthy, oozing hands and forearms raised up on either side of it.

"An alien under arrest!" Joe called out as his brother disappeared into the building. "Take me to your … Damn."

The sliding doors closed between them and he stood alone in the heat and the hum of a summer's early evening.

# Chapter Two
## June 25th

Cleaned, bandaged, and medicated, Kyle again slouched low in the Camaro, finally free of the blessed helmet and dressed in the T-shirt and khaki shorts Joe had brought him.

He'd been checked for broken bones, concussion, internal bleeding, and subjected to a scolding that, under any other circumstances, would have stoked his temper.

One ER doctor had drilled home how lucky he'd been to have only met the road and not traffic or a tree. She'd described in stark, matter-of-fact language the shape he could be in right now and how many less fortunate road rash victims landed in the burn center awaiting skin grafts. It had done the trick; he'd begun to feel relieved and grateful, so glad to have his head and spine intact that he'd stopped obsessing about his hands.

Until now. He stared at them, temporarily useless clubs resting on his bandaged thighs, knowing how close he'd come to seriously screwing up his life, to maybe never painting again.

He swallowed the bile rising in his throat and glanced to Joe for distraction as they pulled away from the hospital in silence, windows down, and the radio low—almost inaudible.

It felt odd to see his brother at the wheel, lit by the glow of the dash and not only driving the speed limit, but without oldies music cranked high. This had to be a first.

Much as he'd rather not think about what had led to this moment and Joe's gentleness with him, it had become hard not to. The painkillers were working their magic and, with the music so quiet, the world, both in and outside the car, had turned all twilight and crickets—the blue hour. So much like the nights last summer when he'd pick up Maria on the Suzuki and take her to hear music at Shagway or stop by a Little League game. As an art teacher at Ludington's middle school, he'd usually found several of his students to cheer for beneath the gnat-swarmed lights. Afterwards, especially if Ludington's team won, a handful of kids and parents would convoy over to the Dairy Queen with them to review the game under more bug-laden lights.

Maria always ordered something butterscotch, after first putting it to the kids for a vote.

*Should I get a Blizzard, a sundae, or a shake tonight?*

She never got tired of butterscotch.

*I just can't do this anymore. We're done, Kyle. I have to hang up now.*

The car jolted him back to the present.

"Sorry," Joe said. "Michigan's finest potholes. You awake over there?"

"I'm awake." Kyle tried to sit up a little and focus on the view. The neighborhood the car purred through offered nothing to distract him.

"Sorry about Maria."

"Yeah. Thanks."

"The Sound of Silence" started on the radio, blending with the darkness in the car.

"So … did she say—" Joe started.

"Look, okay if we skip this for now?"

"Sure."

Kyle shifted on the seat, his eyes roaming the car's dim interior. He spotted a pair of woman's sunglasses tucked behind Joe's sun visor. "How's Vicky?"

Joe took a beat too long before muttering, "Oh, crap."

Kyle slouched back in place and waited, a smile twitching on his lips as he listened to Joe mumbling to himself.

"She'll be okay," Joe said. "She's good like that."

"You had plans tonight?"

"A picnic by the Curves. I bet she texted and I missed it." Joe dug his phone from his T-shirt pocket and held it out to Kyle. "Can you—?"

"Not at the moment. No." Kyle held up his bandaged hands.

"Duh, sorry!" Joe laughed, dropping his phone back into his pocket. "I'll call in a minute from your place."

"My place," Kyle muttered. Vivid memories of Maria crowded his mind and the car. His compact little bungalow would be the same. Unbearable. "Hey, Joe, did you call Ma?"

"Nope. Why would I?"

"Hell." Kyle angled a glare into the night. "I'm staying with her—"

"Say what?" The car decelerated fast, and Joe gaped at him. "*You* are staying with Ma? Did your house burn down or something?"

"The bedroom reeks. I'm doing … um … some painting in there." Kyle stared outside again as the car picked up speed. "Maria's didn't feel like an option last night … or your weeny little cabin. So, I invited myself to Ma's. Purely the nearest option."

"Well, no, I didn't call her. I was busy getting you clothes, talking to the wreckers, getting your blood off my car seats, haggling with the hospital over your insurance without having your wallet—"

"Still at Ma's."

"… or your phone—"

"Probably crushed on the road."

"Besides," Joe finished, "I'll be your ambulance, but I'm not walking into the lion's den for you. Lioness. Whatever."

"Pfft! A lioness protects and nurtures her young. Go with lion." Kyle leaned forward again. "So. Maybe you and I go hang out somewhere till her place is dark? Grab a beer. Or ten."

"You know I'd usually be right in with that but … are you nuts, man?" Joe said. "You're zonked on pain meds, dealing with … everything else. Not to mention, hell, you're twenty-eight years old, Kyle. Screw Ma."

"No, thanks." He grinned at the sound of Joe's laugh, something between a burst and a bark, like his own. Blue-gray eyes, also like his own, leveled a quick look his way.

"You know? Why not come to the cabin?" Joe said and without waiting for his answer, flicked the blinker over and turned east. "I'll stay at Vicky's. You can look after Doughnut."

"Who the hell is Doughnut?"

"Wow. You still haven't met her? She's this skinny little stray cat that adopted Vicky and me last month. She's only got one eye."

"What the hell kinda name is Doughnut?"

"I thought by calling her that I'd learn to like her quicker."

"Did it work?"

"It did. She's a very cool little cat. You take care of her tonight. Let her sleep next to your head."

"Seriously?"

"Seriously."

"Man." Kyle shook his head, feeling lighter than he had all day.

In the darkness of the car, he could feel Joe grinning. His own smile slid from his face as they drove into the offensive curve in Jebavy Road. Neither of them spoke.

Kyle suspected even in daylight there'd have been nothing to see; the wrecker's truck had picked up the Suzuki long ago. But he could feel and hear crunching as the Camaro passed over rough tracks of dried dirt.

*The tractors going in and out of Gillian's farm … There's the answer.*

He made mental notes to revise his conversation with Rusty. Joe's former classmate and former drinking buddy, but now Mason County's youngest—and shortest-ever—state trooper, Rusty had probably heard it was Kyle and asked to be sent to take the accident report.

*"Too fast? Were you speeding?"* Rusty had asked, pen poised above a little notebook, looking up at him from under bushy eyebrows as he was being released. *"Alcohol?"*

*"Doubt it. No and no."*

Joe had cut in then to back him up—*"Kyle's a careful rider, Rusty"*—and probably even believed what he'd said.

After flicking the notebook shut and giving Joe a friendly shove, Rusty had taken off and Kyle knew he'd lucked out getting such a short grilling; Rusty had to know their dad's reputation with the booze, either via Joe, or through living in a town where anyone's business was everyone's business.

Now Kyle felt the silence under the music in the car change tone as the old Camaro left the curve and passed Gillian's farm. Ahead just a quarter mile, a simple frame house interrupted the darkening horizon to their left.

*How many times have I seen that sight?* he wondered. *Arriving home on the school bus in winter as a kid or, in high school, riding my bicycle back from summer cruise nights or the beach.*

*Outside there would be no light other than the pale stars; but inside—yes, there!—in the window way at the back, the unmistakable glow of an ancient, tube-style television.*

He pictured the TV exactly: crammed like an afterthought into the corner of a memory-filled den and surrounded by plants and bookshelves.

"Windows, man." Kyle lowered his voice as they drew closer.

The tiny red light moving on the front porch would be a cigarette slowly burning, unsmoked as always, down to their mother's fingertips.

With a questioning look his direction, Joe slowed and reached over to raise Kyle's window, but left the driver's side down.

"Watching fireflies," Kyle said, rolling his eyes at the open window. *If Ma hears us, it'll be Joe's fault.*

"Yeah. Or stars."

"But never the TV." As they passed, he peered at the side window where a net curtain did little to disguise shifting, flickering images inside. The tiny red light on the porch had stilled in mid-air. "So, why's she always got it on?"

"Noise?"

"Funny, right? She griped about too much noise when we were all there." *I should have said she perpetually griped. About everything.* Before he could amend his comment, Joe spoke.

"She misses him. And us, I guess. Or maybe us as kids … younger years …"

"She'd have to be digging deep for any good memories."

"Yeah." Joe shrugged. "Still … they were together—what … close to thirty years?"

"It should have been three. Maybe. Heard from him at all?"

"Not since before Thanksgiving." Joe reached across him to roll the passenger window down again.

"That long! Seriously? I thought he was only ignoring my messages. Nothing at Christmas even?"

"I told you last time you asked: 'no' … *no*, Kyle. He's avoiding me, too."

"What is *up* with him, anyway?"

"Can we not get into this tonight?" Joe said. "Try asking Ma."

"I have and all I get is … standard *Ma*: Ma *evasion*, Ma *avoidance* … typical *Ma—*"

"Okay. Okay."

Kyle dragged in a lungful of night air, then another. Joe almost never offered any fuel for rants against their parents—if anything he took their side—and tonight ranting alone just seemed too much work. When his jaw relaxed, he started over. "So, with Dad out of the house, you and Ma hang out some now?"

"Not really. She feeds Doughnut—"

"Doughnut." Kyle didn't try to hide the smirk in his voice.

Joe kept talking, "—if Vicky can't for whatever reason and I'm away overnight getting a car to a client or chasing one up. I try to drop off some kind of thank you when I get back. If she needs the gutters cleaned or her oil changed, she'll give me a call. Stuff like that."

"The good son." Kyle raised a hand to poke Joe in the shoulder, looked at the mitten of bandages his fingertips emerged from, and reconsidered.

"I don't know."

"She never asks me for help." Kyle shifted on the seat and yawned, then added, "Hell, maybe I should stay there tonight after all." He sat up, startled that he'd think, much less *say*, that. He shot Joe a "*what kind of drugs did they give me?*" look.

Joe ignored the look.

"Look, Kyle," he said, "you'll seriously freak her looking like you do right now."

"Bah! I seriously doubt that." *You don't freak over someone unless you care,* he thought. "But it suits me fine not staying there, hearing her two cents about Maria dumping me."

"How would Ma know about it already?" Joe asked.

"She stood and listened to the whole phone call. You know she would've been on me about it if I hadn't taken off."

"Maria gave you the chop *over your phone?*"

Feeling his eyes start to fill, Kyle turned to stare at the night outside his window.

Several seconds passed before Joe's voice came into the darkness of the car again, his tone softer.

"I'm not dissing her, man. It's just … you know. You were together awhile."

Kyle cleared his throat and looked ahead at the road, blinking his eyes dry. "Maybe a year—not long for her. I guess."

"Long for you though, eh?" Joe said. "By what? Something like ten months."

By the light of the dash, he saw Joe grinning, needling him.

"Quite a track record for a guy your age."

"Bite me."

"Hey! I can ask Vicky to call Maria if you th—"

"Shut up, Joe. Okay? Just shut up."

"I'm just saying …"

"Shut. The. Hell. Up."

Silence billowed between them, its volume seeming to grow as the murmur of the ten o'clock news began.

Taking care with each word, Kyle said, "I'll feed Doughnut and let her sleep at my pillow, but … you know … just shut up."

"I've shut up." Joe mumbled as if talking through sewn together lips.

The Camaro turned onto a dirt road, grooved and rough to travel. Soft-needled pine trees brushed the top of the car from both sides as it crept ahead, moving at little more than a crawl. In unison with Joe, Kyle automatically leaned into the car away from the fragrant boughs that folded in then lazily backed out each open window as they bumped along.

He gazed into the unlit lane, markedly cooler than the road they'd just left, and breathed in its scent of earth and of green, wondering if Joe would ever bring it into the 21st century. The car headlights shone on, then moved past, quiet grasses and sun-starved saplings.

As they crept along, carrying their own tunnel of light with them, Kyle felt they'd darkened the night behind them. Everything looked and felt exactly as it had when their grandparents lived in the cabin. Just more overgrown. He liked the feeling.

Sensing Joe was listening hard to the quiet still separating them, he felt his own crooked grin start.

"What?" Joe asked.

"I thought you had shut up?" Laughter simmered at the edge of both their voices.

"Done with that. Say 'thanks.'"

"Thanks, man." Kyle looked to Joe and nodded. "You're right. Thanks."

"No problem." Joe drove onto a pebbled driveway that led to an old-fashioned, dark red barn and bordered a grassy clearing ringed with cedar ash and more evergreens.

As they emerged from the overhang of trees a single security light mounted on the high eave of the barn flooded the clearing with light. Nickers and whinnies started up behind the massive double doors.

"Hey, girls! Hey, Bingo!" Joe called to the sounds, paused to listen, then grinned at the volley of replies, and went on, "Hey, Kyle, how are you gonna do anything with your hands like this? You can't even feed yourself."

"Hell, it's only road rash, I'm not in a body cast. Undo my seatbelt and I'll manage from here."

"Hang on. I'm parking her away from the trees until I get her into the barn. Washing off bird crap constantly gets old fast." He turned off the ignition and climbed out, running his hand across the rosewood dash.

"You've never been much into washing." Kyle said, his arms kinked into a tin soldier position, as Joe released him from the seatbelt. "Poor Vicky." Shifting with care to the edge of the low seat, he unfolded from the car.

"She doesn't complain." Joe held the passenger door for him, free hand darting around, inserting itself anywhere he might otherwise have bumped a bandaged limbs or shoulder against a hard edge. Fussing like that would have driven him nuts any other day. Tonight though, he appreciated it.

He sensed Joe right behind him, probably with hands raised, ready to catch him if he stumbled. They crossed the patchy yard to the unlit log cabin on the far side of the clearing.

"She may complain tonight. Get gone man." Buoyed on painkillers, Kyle strode up the familiar wooden stairs and managed to toe open the porch's screen door. He stopped at the cabin's main door, staring at the brass knob. "You could maybe heat me some soup or something first."

"And what? Put it in a Sippy cup?" Joe thrust an arm past him and opened the door. "Outta the way."

Kyle turned sideways as Joe squeezed past, saying, "Take a load off. I'll be right back," then disappearing up the stairs to the sleeping loft, taking them two at a time.

*On a mission of mercy*, Kyle thought. Alone in the dark living room, he tried to find a part of his body he could use to flip the light switch beside the door. After failing with his right shoulder, he'd almost succeeded using his chin when light spilled down from the loft above, carrying Joe's voice with it.

"Sorry. I forget you're not as used to this place."

Kyle offered the light switch his opinion of it and turned to the view from the window above his brother's roll-top work desk. With eight panes of glass reflecting the room he was in, there wasn't much to see of the outdoors.

*Fireflies, the eyes of a possum, maybe? Or something … Doughnut?*

The name had no sooner crossed his mind than he noticed the scrawny yellow cat seated primly at his feet. She stretched her front legs high as if preparing to claw her welcome into his bandaged knees.

"*Shitcakes*, cat!"

"Baby Doughnut! C'mere." Footsteps pounded down the loft stairs as a blur of fur dove beneath the quilt-covered couch. Joe knelt beside it, making soothing noises, then pushed his arm deep underneath and extracted the scrap of a cat. "Sorry, Dough. You best leave the mummy alone."

Stroking and cooing, Joe wrapped her around his neck, strolled out of the front room, and disappeared through the kitchen doorway.

Kyle followed. "I see why some cultures eat them."

He watched Joe moving from cabinet to sink to stove, muttering to the cat still wound around his neck like a collar.

"Eats 'em!" Joe told Doughnut. "Eats 'em whole."

"If she's the doughnut, you're the hole," Kyle said.

"We like this. It gets her purr on." Joe shot him a grin.

Kyle blew air between his lips and stepped up to the stove. "Look, I'll do this now. How hard can it be? You go."

"Nah. It's all good. Vicky's on her way over."

"What?"

"I called her from upstairs. We're camping on the porch couch. She likes that." Joe turned back to the stove with a wink. "It gets her purr on."

Kyle grinned, toed a chair away from the scarred wooden table, and positioned himself to sink into it.

"Nope," Joe ordered over his shoulder. "Don't sit here. You haul your ass upstairs. The sheets are now clean. I'll bring you a mug with a straw. It's tomato soup."

Alone in the dark sleeping loft after sucking up his dinner and settling into Joe's bed, Kyle realized how cool his brother had become—thoughtful. He'd brought up a shot glass of mouthwash with a stirring stick for a straw, apologizing—even though Kyle couldn't have managed one—for not having any spare toothbrushes. Being with Vicky forever meant none of those opportunistic overnighters most guys bragged about. Then while stripping him of his clothes, Joe had made a brief raunchy joke, disappeared, and come back to lay out pain tablets and a battered plastic cup.

"Water. I only found that one straw so you're going to have to recycle it. Lick the pills up when you're ready for your next dose if your fingertips don't work well enough. I'll leave the bathroom door open up here. What else? Fan's on. Window's open. It'll get cooler once the breeze starts in off the river."

"Where'd you learn all this cozy stuff, Holly Hostess?" Kyle asked. "Not from Ma."

"Dunno." Joe shrugged and looked around the space, as if the log-style furniture could supply the answer. "Vicky, maybe? Grandma?"

A small lamp with a yellowing paper shade stood on a rough shelf built into the back wall of the cabin. Joe pulled the light chain and night flooded the room.

"Good night. Don't dream."

"Ha, right! Good night. Don't dream." Kyle chuckled in the dark, remembering. It's what they'd told each other every night in their shared bedroom. He'd twist in the top bunk to poke his crew-cut head upside down over his mouth-breathing little brother. He had no idea where the saying had come from, but he'd started repeating it just to be smart and, as usual, Joe had joined in.

*When had "don't dream" become good advice? And when did good advice harden up and become … whatever it was now?* He didn't want to think. And he didn't want to dream, just to sleep. He welcomed the steady slide into velvet blackness and stopped thinking.

*Can I fix that for you?*

*Fix what?*
*That grin. It's crooked, see? She touched the corner of his mouth.*
*No, best leave it. No one should be completely perfect, he told her.*
*She laughed. The most delicious sound he'd heard in his entire life.*

A happy bark woke him, his own laugh. He lay for a moment taking in the unfamiliar shadows and sounds around him, remembering where he was and why. Easing closer to the edge of the bed with a wince, he propped himself on his undamaged elbow and licked up two pills from the wooden shelf, ignoring the cup of water. He inched back down onto the sheets and let his eyes wander to the large square of starlight visible through the window beside him.

"Ridiculously busy and cheerful up there," he muttered, addressing the hard points of light. "What have you got to be so chirpy about?"

With the glow from the stars and an ancient Daffy Duck night light Joe had stuck into the wall outlet, he could easily see over the split-log railing at the edge of the loft. Raising his head to concentrate, he wondered about the soft noises he could hear: Vicky with her purr on? Or just the river in the ravine beside the house? He craned his neck, focusing his ears toward the porch and felt the bed move slightly. A shape crossed his view and something brushed his cheek.

"Ah. Doughnut. You've arrived." A soft plop, the sigh of a pillow, puffed below his ear. "Hey girlie, what gives? Don't go settling down here! Your dad may be willing to share his pillow, but tonight's an unusual case … Go to the porch and show Vicki how to get that purr on … You're doing great with that purr … So loud for such a scrawny cat, you are … Sounds like you need a tune up … Okay, Jelly Doughnut, you take that side of the pillow … Since you already have … I'd rather not have the tail in my face though … Okay, that's good … Good night, small Doughnut. Don't dream."

Kyle relaxed back onto his quarter share of the pillow and, against a backdrop of ragged purring, finally gave in to remembering.

*Maria's voice on the phone—was it just a few hours ago? Her tone had been different from how he'd ever heard her before. Desperate almost? Or disgusted?* The actual words didn't matter, he had the gist. And the final statement. He'd made sure he got in first to cut off the call, then stood staring at the phone in his hand until Ma made a little noise from her kitchen door. Grabbing his helmet from the table and jamming it on, he'd slammed outside and onto the Suzuki before she could start.

Some kind of owl's call brought him out of the memory and back to the loft and the pillow he shared with Doughnut. He shifted his eyes again to the craziness of the stars within arm's reach.

*If the keys to the Suzuki hadn't been in my shorts pocket, if the bike hadn't started, if I'd kept my head ... that's what Maria would say.*

*"Temper, temper." Or, "Chill, bub—just chill." Always with a grin and a nudge or a hug, till lately.*

He couldn't place when he'd noticed the change in her. He did remember—because it had struck him as odd—she'd once told him he didn't own her.

*If only. If only I'd owned her. Not like some creep who wanted to lock her in a room forever ... just somehow to keep her from giving me the boot.* He searched the night sky, hunting up a constellation of her Barbie doll arms curved above her head as she slept ... trying to find the outline of her smart, clever mouth.

Her combination of sweet and sassy ways had him chasing her from the first day she'd flirted with him on the edge of the school sports field. He'd been waiting for the bell to ring so he could order his class back inside and she'd wandered past; later he'd learn she'd just finished a half-day stint subbing for a sick teacher. It turned out the illness was unrelenting morning sickness and Maria found herself hired on.

That first day though, with her cute nose stuck in a book, she'd walked right past him without watching where she was going. Or noticing him.

"Now there's good multi-tasking," he'd said. "You could teach the men of the world."

Then he'd gotten his first view of those big, brown eyes. She'd looked over the edge of her book and delivered the line that she'd say in some form for months afterward, about letting her fix that crooked grin.

Within hours, on that same afternoon, she must have decided brushing her full lips, tinged with Dairy Queen butterscotch, across his crooked grin could help straighten it. And it had. It had wiped it right off his face. She'd floored him.

She'd dipped her head low and laughed; the final nail in his coffin—her incredible laugh. That very first time he'd tried to capture it in his mind, an image he could someday paint: rich soft moss or the froth of sea over pebbles. Had he ever done that though? Painted her laugh?

He didn't realize he'd groaned aloud till he heard Joe call from the living room door.

"'Y' alright up there?'

"Yeah. You alright down there? Keep the noise down."

In his mind, he saw Joe's answering grin, as real as if he stood beside him. He also thought he heard sleepy mumbles—the feminine sort. Vicky sounded so like Maria. Yet women didn't all sound the same. Pillow talk used to annoy him in the past, but Maria's never had. She could even laugh off the times he'd accused her of snoring: "Maybe if your ears weren't so big? Stop listening so hard when I sleep. Are you watching me again? Go to sleep, you."

Kyle maneuvered his aching body lower into the bed and felt Doughnut adjust herself around the top of his head. Her tail curled around one of his "big ears." The ears he'd inherited from his dad. He'd often wondered if his looks and his ears were all he'd gotten from the man—always *there*, in the house, as he and Joe grew up, but … not really a *dad*. And now … this big, cold-shoulder thing to both of them? *Why?* It could *really* bug him if he let it …

"Sleep," he ordered himself. "Don't dream."

# Chapter Three

## June 26th

"Hey, Sleeping Beauty, can you handle coffee with a straw or should I run out to get you a juice?" Joe stood beside the loft's bed, looking down at Kyle making full use of the queen-sized mattress and Doughnut curled around the top of his head doing a great imitation of a bad toupee.

There wasn't a lot of bed left over. It never felt too small for Vicky and him. She was slender but tall and he wasn't any less built than Kyle nor, at six-foot-two inches, any shorter. Maybe it came down to how he and Vicky usually twined together in the middle, spooning rather than sprawling.

Kyle opened an eye partway and slurped up a trickle of drool. "Getting old, this looking up at you stuff."

"Well, I could've sent Vicky," Joe said. He crowded a steaming Green Bay Packers mug in beside the pills and the lamp on the little shelf, then ducked into the closet-sized bathroom behind him. "But I figured if she got an eyeful of you buck-naked, she'd never come back to me."

He pulled a T-shirt from the hook on the door, yanked a once-familiar wad of terry cloth from an overstuffed cabinet, and stepped back to the bed. Doughnut now sat on its edge, paws pressed side by side, looking from him to Kyle and back.

Kyle grinned against his pillow. "Yeah, man, I see your point."

Joe tossed the T-shirt on the bed for Doughnut to inspect. "Well, I don't want to see yours—"

"Har, har."

"—so this relic is for you." He held up the tangled white towel, studying Kyle's expression. Seeing him swallow hard through gritted teeth and struggle to sit up, Joe felt the pain himself. "Bad this morning?"

"Worse than last night; stiff and sore." A sharp wince punctuated Kyle's attempt to shrug and Joe grimaced. "I just need another one of those magic tabs there."

He snatched up a pill and poked it between Kyle's lips. "Stand up. I'll get this towel-skirt thingy on you."

Doughnut abandoned the T-shirt she'd been kneading and stepped closer to sniff a bandaged thigh as Kyle eased up from the bed, his lips pulled tight. What started as a suppressed groan turned into a bark of laughter.

"Hey, Joe, remember running around naked after our baths when we were little? And Ma chanting: 'Nudey boy, nudey boy!' while we ran?"

"Nope. When was that?" *This towel looks odd; is it inside out?* he wondered.

"Heck. I don't know. If I was six or seven, you'd have been two or three? Maybe we were older."

The Velcro waist seemed stuck to the hem. *No wonder nothing has Velcro on it anymore. Except maybe kids' shoes.* "That couldn't have been me, man," Joe said. "Unless it was Grandma and you were here. I didn't come back home till I was four."

"Right." In Kyle's mouth the word had several syllables. "The first of many Carson family mysteries: sent into baby exile at age one—"

He cut Kyle off. "It was hardly baby exile. I loved living with Grandma and Grandpa."

"Why did you, though—live here I mean? With all the secrets Ma and Dad have shoved under the carpet over the years, their living room should look like a mogul field."

"Yeah, well … no nudey escapes for me, and I think I'd remember."

"But you do remember the day Dad brought you back, bawling all over you?"

"Let's not dig that up, Nudey boy." Joe kept his eyes on his task. He pooched out his lips in a kind of mouth shrug and thrust the half-towel to Kyle. "Finally! Here."

"Where'd you *get* this thing?"

"Vicky. Her presents have gotten better."

"A towel with a Velcro waist?"

"It's from a while ago. Think of it as … a white kilt. After all you're going commando. And don't tease too much … she's downstairs right now making you a banana smoothie for breakfast." He grabbed the T-shirt and shook it out. "Here, stick your arms up. This is pretty clean, I think."

"This isn't yours. The armpits smell good."

"Ha. That's Old Spice deodorant; reminds me of Grandpa." Joe plucked Doughnut from her new nest of tangled sheets and arranged her around his neck. "There's your coffee. See you downstairs."

He raised the cat's paw between his thumb and index finger in a farewell salute, and she rode his shoulders down from the loft to the kitchen doorway where he stopped with a grin. A warmth spread through his stomach as he took in the scene. If it weren't for that messy-haired beauty in a flannel shirt and riding boots, the whole cabin could have been lifted from a Norman Rockwell painting: paned windows everywhere, open-front wooden cabinets, and a round, scarred oak table. But Vicky, straight from feeding the horses—her mop of dark hair, still flattened from sleep on one side, kinked in a wing on the other—she was the best part of the cabin and his life.

Grandma was easily a pretty close second, though she'd not been in the cabin for two years now.

That realization fractured his contentment and he slammed the door on it. Walking to within inches of Vicky, he leaned in closer. Doughnut turtled her neck to reach Vicky's hair, hooked a paw around a lock of it, and took a nosy sniff.

Vicky turned with a smile and tipped her forehead against the cat's. "Good morning Doughnut, you traitor, we missed you last night."

She turned back to lift the blender off its base. "I don't think we've ever used this for anything besides margaritas. Joe, did you see what came in the mail yester—"

Pierced through by the shriek of an old fashioned wall phone, they both jumped and clamped their hands over their ears.

Doughnut let out a truncated yowl. Her eyes wild, she shot off Joe's shoulders and between Kyle's feet as he stepped into the kitchen. His bandaged hands shielded his ears.

"Holy Christ! What the …?"

"Wow, Joe! Ow! Are you ever getting rid of that thing? Oh my God, Kyle. Look at you."

Joe lifted his hands off his ears just enough to hear himself say, "It's good to have a back- up. What if a client couldn't reach my cell for some—"

"Ha! Vick, you know this cabin'll always be a shrine to Gran—"

"Well, grab it, grab it! Before … Oh, ow!"

Joe yanked the phone from the cradle mid-ring. "Hello? Oh Ma, hi." He watched Vicky glop some banana smoothie into a Mexican glass tumbler. "Yep, he's here."

Vicky approached Kyle, shaking her head, and touched the edge of the tumbler to his lower lip. Her gray eyes roamed the multitude of bandages on his limbs.

Kyle drank noisily for several seconds, tipping his head back little by little as Vicky reached up to follow his mouth with the tumbler, then nudged it away with his lips.

Joe tilted the heavy, black receiver toward him, nodded at his quick frown, and told Ma, "He's in the loft; snoring the roof off." He bobbed his chin in response to Kyle's grin then tried to concentrate on the phone call. "So, Ma, did you guess … oh." He hunched his shoulders and mouthed, "she saw us drive by."

"Oops." Kyle grinned bigger and laughed at Vicky's "tsk" as she turned back to the blender.

"Well that's good." Joe tuned in to both conversations, a trick he'd perfected while living at home. He could follow an entire TV program in the den yet, if their parents' after-dinner conversations turned sour, he'd vacate the house before the shouting started. "Because, we didn't want to bother you, so … you saw Rusty's wife where?" He looked back at Kyle and held his eye until Vicky returned with the refilled tumbler to start round two.

"Ah … yeah, Ginny's right. All the caked mud on Gillian's corner probab—"

Kyle wiped his mouth on his good shoulder, shot Vicky a grin of thanks, and turned back to Joe.

"What? No, his cell was crushed on the road, besides he bunged up his hands a little, too … yeah, I should have … sorry." Kyle and Vicky stood together, watching him talk.

"No, it's cool having him here, Ma. Let's leave it like this since he's already here and … right … comfy."

Kyle raised one eyebrow and mouthed, "Comfy?" and Vicky chuckled. She flicked Joe's shoulder as she stepped up and reached around him for an open box of doughnuts on the counter.

"Sure, Ma, yeah, if anyone calls looking for him, give 'em my cell number … No, I'm not sure how long, but it's no trouble having him here. It's fine … okay, I'll tell him. Thanks for calling. Yeah I know… I should have … yeah. I do know better … sorry … yeah. Bye, Ma."

"Tell me what? I'm a shithead?"

"Feel better," Joe said.

"Really? You liar."

"No, really, 'Tell him to feel better,'" Joe insisted. "That's what she said. And she asked if you were comfy."

"I wonder when I'm going to hear: 'hothead,' 'bat outta hell,' 'what did you expect?' That sounds more like her," Kyle said.

"Ouch, really?" Vicky asked, holding out the box of doughnuts. Joe pulled out his favorite, toasted coconut, and offered a chunk of it to Kyle.

"Joe's fifth basic food group—tied with beer. No coconut for me … frosted, please." Kyle surveyed the selection as Vicky went on.

"I could imagine your dad talking like that if he'd been drinking, but I've never heard Sylvia say anything like that." She pointed into the box and smiled at Kyle's enthusiastic eyebrow waggle as she broke a maple-frosted doughnut into pieces; she touched a chunk of it against Kyle's lower lip and glanced at Joe. "Granted, maybe she used to, but not in the nine years since we've been together, has she Joe?"

Kyle answered around his mouthful. "Maybe not in public, no—but you bet she used to." He made a show of swallowing and turned to Joe. "Who does Ma think's going to call *her* to find *me*?"

"I don't know? Maria? She didn't say." Joe poured himself a coffee and raised the pot to Vicky in invitation, but found her staring at Kyle's towel-skirt. He clattered the coffeepot into its holder louder than he'd intended. "You heard the conversation. Except she also said she'll bring your things by later."

"Come to pass judgment on the damage more like."

Joe shrugged and took a swallow of coffee.

"I thought I recognized Joe's old present; it sure looked better on him," Vicky said. "But anything would look better on anyone besides you right now, Kyle."

"Ha. Thanks." Kyle reached in the direction of the Velcro waist as if threatening to rip it open. "Want to see the worst of it?"

"Egads. I don't think so."

"Lucky for us, your paws aren't working just at the moment," Joe said in a dry voice.

"They said it won't be long, though." Kyle looked at his bandaged hands. "My right hand's not as bad. That was lucky."

"Whew. So there's still a chance of a Picasso in the Carson family." Vicky offered another piece of doughnut and Kyle reached for it with his fingertips. "So, once you're healed will you be covered in scars?"

"Nah, nothing that exciting." His doughnut fell to the table, frosting side down. "Damn. Sorry."

"Want a plate … or a bib?" Joe wiped the table as Kyle went on.

"The ER doc last night said she's got souvenirs of her own from a ride twelve years ago. They rate road rash like burns. Mine is first and second degree. Where it's worst, I'll probably scar, she said—my left hip, shoulder, and hand. Otherwise I should be okay by end of July latest and the rest in just a couple weeks. I have to be careful in the sun while the new skin heals."

Kyle fixed his gaze onto the last bits of Joe's second doughnut, nodding, and tipping his head back, mouth pulled wide open like a baby bird.

Joe obliged, drained his coffee cup, and turned to start the dishes. "I'm off to see Grandma in a few minutes. Join me, Mummy?"

"Looking like this? Don't think so. I'm already Pizza Boy to her."

"That was one time, Kyle—and what?—at least a year ago. But you're right; she probably wouldn't know you in all your bandages." Joe glanced over his shoulder. "Vick? Want to come? We could head straight to Grand Rapids afterwards, and you could visit your mom and sisters or Penny while I'm at the car fair?"

On her way to the deer antler coat rack in the hallway, Vicky paused. Joe turned to watch her twist her hair into a quick ponytail and consider his invitation.

"Hmm … a whole day out? That won't work. I'd love to see Grandma, but my first client's in a couple hours, and I still need to exercise Bingo and turn out the others before he gets here." She plucked a matte black riding-helmet from the antler nearest her. "Given how long it is to Muskegon and back, I really can't. Sorry."

"Okay, then. I'll give Tommy and Jocko the day off and just head straight to the fair after seeing Grandma—puts me an hour closer. If I get any bites from buyers there, I might stay over at your mom's, and head home tomorrow." He flicked soap suds in Kyle's direction. "In time to help you scrub up."

"Forget that. I can handle a Triple P." Kyle waggled the visible tips of his right hand fingers.

Vicky stepped back into the kitchen and finished strapping on her helmet. "Dare I ask, what's a Triple P?"

"Just the essentials: pits, pecs, and package."

"Lovely." She grinned, shaking her head. "Joe's favorite sort of shower."

Joe held his arms open as she came to him, kissed his mouth, and leaned back into the circle of his hug.

"Give Grandma my love and good luck in Grand Rapids, smooch. Let me know." Her warm expression turned serious. "And be sure to look at yesterday's mail. It's on your desk."

Joe swatted her back-side as she turned to leave and left a wet handprint on the butt region of her flannel shirt.

"You, mister, are Joe's patient!" She stopped to peck a kiss onto Kyle's cheek. "But if you need anything and presuming you can manage that phone, my cell and the barn phone are both on speed dial—then I'm with clients and off-line from eleven." In a quieter voice she added, "I'm really sorry about Maria. I really liked her."

Kyle's chin came up, but he said nothing.

Joe turned back to the dishes, listening to Vicky sweet-talk Doughnut out from beneath the living room couch and begin instructing her on being a good barn cat. The screen door banged shut and he chuckled.

"She loves letting that door slam. Childhood revisited, I guess." He dried his hands, dropped the wadded towel on the counter and went to the roll-top desk in the living room. As he passed Kyle, he put on a getting-down-to-business voice. "No Triple P for you ... the ER doc's orders were to gently scrub all over, put on the antibiotic cream, and bandage up again. Twice a day."

"Sadist. Shit."

"Yep. And how's that going by the way? Hope you're not needing help with that end of things."

Joe returned to the sink, leaning against it to flick through the handful of flyers and envelopes in his hand. He glanced up at Kyle.

"Hell, *no*. The fingertips work well enough for that." Kyle waggled them at Joe. "And even if I *did* need help, I wouldn't."

"Got it." Joe went rigid. Chewing the inside of his cheek, he stared at a bent and smudged square envelope addressed to his father, then tucked it inside an advertising flyer, and straightened to his full height. "So, that shower, now?"

\*\*\*

"Joe, does Grandma actually even notice you," Kyle asked, "much less still *know* you?"

He followed Joe through to the cluttered mudroom at the back door and into the bathroom, then stopped and took in the room: plain vanilla now, but soon to be an S & M chamber.

Above a single wooden towel rail crammed full of towels, a framed selfie of Joe and Vicky hung. He studied the lop-sided photograph: an exuberant but discreet shared bubble bath, they threw and ducked handfuls of bubbles, their faces and mouths open with laughter. He thought of his last shower with Maria—not a good move—and snapped his focus back to the S & M chamber.

Other than a Betty Boop shower curtain and a tiny orange vase stuffed with silk violets—which had to have both come from Vicky—the room begged for color. Any color. He imagined flinging a brushful of hot orange paint across a wall up onto the ceiling or—

"She notices me, sure. She's got Alzheimer's; she's not blind." Joe lifted and sniffed two towels before extracting one. "And yeah. She knows me."

Kyle raised his arms above his head, trying not to feel like a kid as he waited for Joe to pull off his shirt.

"You see her every week, still?" he asked.

"Usually three times."

He sniffed again at the scent of Old Spice as Joe raised the shirt over his head and heard Joe doing the same.

*What a guy ... how many men would choose their deodorant in remembrance of their dead Grandpa?*

The shirt's neck hole caught on his chin; through the thin fabric, he heard Joe continue, "I hate to admit it, but I'm not sure I'd be visiting Ma that often if she got dementia."

"Oh, nordy boy!" Kyle talked through the shirt as Joe worked it past his chin. "Who'd really notice any difference in Ma, though? It's not like she's ever shown a lot of interest in us and half the time she sounds demented anyway." The shirt caught on his nose, then sailed over his head and onto the floor. "You'd think *she* was the drunk."

Joe's skeptical look mirrored his own thought: *but it's not like we were ever cozy with Dad, either.* He offered Joe both bandaged hands and watched him unwind the gauze, releasing a finger at a time from their cotton cocoon.

"Have you noticed Ma seems different lately?" Joe said.

"Different how?"

"I don't know. Less caustic or something. Nicer."

"I couldn't tell you." Kyle tried to position his arm to make it easier for Joe to untwine the shoulder bandages. He looked away into the corner of the metal shower stall as Joe undid the half towel. "Until I went to stay there Saturday, the only time I've seen her since Dad started this total cold shoulder campaign, was ... wow, at least two months ago. She was coming out of Book Mark. You'd think a librarian would get her fill of books at work."

"She's big on supporting local."

"Is she? Anyway, we hardly talked. I told her I still hadn't heard from Dad and asked if she had. She went all cagey and fidgety—like she'd bunged him under her house in a shallow grave. She took off without answering."

He wasn't about to explain that, since meeting Maria, he hadn't given either parent much thought, other than raising a toast last September when Joe told him their dad had finally moved out. Having Maria as a buffer and a focus the past year had dulled the sense of insult both parents engendered in him. Though she'd never asked about it, she always seemed baffled by how little he interacted with either of them given they only lived a few miles apart. He'd never told her the contact was mainly a one-way street, with him doing nearly all the driving. Other than the annual birthday card or an email invitation to a random holiday dinner, usually sent last minute, he couldn't remember a time Ma had initiated contact with him—and their father, never.

Kyle knew most of the town saw his family as a little weird. They had no idea the extent of it. Vicky didn't seem to. Joe did, of course, but had always had an irritating way of ignoring the dysfunction and just about anything else that would drive any sane person nuts.

"She acted that way when I asked at Christmas, too," Joe said. "Um … remind me when I'm back from Grand Rapids, and have more time, to show you something from yesterday's mail."

Kyle nodded then snorted. "Sounds like maybe Ma's got another secret." As he surveyed the stained bandages accumulating on the bathroom's tan and white tile floor, he tried to pinpoint the last time he'd actually talked to their dad. He'd skipped the latest family Christmas; snowshoeing in the U.P. with Maria sure beat that annual charade.

*But … with Dad not there, Christmas at Ma's could have been different … could've been fun to needle her for her cagey ways, too. Did she finally cut Dad loose? Or … hop back in it with him and can't admit to it?*

"Well, you'll get your chance for a nice ol' visit later today." Joe twirled the last bandage free and, with a quick wince at the sight of him, dropped it on the pile.

There was no other dude alive he'd stand in front of naked; yet, Kyle still had to resist a strong urge to clamp his hands over himself, fig leaf-style.

"Jesus," he said. "Last time we showered together would have been summer camp when you were seven."

Standing there naked and raw, he peered at his own angry-looking limbs. Even his penis looked defeated.

Joe shoved Betty Boop aside, turned on the water and, with a goofy grin, stripped down to a pair of navy blue boxers.

"Okay, here we go, big, ugly brother," he said. "In a minute that road rash of yours is going to be road rage."

"You better not turn this into payback for anything I ever did to you."

"Would I do that? In we get."

# Chapter Four
## June 26th

"Hello?"

Kyle raised his head from Joe's pillow, blinking at the bright midday sun. Had he just heard a voice?

"Hello in here! Where is anybody?"

*Oh great.* That *voice.* "Hang on, Ma. I'm in the loft."

"Well, I'm not coming up there."

"I didn't ask you to. I said hang on." Because he was still groggy, it had come out sounding civil. The screen door banged and he rolled his eyes.

"Off to a good start," he muttered to Doughnut. Lying so close that her fur brushed his forehead, she commiserated with a slow blink of her only eye. He leaned close to study the other one, seamed shut as if she'd never had use of it, and trailed his fingertips down the pronounced bumps of her spine. "Stay here and enjoy the sun, scrawny one. It'll be a lot nicer than listening to this."

On the porch, he paused at the sight of his mother waiting for him at the far side of the yard. She had settled, cross-legged, into one of the two big red Adirondack chairs facing a gap in the trees that lined the riverbank. The chairs, the pines, and his mother's pale green sundress evoked a brief image of Christmas, erased immediately by the implications of the deep-seated matching chair beside her. Torturous and empty, it also waited for him.

Kyle pictured first trying to lower himself into the low-slung chair while Ma watched then, worse, trying to exit it. Standing beside her wouldn't work either. He'd just have to perch on the wide arm. And hope he didn't go ass over teakettle.

He toed the screen door open and made his way down the wooden stairs to the yard, concentrating on walking as naturally as his stiff limbs allowed. The grass underfoot presented a patchwork of greens, yellows, and browns, lush here, burned or worn there. His grandfather had called it a working yard, and Joe kept it the same: driving or washing cars on it, letting horses pee on it. Today it felt way too big.

Kyle wondered how long he'd been sleeping and when he'd last had a pain pill. Pausing at the picnic table, his fingertips pressed to the weathered wood for balance, he glanced up to see his mother attempt to stand up from her chair. On her third try, she rose to her full height, collected up her huge purse and a small white bag, and came to meet him.

"I love the look of those chairs," she said, "but they're ridiculous for tall people. Let's sit here instead; it might be easier."

Kyle took care to keep the relief from his face as they sat.

"How are you?" he asked.

Though he knew she had turned fifty-three a couple months earlier, he thought most people would guess her to be early sixties or more, but that they'd also still call her pretty. As a kid, he'd privately sketched her face, the archetypal artists' oval, amazed at her defined cheekbones and brow line. The same looks Joe had inherited. If Ma were anyone else, he would've asked her to sit for him as a model years ago.

"Good, Kyle. Better than you."

She fished around in her yawning handbag and pulled out a soft, yellow canvas sunhat.

"What can I say?" *A mistake; she'd certainly offer her ideas.*

She ignored her chance and pulled on the goofy hat. "I brought you some scones."

"They smell fresh." He pointed his nose at the little paper bag. "The bakery in town?"

"I made them."

"You baked?"

"Apparently—if a mix counts. But I used chai tea instead of water. To bring out the flavor."

"So that's what I smell. Nice."

"Have one. They should still be warm. I brought butter, too, in case Joe only has margarine."

"I won't now, thanks."

"Go ahead."

He fastened his eyes on the view of the riverbank, over her shoulder. "I'll have them with Joe and Vicky later."

"They won't be as nice later." She held the bag close; inches from his chin.

His salivary glands kicked in, but he focused instead on the green and white dappling of light through the yard, and pictured how he'd paint it. *Maybe in abstract … sharp shadows and gashes of sunlight, bright red splotches for the chairs, patterns playing over them.* He heard her withdraw the bag and set it on the picnic table.

"Oh."

At her odd, neutral tone, Kyle shot Ma a look and found her studying his bandaged hands. *Please, God,* he thought, *don't let her offer to feed me a scone.*

"So, where have Joe and Vicky got to?"

He stifled a second sigh of relief. "Joe went to visit Grandma earlier, then off to a vintage car fair. Vicky's shoveling poop or riding a horse or something."

At the mention of horses, his mother sneezed. A tiny knot exploding. Once. Twice. Three times.

"Bless you."

"Thanks."

A robin sang overhead and they both searched to find it.

Kyle took the plunge, glancing at her. "Maria sneezes just like you. Girly."

Ma smiled, her eyes still searching the branches of a cedar ash. "I like Maria."

"Well, you heard yesterday. She's a Christmas card kinda chick now."

"She's on my card list already, but … I'll see her."

Kyle stared at her, but now she refused to make eye contact.

"We had coffee this morning," she added.

"You did? Why?" He knew he sounded like a teenager with a crush. It annoyed him. "To talk about me?" Hearing that pop out annoyed him even more. He caught Ma's sideways glance and pressed his lips into a hard line.

"No … to talk about her. Me. Lots of things."

"And what do you mean, you'll see her?" The neediness in his voice ramped up his irritation to another level. He watched her fidget with the soft edges of her hat as she chose an answer.

"We have a lot in common."

"Pfft! You and Maria?" Kyle bit off each word. "I don't think so."

In the crackling silence between them, his mother raised her chin several notches, her face closing further with each lift. "I left a bag on the porch with your wallet and clothes and things." She got up from the table.

Silent, Kyle sat and watched her walk to her car and bend to unlock it. *She locked it?* he thought. *Out here—in Joe's driveway?*

She didn't look back at him or wave as she turned a tight circle in front of the barn, her tires running over the grass, then disappeared between the rows of soft pines.

*Good riddance.* He scowled at the little bag sitting in front of him leaking butter. Saliva sprang up again.

"Screw you," he told it and wished he had a way to knock it to the ground.

Ma didn't even ask how he was? Say she was sorry about Maria? Offer to tell him what Maria said about his crash or whether either of them worried about him being hurt?

*Would she bother to tell Dad about the crash—if she ever talked to him?—or volunteer any reason why he never answered emails anymore.*

Kyle struggled to get up from the rough bench and, once standing, to decide where to take himself. Going back to nest in the sun with Doughnut didn't feel like an option after Ma.

Despite wearing only a thin T-shirt and another pair of Joe's baggy shorts, the punishing sun and his cocoon of bandages made for a sweaty combination. He pictured the cool and quiet inside the barn and marched across the yard to the big double door.

*Stereotypical peeling paint; does any barn in the whole Midwest have a frickin' decent paint job?*

One of the big doors stood ajar just enough to stick his heel into the gap; he pushed hard against the thick wood until he could squeeze through without grazing the edges. Inside, heavy gloom blinded him. Waiting for his eyes to adjust, he smelled hay. Motor oil. Car polish. Horse manure. He heard a soft rustling just to the left of his foot. It stopped. Above him, the anxious, urgent cheep of a bird. He felt his calm returning. Then from farther into the barn, beyond the hulking shapes of various vehicles, came a rich, deep male voice, followed by a quiet, feminine voice—*Vicky's.*

He stepped forward, feeling his straitjacketed fingers trying to curl into fists. *That's not Joe with her back there.*

He strained his eyes open wide. His forehead ached. Down the main aisle, silhouetted black against the sun white of the doorway to the exercise arena, was a large irregular shape. As he watched, the shape split into two figures. A massive, broad-shouldered man straightened, and ducked through the door into the arena, his frame filling much of the wide opening. The remaining figure, unmistakably Vicky, stood motionless for several seconds. Then punched her fist in the air and let out a quiet "woohoo."

Kyle tasted bile in his mouth. Not caring if she heard, he spat hard into the sawdust at his feet, then followed the strip of light across the floor and out of the barn. He fumed across the blazing yard and stomped up the porch stairs. With the tip of an index finger latched under the screen door handle he jerked it open, not caring that the hot metal burned. Two strides through the porch, four to the stairs and he was back in the loft. Ignoring the pain, he stretched across the bed on his back like a teenager. *Again.*

As if drunk from the sun, Doughnut stumbled over and stood squinting down at him with her single eye. He stroked her with his thumb and glared into the wooden rafters overhead. Cobwebs and knotholes.

Doughnut pushed her nose into his cheek and started to purr.

"You didn't see what I just saw: yet another woman jerking a Carson man around," Kyle told her. She pressed against his mouth and revved up louder. He turned his face free. "Heck, Doughnut, it's an oven up here. And dead quiet. Why do you want to be up here?" He nuzzled into her back to make up for his harsh tone and found he'd wetted her fur with angry tears. "Look at that! Your mom made me cry. *My* mom made me cry. I haven't cried since Hairy died."

He shut down the memory of howling on the roadside.

Doughnut eased back against his cheek and settled into rhythmic breathing.

"You're sleeping again," he whispered, his breath parting her fur. He studied the downy underfur. "You're as bad as me. You'd think you were the one drugged up on pain meds."

There was no answer.

"Okay. I'll be quiet."

***

"Hey, Kyle! What would you like for dinner? Did you have any water today? It's awfully hot."

Kyle opened his eyes and missed Doughnut. He felt a chill where her body had just been soft and warm against his cheek. Knotholes blended now with the shadows above him, the cobwebs already consumed.

Muffled, below the loft railing, Vicky went on, "Hey, Baby Doughnut. How you been, my one-eyed pirate?"

Doughnut meowed.

"Ooo … shhh…keep it down. I think your uncle's napping again. That's good, eh? Healing all those owies."

Another meow.

"What's that, sugar paws? Meowy? No. Owie. You try."

A rumbling meow. Purring mixed with this one.

"Close enough."

Kyle lay still and listened to Vicky moving away from the loft stairs and through the living room.

"Cat does not live by cuddles alone. Come let me feed you. Oh my, I think you've put on half an ounce. Good for you."

The kitchen radio came on, low, songs from the '70s and '80s, as usual. Kyle listened to Vicky sing along to Michael Jackson, Madonna, and Springsteen—in a pretty decent voice. He heard her running water and chopping things. Then she padded into the living room and snapped on a lamp. The shadows above him eased a little. It brought to mind movies he'd seen depicting overnight air travel with flight attendants gently waking passengers by slowly turning up the cabin lights.

"Kyle?" She called again in a soft voice, this time a couple steps below the loft. "Come get something to eat. You must be starving. I've made a cold pasta salad and a fruit salad."

At the mention of food his stomach grumbled. He figured the horses could have heard it in the barn.

Vicky laughed as she retreated down the steps and, in a louder voice, said, "Well, clearly part of you is awake. Come get some cold water."

He eased from the bed and followed her as far as the kitchen doorway. Her smile melted away at the sight of him. The Eagles song she'd been singing died from her lips.

She raised one eyebrow. "Wow. It just got really cold in here. What gives?"

"What the hell is going on?"

Her second eyebrow rose and she faced him, holding his gaze. "You got me, Kyle. But I sure hope you'll tell me."

"I saw you and that marine-looking guy in the barn."

"Wha…? Oh!" Her face relaxed and, turning back to the table, she began dolloping large spoonsful of fruit salad onto two heavy paper plates. "So you were spying on my session."

"Pfft. That's what you call it: a session?"

"Yep, that's what I call it." She sounded normal, all light and natural. "He'd just finished and … hey. I'm not going into his business with you. It's private."

"Yeah, it looked private!"

She paused and turned to him, her wooden spoon dripped juice onto the marked and dented table. "Okay, Kyle I don't like your tone. You screw your head back on. I—"

"Vicky?" A woman's voice and the sound of a quick tap traveled to them from the porch.

"Coming, Mel!" Vicky called. She stabbed her spoon into the fruit and shook her head at Kyle. "Hang on a sec."

He turned sideways to let her pass.

"Hey, girlfriend! All done for the day?" Vicky's warm voice wafted back to him.

Kyle stepped backwards toward the living room and tried to listen but could only hear half the conversation. "You want to come in for some dinner? … Oh, gotcha. Yep, leave Bingo here overnight. Everyone's fed and watered? Ready for tomorrow?"

He couldn't make sense of Mel's muffled answer.

"You're bringing Bonnet, and you'll be here at six, right?" Vicky said. "That'll give us plenty of time to load up and get up there before the heat kicks in. I'll be ready."

He missed another murmuring answer but caught Vicky's enthusiastic reply.

"Oh yeah, such a good session! It felt great, didn't it? He must have had a real breakthrough. And after what—only three sessions? That pattern you picked up on with Bingo seemed to really trigger something with him. I guess we'll never know what though. I have a feeling we won't be seeing our Marine again; I think that'll be his last time."

More murmuring from the visitor and Vicky replied, "So true! Anyway, you get home, Mel. See you at six! Thanks for another awesome day. High-five … Ha! You're right, high-five to Bingo. He and the girls, the stars of the show—as it should be. As long as we get out of their way."

Knowing he'd miss his chance in a second, Kyle swerved around the kitchen table. From the corner window looking onto the grass driveway, he saw a tall, ponytailed woman walking, loose-limbed and confident, toward a baby blue pick-up. At the sound of footsteps he turned back to the table, feigning nonchalance and trying not to smile.

"So …" Vicky threw him a teasing glance. "… did your eavesdropping clear up the concerns you dreamed up by spying?"

Shaking juice from the serving spoon, she dug into a bright yellow bowl mounded high with cold pasta and veggies.

Kyle tilted his head in apology. "Not exactly eavesdropping when it can't be helped in this shoebox." He slanted a grin toward the table. "And not exactly *spying* when all I did was walk into the barn and there you were knotted with some huge dude."

A genuine laugh burst from Vicky. "Knotted, eh?" She flicked the spoon at Kyle. He turned his wrist over to dislodge a piece of yellow pepper that landed on the bandage. "Sure, 'there I was' in the barn, Kyle, because I work with *horses*. As you know, *dufus*. We'd just come in from the arena."

"What do you do anyway that gets your clients hugging you at the end of a session …"

"I usually don't get hugs. Usually the horses do."

"Don't tell me that Marine hugged a horse."

"I'm not telling you anything. Client sessions are private. You didn't see the sign on the door of the barn?"

"Nope. I did not."

"Well. I better hook it on better. No one comes in when we're in session, unless the client gives permission. Okay? Please remember next time." She loaded cutlery, two re-useable water bottles, and the heaped plates onto an old Formica tray edged with stainless steel rails. "Let's eat at the picnic table. I used the stove, so it's going to feel cooler outside than in here now."

As he followed Vicky outside, Doughnut streaked past them.

Kyle cringed. "Damn! *Straight* to those birds." At the edge of the yard, chickadees and wrens picked through fallen seed at the base of the rough-hewn feeder.

Vicky carried on to the picnic table and started unloading the tray. "The birds will win. Doughnut's a lousy hunter, I'm glad to say." Her skyward glances suggested she wanted to catch the sun as it dropped behind the trees. "Maybe it's having only one eye. Or maybe her sweet heart isn't really into it."

Watching until all the birds settled on branches just above Doughnut's leaping reach, Kyle nodded. "I'd say it's the latter."

He scanned the area around the picnic table for any sign of Ma's pathetic peace offering, but found nothing—and if Vicky had, she didn't mention it. *Good.* He wondered if chipmunks feasted on chai flavored scones and buttery paper somewhere by the river.

"So hypothetically speaking …" He slotted himself limb by limb onto the rough bench seat, feeling more curious than pissed off now. "… a Marine sort would hug—who was it—Bingo?"

"Bingo gets a lot of hugs." Vicky set a lime green water-bottle in front of him. "I found these stuffed in the back of a cabinet."

"Ah. Hands-free—nice." He leaned forward and took a long suck from the permanent straw.

"Bingo gets hugs and he gets a lot of tears."

Kyle thought of his crying onto Doughnut earlier. *What is it about animals?*

After a long drink from her own bottle, Vicky continued. "He's even gotten the occasional Christmas card."

"You gotta be shi— "

"Hey." She pointed her fork at him. A bobbing, bright red triangle of watermelon punctuated each word. "Come with us tomorrow; you can see what it's all about. In a *legit* way."

"Can't you and your watermelon just tell me now?" He leaned over and bit the fruit off her fork.

"I'd rather let you see for yourself—it's more powerful. Come along. It'll be fun."

"Looking like this?"

"Wear light clothes. You won't need to do anything but sit and watch. It's a demo." She knuckled his good shoulder with a fist. "So watching's allowed."

# Chapter Five
## June 27th

Tossing their regal heads and snorting, both horses set off at trot, muscles sliding beneath glossy hides, feet precisely lifted and placed. After several dozen yards, the pair, a palomino and a chestnut, slowed, then stopped a few feet from Kyle and stood very close together, playfully mouthing and nuzzling each other. Seconds later, a fat, cream-colored, mini-horse jolted to a stop near them and stood watching something in the distance that only it seemed able to see.

The trio ignored the humans in the arena. Until a moment ago, the man and woman had seemed on the verge of capturing them with rope tethers. Now they simply stood, feeble grins on their faces, looking abandoned in the middle of the baseball diamond. An ankle-high cloud of fine dust settled over their shoes as they stared after the horses.

Kyle paused before climbing onto the bleachers at the edge of the Manistee High School playing field, trying to come awake and to gauge how much of Vicky and Mel's demo he'd slept through. The rhythm of Mel's truck over the smooth highway and the murmur of the two women's voices had lulled him to doze as they drove the half hour north from Ludington. He'd woken to find himself alone in the front seat, an unfamiliar red sweatshirt balled up as a pillow between his head and the window.

Closing his mouth against a yawn, he eased onto the wooden seat, aware of a balmy breeze lifting his hair, and of someone staring at him. One row behind him, the plumper of two very plump, forty-something women went a little pink when he met her eyes.

"I'm late. What did I miss?" Kyle said and saw her relax, but her gaze swept over his bandages once more before she answered. He gave her peony-printed caftan the old up and down in return.

She had the decency to blush. "Well, we just got here ourselves. So we missed most of the first demo, too—it was a young boy they called Gordy. My sister's …" she leaned into the woman beside her for a moment, "…little neighbor and our nephew, both go to school here." Her sister stayed focused on the action in front of them. "It's an *Eagala* demo—that's 'Equine Assisted Growth and Learning Association.' That's Janet and Gene out there. She's the guidance counselor here and he's the vice principal."

Kyle turned to look at the field. Out near the pitcher's mound, with a laughing glance over her shoulder as if urging him to follow, Janet beckoned to Gene. Gene nodded, with an exaggerated squaring of his shoulders that announced: "I've got this." Together they marched toward the horses. Both of them gripped a tether, holding it high as if ready for immediate use.

"Why are *they* trying to catch the horses instead of Vick—um … the women in charge of the demo doing it?"

"From what I gather from those kids," she tipped her head toward a teenage couple in cut-offs and tank tops, tangled together on the top bleacher, "of the two women leading this, the taller woman is the horsey one, and her job's keeping everyone safe and tracking how the horses behave. And the pretty, dark-haired one is a mental health something or other, and *the whole idea* of the therapy is about how the people taking part and the horses *interact*. And what they—the people in the arena or in this case the ball diamond—*make* of it all. Supposed to help them grow and to solve their own prob—"

Her sister interrupted in a sharp voice, "'Grow and come to awareness around their issues. Using metaphor.' *Shhh!* Just watch."

Kyle's new friend lowered her voice a notch and leaned closer, the bleacher creaking beneath her. "Janet and Gene were just told, 'go out, catch the horses, and bring them in' and to take as long as they needed to do it. Well, as you can see," her quiet chuckle turned her eyes to slits, "they're really getting a run for their money! Charging around in the dirt out there …"

And all this time he'd thought Vicky gave horseback riding lessons.

"Shhh!"

Shooting his informant a grin of thanks, he turned back to the ball diamond and settled in to watch.

Janet, stocky and thirty-ish, had a copper-colored helmet of hair. Her boss, Gene, looked oh-so-sincere and, despite a little paunch, very tidy in his button-down shirt and tan walking shorts. Though he was head and shoulders taller than Janet, he had to quick-step to keep up with her arm-pumping gait as she strode toward their quarry.

Still clustered in a loose trio near the bleachers, the horses looked more wound up and uncatchable than minutes before. The palomino, compact and sleek, kicked her rear legs out in response to repeated nips from the chestnut while the fat little mini circled and tossed her head like a ringmaster egging on a show.

*I know your sort,* Kyle thought as he watched. *Troublemaker, stirring up shit and keeping far enough away to not get any on you. In grade school, before I got hooked on art, you and I would've had a lot in common. And … what are all of you frowning at?*

Several of the random twenty or so people seated on the bleachers around him shot sideways looks his way, and he realized he'd been chuckling under his breath. The surreptitious glances struck him as even funnier.

Shifting on the hard plank, he wished he'd brought a charcoal or chalks and a pad with him—then remembered he couldn't use them anyway. Cream, golden, and chestnut horses moved beneath a stark, Caribbean-blue Michigan sky; he studied the kaleidoscope it created and his fingers ached to capture it. The palomino had an uncontrolled forelock that reached nearly to her muzzle. Catching glimpses of her dark eyes beneath the moving sheets of blond hair, Kyle found himself thinking of the smoky looks Maria would throw his way while crawling across the bed to him.

*Screw that!* That was not an image he wanted when the dumping Maria had delivered wasn't even cold yet. He turned to memorize the glossy power of the chestnut, studying the lines, the color, staring at new moves the horse was trying on the palomino: nudging a cheek against the mare's forelock, matching his blaze to where hers would be if it weren't buried under all that silky hair. The palomino repeatedly dipped her golden head and rubbed her forehead across the chestnut's up-stretched neck. Both ignored the circling mini now, seeming oblivious to anything or anyone else on the playing field.

Yet, as if on cue and choreographed, just as Janet and Gene seemed close enough to touch the larger one, both horses wheeled around and cantered to the far edge of the playing field, the mini close behind.

No longer grinning, the man and woman stopped in their tracks. Shoulders hunched and heads jutting forward, they stared after the animals for a long minute then started plodding toward them, rope tethers dangling now and dragging in the dust.

"Can I sit here, Mister?" Kyle looked into the open and eager face beside him. The bleacher beneath him shuddered as the boy, about eight years old, dark as cola and built like a cube, dropped onto it, then squirmed to get comfortable. "I got to tell someone this! Did you *see* that? Did you see me out there with that yellow horse?"

Before Kyle could explain he'd pretty much just sat down, the boy launched into his story, swinging his feet and kicking the toe of one dust-covered leather shoe against the bleacher in front.

"I went first, they asked for volunteers and someone hasta be first, right? So, why not me?" He stabbed a finger at the palomino in the distance. "That horse, she *talked* to me. In my head!"

"'She talked to you, did she?" Kyle grinned and fixed his eyes on the lively face, prepared to listen closely. This kid was great.

"Yeah, man! For *real*. Not like crazy or nothing. You just kinda *hear* what she's thinking. You know?" He shook his head and, eyes wide, stared at the ground ahead of the bleachers. "Man. It was wild. That horse knows my momma! She's got to for all the things she sorta told me—once I stopped chasing her around, yelling at her. I know why I make my momma so *mad* now. She calls me a brat most *all* the time. That horse, she told me, 'yep, you're acting like a brat with your momma.'" He shook his head again, slow and deliberate. "But she told me in a *nice* way, ya know? Just a fact." He delivered a smart pat to Kyle's knee and seemed not to notice Kyle flinch. "Then she said, 'Gordy, you jes' stop being a brat.'"

The boy turned to fix huge eyes on Kyle's face and reared back stiffly, burying his chin in his neck. "So, I'm gonna, man." He nodded. "I'm gonna. How do you say 'no, I ain't' when a horse tells you '*do it*'? You jes' don't."

He looked back at the dirt in front of them, shaking his head, his eyebrows pulled up as high as they'd go. Leaving Gordy to contemplate, Kyle raised his eyes to the sports field and found the Vice Principal and Guidance Counselor now tiptoeing quite close to their quarry. Imminent triumph in their body language, they rushed to close the distance. In a squall of hooves, tails, and manes, the horses relocated yet again, heading back toward the bleachers.

Janet turned with a loud groan, flung her arms high for a moment, and carried on in red-faced pursuit, leaving Gene to puff after her in a slow jog.

"Man, that stuff is something. That yellow horse, she is *smart*. She saved my bacon." Gordy spotted a cocooned hand lying against Kyle's bandaged thigh. He reached across and planted a backhand high-five on the exposed fingertips and, with a loud heave, got up and shuffled off to the vending machine beside the bleachers.

Kyle sat and watched him buying an orange pop, glad the kid had been too full of his own story to launch a quiz about all the bandages. Relieved, too, his farewell slap had only connected with fingertips.

Digging deep in the pocket of his hot orange board shorts and then peering closely at the coins, Gordy stabbed them one by one into the machine, and stood back, hands fisted on his hips, to await his delivery. Instead of coming back to Kyle, he plopped down on a bleacher beside another spectator, snapped open his drink, and clearly began telling his story again, all eyes and animation.

Kyle turned back to the antics on the playing field. Amusement—and more than a little genuine interest—laced through his skepticism now; without a doubt those horses were affecting people big time. He remembered yesterday's Marine and wondered what awaited old Janet and Gene out there. Whatever happened, the show had been a laugh so far, especially the horsey foreplay a few minutes ago.

He shot frequent glances Vicky and Mel's way, expecting them to help the two poor suckers flailing around in the sun—maybe offer tips on how to wrap up the Abbot and Costello routine. Far from having luck using their tethers, Janet and Gene had only managed to brandish them in the direction of the smarter, four-legged participants in this farce. Yet, Vicky and Mel just stood near home plate, watching, now and then directing a brief comment into each other's ear and nodding.

Finally, ten or twelve yards from the horses, Janet came to an abrupt halt and just stood, hands limp at her sides. The intensity of her stare over his head, somewhere beyond the bleachers, made Kyle itch to turn and search the sky. He heard the two sisters behind him squirming.

Head down, Gene trudged to a stop at the edge of the infield, kicking up dust with each step like a sulky teenager. He seemed unaware—or maybe past caring—that twenty-some sets of eyes focused on him; he just stood, staring at his shoes for a bit before shuffling over to Janet.

After a short, quiet confab, the two turned and locked eyes on the three rumps in front of them.

*Show's over, they're giving up*, Kyle decided. Squinting from the sun, he looked to see Vicky and Mel's reaction and saw a quick grin flash between them, a subtle nod. *And those two don't look bummed at all.*

Janet and Gene exchanged a low fist bump and started wandering to where the horses stood, again clustered near the bleachers.

"Well. Will you look at their faces now!"

"What just happened there?"

Without turning to the loud whispers behind him, Kyle muttered, "Exactly."

Tethers dangling at their sides, Gene and Janet strolled closer still, chatting too low for Kyle to make out what they said.

He checked Vicky and Mel's reaction again—they seemed to almost vibrate where they stood now—and scooted to the edge of the bleacher.

The mini had just dropped her ringmaster act to nip grass from the infield; the chestnut and palomino stilled, then turned and stood, flank to flank. Their dark eyes riveted to the slowly approaching pair, the two larger horses exuded a curious innocence, nostrils wide as if inhaling the smiling man and woman.

Kyle held his breath and felt a grin spread across his face.

Leaving the mini to graze, both horses took a step forward … and another. Almost as one, they ambled on to an arms-length from Janet and Gene then accepted having the tethers loosely looped around their gleaming necks. Kyle thought he heard Gene gasp, but Gordy drowned it out.

"Whoa *hoe*! Did you just *see* that?" Half standing, he addressed the bleacher crowd. "They caught 'em! The horses *surrendered*."

Around him a surge of delighted giggles and chatting broke the tension. Kyle glanced at the sisters behind him; the crabby one rubbed goosebumps from her fleshy arms, the other swiped at tears. A chuckle started deep inside him, bubbled up, and burst. With it came an intense stab of missing Maria; she would have cried over this and—wanting to hug everyone involved—would have been hugging him.

But the show hadn't quite finished. The crowd grew quiet again, watching as Janet and Gene, each leading a horse, headed over to the mini. She looked up, blinked, and kept chewing for a beat or two before raising her head—as if waiting for the horses and people to reach her. She didn't flinch when Janet reached to stroke her forelock then slid the tether around her neck. Kyle shook his head. *Bizarre.*

Beaming, Janet and Gene led all three horses across the ball diamond to where Vicky and Mel waited, their faces alight.

"So, how was that?" Vicky must have raised her voice for the spectators' sake. Gene took her cue.

"That was … gosh … amazing." He lifted and dropped his free arm like a wrung-out rag doll and turned a begging look to Janet.

"Beyond amazing." Janet gave a watery laugh, raised a shoulder and smeared her wet cheek across it. "I'll go further and say these three horses just taught me in twenty minutes what nine years in my career failed to do—sorry, Gene!" She grinned at her boss. He nodded and lifted then dropped his arm again, helpless.

"What did you learn, Janet?" Mel asked.

"Well … attempting to force my solutions, my agenda, has often cost me a lot of heartache for very little—well, really—*no* gain. It just all of a sudden became so obvious: we had to chill and meet the students—I mean the horses—where they were at, not push our approach down their throats. Respect them, really. That's the best, the *only* way, really. *And* we had to spread our calm out." She looked over at the palomino and down at the mini whose leads still lay across her palm; the horses stood, looking as receptive as actors absorbing their critics' reviews.

"Thing is, I've experienced this before, with real students." Janet laughed. "But the lesson never really hit me between the eyes, you know? Like it just did here."

Gene had found his voice and Kyle leaned forward to listen. "*This*, Vicky, Mel, what you've got here is dam—uh, sorry—really powerful stuff. Janet articulated it very well. All this time ... right?" He threw a glance at Janet and emitted a gurgling noise. "This lesson, if we'd got it earlier, could have saved us and the school, a lot of people—including so many students—a whole lot of grief. I don't know yet how those horses managed to get all that across, and I'll need to understand that—we have to explain it to get any money from our funding bodies—but I get that it *does* work. By Jove, it does! And you all *saw* how *fast!*"

Throwing his free arm wide, he called out to the couple dozen spectators.

"Next! Come learn your lessons! It doesn't hurt a bit." Laughter rippled through the crowd and Gene turned back to plant a vigorous, open-palmed pat on the chestnut horse's massive shoulder.

"Please contact Janet so she knows how we can access sessions for our staff and our students," he asked Vicky as he reached out for hearty handshakes with her and Mel.

Vicky nodded, gave a little whoop, and grabbed Gene's hand with both of hers.

Mel accepted the leads the pair handed her as they turned to leave, flashing each of them a big smile, then laughed out loud when Janet rushed back and hugged her and Vicky hard.

Kyle shook his head and looked at the people around him, nearly every one of them grinning like a fool, including him. He still had no clue what Vicky and Mel, or more to the point, their horses, actually *did* or how they did it. *Voodoo?* Raking his fingertips through his hair, he imagined Maria crowing, "*It's magic!*"

He did know one thing more than he knew yesterday: he wanted that voodoo worked on him.

*Not in front of this crowd ... but curious? Hell, yeah.* He had some questions he'd take back to Joe's, to see if that palomino or the chestnut had something to tell him.

# Chapter Six
## June 27th

"Chuck Wagon pizza and beer at the picnic table," Joe said. "The official start of summer. Well, after opening day at DQ, that is." He looked around him thinking this was his idea of heaven. Fresh from a quick shower, Vicky sat next to him in a red-striped sundress, smelling of baby powder. Across the table in a navy tank top and a pair of cheap sunglasses, Kyle could have starred in a Coke commercial, if you ignored all the bandages. A breeze nudged the grasses and the highest branches of the pines that edged the river beside them and, although the sun still shone, fireflies rose up here and there, dotting the yard with golden winks.

Vicky raised her slice of pizza to his and they touched the sagging tips as she toasted: "To summer, to super pizza, and to …"—the look that came over her face reminded Joe of a toddler tasting chocolate for the first time— "… *horse power!* Your sort and mine!"

"Hear! Hear! Two scores at the car fair, a '55 Chevy Belair and a '56 Olds convertible—exactly what my clients ordered—" Vicky pressed a spicy kiss to his mouth before he went on. "Plus a kickass deal on a Mercury Monterey convertible. The *craziest* part: three new clients put in orders."

"Way to stick a fork in it, Joe!" Kyle said.

*A mighty fine fork,* Joe thought. *That Mercury should sell pretty quick and ring up a nice profit, but three new clients? I never expected anything like that. Especially since that one guy's a collector and likely to be around for the long haul. Well, safer to say could be with me for the long haul—who knows? —best not to count my chickens.*

"That is so great! And for me and Mel—" Vicky interrupted herself to call out her thanks to the absent Mel. "We signed up two schools and a park district as ongoing clients, plus a Boy Scout troop is scheduled for several full morning sessions starting in a few weeks. Who knows where that might lead?"

"Well done, my wild-haired entrepreneur." Joe nudged her shoulder with his, hoping his eyes conveyed his intense pride in her … so he wouldn't have to articulate it.

He'd always thought of her as the go-getter between them and had never had a problem with that. Lately, though, she seemed more annoyed than pleased if he said as much.

"Why didn't Mel stay for pizza, Vick? Where was she roaring off to when I got home?"

Vicky raised her hand in front of her mouth and talked around a bite of pizza. "The train station. She's picking up our summer intern, Juliet, from Illinois. Did I forget to tell you? She'll be the third in our people team starting tomorrow morning. We gambled that today's demo would bring in enough work to warrant taking her on. And we bet right."

Joe noticed Kyle had dropped out of their conversation; seeing the reason why, he chuckled. "Dude! He won't eat much."

Intent on lifting something out of a blob of sauce on his paper plate, Kyle's grimace read: "busted."

Vicky grinned. "Rescuing a gnat?"

Kyle made a grab at Joe's T-shirt, as if to swipe his fingertip clean on it. "Last swim for that poor sucker."

Joe leaned out of reach and took a long swig of beer. "Nuh-uh. Not on Jimmy Buffett you don't! Use your own."

Kyle did, twisting his finger in the hem of his shirt, eyes wide with mock innocence behind his sunglasses.

Vicky groaned. "I remember when you'd have just called that extra protein. Did Maria turn you veggie?"

Joe knew that tone. Teasing or not, she hoped to get Kyle talking about the break-up. Neither of them had broached the subject. He figured Kyle would talk when, and if, he wanted to—emphasis on if—and figured they should leave it alone which was pure torture for Vicky. Probably to be expected given the work she did. Though, if he saw someone driving a rattletrap vehicle around town and knew he could fix it—well, he figured that'd be their issue, until they showed up out here asking for help.

He squeezed her bare knee under the picnic table, but she kept her gaze on Kyle.

Kyle steepled his bandaged hands together. "Namaste. I'm half Buddhist now … meditating on this pepperoni." He narrowed his eyes at the last bit of pizza on his plate. "Balancing my good and bad karma.

"You're way outta whack in the karma stakes, big brother."

"Okay, I'll earn some good karma. I'm calling Dad with all this good news— hell with emails—we'll check up on him, too. Dial his number, Joe."

Joe tensed, remembering the envelope he'd stuffed into his shorts' pocket. He wished he could rewind and erase yesterday's shower session conversation; since then Kyle seemed bent on forcing contact with their father.

Hoping for the best, Joe punched in the number, set the phone to speaker mode, and stood to pile greasy paper plates inside the empty pizza box.

Vicky nudged him away. "You got dinner. I'll do the cleanup."

As he planted a kiss on her sun-warmed shoulder, his phone announced: "You have reached a non-working number."

Kyle raised an eyebrow.

"Weird." Joe grabbed the phone and dialed again.

"You have reached a non-working number."

"What did I say?" Kyle jabbed the off button with a fingertip. "Shallow grave."

"Hmm." Joe frowned. "This makes it weirder." He pulled a bent envelope from his shorts' pocket and handed it to Kyle.

"What's this?"

"The birthday card Vicky and I sent Dad a few weeks ago … returned, address unknown."

"So now, no phone *or* known address," Vicky said.

Joe nodded once, watching Kyle and steeling himself for a full-blown rant.

Kyle shot him a sharp look. "Thanks a lot for telling me."

"I only saw it yesterday, Kyle. I was going to show you. Now's the first real chance I—"

"Ma would have known, too. And never bothered saying anything." Scowling at Joe's "par for the course" expression, Kyle poked the phone lying on the table between them. "Look him up online, Joe."

"I already did," Vicky said. "Yesterday when I saw our card was returned. Not one single thing came up on him … he's not even on Facebook." Joe caught the flicker of concern that crossed her face before she added, "Just ask your mom, you guys. What's the big deal?"

"That's how things *should* work, Vick … in a normal family." Kyle stood.

"Well, I planned to stop in at Ma's after we ate, anyway." Joe gestured toward the Super 88 convertible parked and glistening in front of the barn. "That goes to a lead she brought me. Tommy and Jocko raced down to get this one. Come for the drive and ask her yourself about Dad."

"There you go, Kyle," Vicky said.

"If we stop at my place on the way back?" Brows knitted, Kyle frisbeed his plate into the box Vicky held. "So it's not a wasted trip."

"Sure, why not?" Joe sounded too eager, even to his own ears. He dialed it back. "Don't worry about digging out your key. I've still got your spare from your trip at Christmas."

"Steer clear of DQ, though. Okay?" Vicky said. "Tonight's perfect for ice cream and Hershey's out here when you get back."

Joe gave her a thumbs-up then privately crossed his fingers. He drained his beer, took a deep breath, and beckoned to Kyle. "Let's go, dude." As they crossed the grass together, he started talking. "You'll have to trust my driving; this car's a '56, too old to have seatbelts."

Still frowning, Kyle raised one shoulder. "You might've noticed motorcycles don't come with 'em either."

"I wonder if the new owner will ask me to install them. I get that it's safer but ... helluva shame to change anything about a classic."

Kyle didn't answer, but at the car he reached out to run a fingertip along one of the fins.

"Wind in the hair would be great." Joe cranked and guided and snapped till the top was in place. He watched as Kyle strolled around the red-and-cream colored car. "But tonight, with the roof down we'd swallow a thousand gnats."

Kyle squatted to glare at the gleaming white walls and Joe tried another angle.

"They say the first licensed Batmobile had an Olds 88 chassis, the Rocket 88." The glare seemed to soften; relieved, Joe went on. "A guy my age did the custom work on it in his family's barn. In 2008 someone found it abandoned in a field in New Hampshire."

"Who's got it now?"

"You could." Joe swung in behind the wheel and pushed Kyle's door open. "It was on auction in Biloxi last October but the owner turned down the high bid —$1.35 mil." He tuned the car's radio to the True Oldies Channel.

"Do you ever listen to anything else?" Kyle asked.

"Why move on from the best?" Joe eased along the lane to avoid the low-hanging branches and protect the car's suspension. "Grandma got me into it. It's her favorite station, too. Even now."

"So of course it's yours." Kyle jerked away from the open window and a branch snapped out as they passed. "Why don't you pave this lane? Cut back those trees? You got the bucks."

"You sound like Vicky." Joe turned up the volume on "La Bamba" and shouted over the music. "My all-time favorite. The way Ritchie Valens rocked up 'La Bamba,' and earned himself a place in the Latin Grammy Hall of Fame *and* the Rock & Roll Hall of Fame, I figure if he'd lived past seventeen he'd have been bigger than Elvis."

Kyle just lifted his chin in response, thick hair tumbling in the wind.

*Rant averted,* Joe thought. *Yay.* He sped along the quiet roads, nodding to the music, and rapping his fingers against the steering wheel. This had to be the dictionary definition of bliss. Valens' music got right into your soul and almost made your heart explode.

As their mother's house came into view, he lowered his speed and, once in her drive, lowered the sound.

"Yeah?" Joe grinned.

Kyle's answering smile brought their dad's voice to mind.

*Look at that fool grin.*

Joe had always taken it as if he was being called a fool. For the first time he wondered whether his dad meant him or the grin. Tonight, who cared? He knew he wore the same look: pure wordless appreciation of good things.

He took his time unfolding from behind the wheel, savoring the feel of the heavy door in his grip, the smell of the soft leather under his hand. *Old leather,* he thought. *My favorite smell in the world. And I bet Vicky and Grandma are the only people alive who know that.*

"Ha! Getting better already." Kyle sounded damned pleased with himself as he opened the passenger door using two fingertips and the toe of his flip-flop.

They stood for a minute admiring the car's chrome and curves.

"Good as a bike?"

"Can't go that far. But a car would sure be nicer in the winter. When the insurance for the bike comes in, maybe I'll put it toward something like this."

"Yeah? Cool … four new clients today then." Joe turned and headed to the side door, knowing the den off the kitchen, overstuffed with furniture, photos, and memories, had always been their mother's go-to place.

"Family rates, of course. No commission." Kyle fell into step beside him.

"Cheap bastard."

"Cheap? Sure. Bastard?" Kyle cocked an eyebrow, lowering his chin and his voice. "Don't let Ma hear you impugning her fidelity."

Joe snorted and ducked past him, jostling for position on the worn concrete stoop. Several terra cotta pots, crammed with the laughing faces of Ma's blue and yellow pansies, crowded the tiny space beneath a rusted, dripping air conditioner. Yellow roses climbed a rickety wooden trellis propped against the pale gray siding of the house. Joe breathed in their night scent and was suddenly back to age ten.

*With my big brother, about to leap on our bikes and ride to the Curves for a swim. God, life is good.*

Out loud, he said, "She won't hear anything with this old relic running. The drone of that thing could double as torture."

He pressed the doorbell, then poked his head into the kitchen and his mouth watered at the smell of Italian meatballs.

"Didn't you know the buzzer's busted, perfect son? So we're just going to have to sneak up and scare her." Kyle skirted around him, tiptoeing like a vaudeville movie villain into the kitchen.

"I don't think so." Joe raised his voice to give Ma a heads-up. "You're going to give her a heart att—"

Kyle jerked to a stop in the doorway to the den and thrust his bandaged arms ahead of him. "Boo!"

From over Kyle's shoulder, Joe saw their mother jump and, without looking up, stash a child's stuffed rabbit inside a box printed with toy bugles and drums. She shoved it aside on the couch beside her and dragged a shawl over the box.

"What's up, Ma?" Kyle's voice dropped a gauntlet.

Joe swallowed hard and squeezed past him, watching her arrange her face into something a stranger might've called a smile.

"Hi, Ma. Who's got a baby?" He almost bent to kiss her cheek, but—she wasn't Grandma.

Standing up, her hands stuffed deep into the slouchy denim sundress she wore, she blocked their view of the shrouded lump on the couch. "No one you two know."

"So, what's the big mystery? Try us." Kyle had become a bulldog.

"What brings you guys here?" Sounding perky and false as a bad cheerleader, she wouldn't even look at Kyle.

Joe started, "Just wanted to—"

"Oh, man." Kyle's tone shifted to bitter. "You love your little secrets, eh, Ma?"

*Here we go,* Joe thought. But instead of rising to the bait, Ma fixed her gaze out the window into the back yard. Squirrels played over a faded tire swing hung from the elbow of a gnarly sugar maple; the swing twisted then untwisted on the end of a fraying rope, as if unsure which way to turn.

The air conditioner cycled down with a crash and left a brittle silence, broken within seconds by the slap of Kyle's flip flops on the kitchen floor.

"Wait!" The slaps changed direction and Kyle reappeared at the door. "What's with Dad's phone and invalid address? Where is he?"

Ma's eyebrows quirked high though she kept staring at the tire swing. The quick shake of her head resembled a shiver, as if the question repulsed her.

"I can't help you with that, Kyle."

"Can't or won't, Ma?"

"Last I saw your father was at Thanksgiving. We went skiing. I haven't talked to him since." Her closed face made it clear that was all the answer he'd get.

With a growl, Kyle turned on his heel. Seconds later the kitchen door slammed. As a new silence settled around them, Ma's eyes swung to Joe's, asking him to start over.

"Umm …" Joe chewed the inside of his cheek and tried to claw back some of the nostalgic contentment he'd felt on the doorstep with Kyle. "Just wanted to show you the '56 Olds I got today for your coworker—for Sherri. One of my part-time helpers, either Tommy or Jocko, will bring it by her place or to the library tomorrow, if she's working, whenever it suits her."

"She is working tomorrow, I think."

"Okay, I'll give her a call."

"Thanks, Joe."

Ma stood rigid, bare feet planted on the threadbare Oriental carpet where he and Kyle had played Connect Four on a hundred rainy Saturdays. She didn't bother to make a move toward a window, much less to go outside and check out the car.

After a second, her eyebrows rose as if asking did he have more to say. He turned back to the door, jangling the car keys in his hand.

"Okay, then. Have a good night."

"Yep, I'll do that. 'Hi' to Vicky for me."

Letting himself out of the house, Joe shook his head. *Now that was a classic bum's rush,* he thought. *What gives, Ma?*

In the car, the vibes coming off Kyle turned the evening cold.

"Let it go, Kyle. She told us what she could."

"Bullshit! She knows more than she said. I'm so damn sick of her secrets."

*And I'm going to cop the flak because I'm here,* Joe thought. Silent, he backed out of Ma's driveway and turned toward town.

"She's always got to be hiding something!" Kyle started his rant and Joe tuned him out, concentrating on the happy lyrics of the Turtles biggest hit.

By the time they turned onto Kyle's street, a tidy little lane that would fit well on a Monopoly game-board, Joe had restored his own good mood and begun thinking about home and ice cream.

"Earth to Joe!" Kyle twisted in his seat with a glare. "I said: what could be bigger than not telling us where our father is?"

"It sounds like she doesn't know either."

"Christ, Joe … really? You saw her reaction, my question didn't surprise her. It's not new news to her! She's just not saying. Like about that toy. Everything's a big fat secret."

"She's entitled to her privacy. Like any of us." Joe pulled up in front of Kyle's pale green bungalow and parked. "And I'm not getting bent outta shape about a toy."

In a habit he'd picked up from Grandma, he reached over before thinking better of it, and touched Kyle's bandaged hand. "Why are you?"

Kyle jerked away and aimed a glare at him, then toward the little house beside them.

Joe climbed out and led the way onto Kyle's shallow porch. Unlocking the canary-colored door, he paused. "Why are you so angry at the world, man?"

"Screw you." Kyle glowered past and disappeared inside.

*What a question. Why'd I even ask?* Joe wondered, then realized … *Because I wish you were happier.*

After doing battle with the mailbox and assessing the state of the tiny front lawn, he stepped into the oak-paneled foyer. Grunting and swearing came from the vicinity of the back door.

"Good thing we came by," he called.

*God, the house stank of paint.* He dumped a stack of flyers and bills, many creased or torn, onto a red plastic cube he figured was a table. "I had to yank that wad of mail to get it out. Tore some stuff."

Kyle strode up the dim hallway, a tall and broad-shouldered figure backlit by the evening sun that poured through French doors in the kitchen. Joe watched him pass, flip-flops loud on the shining hardwood floor, carrying a paintbrush and a quart tin of paint with his fingertips, a screwdriver balanced across the tin.

"Come open this for me."

Stifling a sigh, Joe marched down a second narrow hall, this one brightened by a rectangular skylight, and stopped to lean against the doorframe of Kyle's darkened bedroom.

"Hang on. You never answered my question, Kyle." The paint smell was stronger here. No wonder he'd asked to sleep at Ma's. "Not judging. I'd like to know. Why are you always so pissed off with the world?"

"Just open the damned can, would ya?"

"You're going to paint now?" Joe reached in to flick on the overhead light and his mouth dropped open. He took several steps into the bedroom, slowly turning a complete circle. "Jesus Christ, Kyle! You did this?"

"And I'm going to undo it once you close your mouth and open this thing." With difficulty Kyle squatted at the end of his bed and set the tin on the polished floor.

"No way in hell you're painting this out. Man, this is awesome … completely awesome."

As he protested, Joe did another slow turn, taking in the mural that started on the room's east wall with the soft pinks and lavenders of sunrise, traveled up to a darkening indigo and silver Milky Way above the bed, and finished on the west wall in a blaze of brilliant oranges blended into yellows and reds. "You've got to know how amazing this is, right?"

"Get lost. I'll open it myself." Kyle made clumsy stabs with the flat end of the screwdriver, trying to hit the lip of the paint tin.

Joe grabbed the screwdriver. "Dammit! Cut it out, will ya? Grow up!"

"Grow up?" With a glare that could melt glass, Kyle struggled to stand, then came toe to toe with him.

Their faces inches apart, Joe raised his chin a notch, holding his ground and Kyle's gaze. He watched the glare wilt then morph.

"You practicing your 'Dad voice' or planning to become a teacher?" Kyle stepped back, sounding beat.

Grinning his truce and watching Kyle try but fail to do the same, Joe resisted a sudden urge to hug him hard.

"This was for Maria, wasn't it?" Joe backed up till he felt Kyle's bed against the backs of his knees, and dropped onto it, hoping his own sadness hadn't seeped into his question.

Kyle turned from him, going to the window and setting the paint can on its leather-covered, built-in seat.

While he waited, Joe pulled his smartphone from his shorts, lay back on the bed and snapped several panoramic shots. He sat up to check the photos and found Kyle staring at him, face slack, eyes half closed. He swallowed hard, but Kyle spoke first.

"You want to know why she dumped me? We fought about her belly button."

Joe's eyebrows shot up. He forced a neutral expression, watched Kyle's eyes drag across the mural, and waited some more.

"The night before I finished this one, I stayed at Maria's. I woke up early to find her fiddling with her belly button and, one thing leads to another, looks like fun to me, but no, she pushes my hand away. We end up arguing. I leave on the bike, head back here. She doesn't try to stop me, never even tries to apologize. I spend the day finishing this and the fumes stink so bad, I go to Ma's for the night. Next thing I know, Maria calls my cell and says we're done. Her words, her choice. I'm shit, apparently."

"She didn't say you're shit."

Kyle turned back to the window. "What does it matter? It's all shit."

Joe chewed the inside of his cheek, trying to think. He figured Vicky would know what to say now. *Why can't I hear what she'd say?* All he heard was the hard edge to Kyle's next words.

"Anyway. So, help a poor cripple and open this paint." Kyle pressed his fingertips to the sides of the can, brought it over with slow steps, and set it on the bed beside Joe. "Pretty please, with sugar on top?"

"No. I still won't." Joe's voice broke. "Kyle, I'm so damn sorry it fell apart for you guys." He gestured at the walls, the ceiling. "I knew you were into her, but Jesus …"

Kyle's bandaged hand flashed out, held traffic cop style. "Stop."

"Okay. Whatever happened doesn't change that this is … I don't know, a masterpiece. Seriously, man."

"I thought we'd live here." Kyle headed out of the room.

Joe barely caught the muttered "what an idiot" tacked on the end of the sentence. He grabbed the paint and brush and followed Kyle down the hall to the kitchen.

"I was going to ask her." Kyle leaned against a deep granite sink set in front of a tall, paned window that housed an army of jade plants. He tipped his head backwards and added, "Once I finished this."

Joe came close, peering at the walls beside and above the window. Markings, pencil sketches, and short notations stretched around the entire outline.

"She loves nature and crap. The different seasons."

"So do you," Joe mumbled, distracted. "These are so light, hard to make out. They're birds? On skinny little branches?"

"Spring on this side, hummingbirds, finches; winter that side, cardinals and chickadees." Kyle's voice was flat. "Summer green, dragonflies and the colors of fall, pine cones and acorns and shit, in between, above the window."

"You've got a summer project then." Joe stood back nodding and felt the fool grin on his face again. He dumped the brush and paint can on an oak island in the middle of the room. "As soon as your hands heal up."

"Summer? This would take me a few nights, if that."

He watched Kyle extract an iPad and hotspot from a pile of papers on a desk beside the fridge.

"Why bother," Kyle said and headed down the hall to the front door. "Got the keys to lock up?"

Minutes later, as Joe drove by Ma's house, Kyle saluted it with his iPad. "The internet's still more open than she'll ever be."

"How would you know? You hardly use it."

"Give me a sketchpad over an iPad any day."

"So what do you think you'll find that Vicky didn't? You heard her; she searched on Dad and found zip."

"A *librarian* would know where to look for him ... if she cared." Kyle dropped the iPad into the car's foot well and threw a glare over his shoulder. "Ma doesn't need to though. She knows. She drives me *nuts*."

Joe tensed and searched for something to say, then just drove in silence.

Kyle grunted. "You know when she dropped my gear off yesterday? She told me she and Maria have a lot in common, that they'd be seeing each other."

Joe slowed to let a raccoon waddle across the road after flashing a look of dark disdain their way.

"What kind of mother makes a point of hanging out with her son's ex after he's been dumped?" Kyle squinted at the road ahead.

Joe came up blank again. He shook his head and turned into the lane to the cabin. It did sound pretty bad.

"She doesn't care if that same ex, despite knowing there was a crash, involving injuries and a totaled bike, never even stopped by out of simple courtesy. What kind of—"

"Looks like that might not be the case any longer. Look who's climbing off her bike just ahead of us there?" Joe couldn't decipher the expression on Kyle's face—pain? fear? fury?—but knew he wouldn't want to spend time in front of it.

"You get out. I've got stuff to do in the barn after I put this baby to bed." He leaned over and opened Kyle's door, then pulled back from the hissed, "I can do it!"

As he parked the car inside, he sent them both a mental wish for luck. *I think you're going to need it.*

# Chapter Seven
## June 27th

Kyle stayed at the edge of the drive, trying to think then trying not to think. There she stood, kickass legs and curves, in her favorite Hawaiian print shorts and a long blue tank top. She pulled off her bicycle helmet, clipped it to her handlebars, and shook out her hair. His stomach flipped. Then he was angry.

*Here it is Tuesday night. I was in the emergency room Sunday. You're only bothering now?*

He erased his face of all expression and stood where he was, waiting for her to come out of her music world. She tipped her head one way, then another, pulling her earbuds from her ears then hanging them around her neck. He saw the moment she became aware of him there; a look of genuine pleasure lit her face but didn't last long.

She flexed her wrists and pulled at the edge of the tank top. Staring at his bandages, and finally at his face, she came up and offered a quiet hello.

Kyle nodded and kept his eyes on hers, saw her swallow and glance toward the barn as Joe revved an engine. She looked in need of sleep; faint bruising tinged the skin beneath her eyes.

"I came by yesterday morning, but no one was around. Maybe you were sleeping?" she asked, head cocked in that way she had.

He shrugged. "Drugged up." He felt a little leap of satisfaction at the pain that flickered across her face.

"I talked to the admin at school yesterday—Tammy? She said she'd been trying to reach you about scheduling the planning meeting for the fall term, and when she couldn't get you on your cell ..."

"My cell is toast."

"I know. Tammy figured we'd be together, so she called me—"

"Her mistake."

"Ummm ... well, she ... didn't know." She shifted her feet and adjusted her shirt's skinny strap. "When I told her about the accident—not about us though—she wanted to send you flowers, but figured that might be too girly. So ... she wanted me to tell you hurry up and get well so you can ... enjoy your summer."

Kyle resisted making a scoffing noise.

He wondered why Maria hadn't jumped in to announce their breakup but wasn't about to ask that. Her voice was changing as she talked, like water trickling down a drain. It didn't sound like her.

"Since you're pretty much the key player in the art department, she won't set the meeting date until you say you feel up to it. She asked for you to let her know."

"Well, that's good. Thanks for relaying the message." He considered offering his fingertips for a handshake to wrap things up. He thought he might.

"Oh Kyle, that's not why I'm here. Well, partly …" She shook her head.

It looked as if she gave a little shiver. *Why the hell is she frustrated?* He wondered.

"I mean, I wanted to tell you that, but I could have rung Vicky, you know … or had your mother tell you. I knew you wouldn't make it easy. But, there's no way I could know you were hurt and not come see you."

He shrugged as best he could and said nothing.

"I hate that you're hurt." She swallowed hard, her brow furrowed. "It's my fault, isn't it?"

Kyle had to look away from the pain that filled those huge eyes of hers. There was a hard, hot lump of anger and tears in him, all his words clogging up behind it. He had words to hurt her more, words to beg her not to feel bad, to say he was an idiot. And nothing was coming out. His eyes narrowed, roamed the sky and the yard, then flicked over her face again. A movement caught his eye.

"Doughnut!" Sauntering out of the barn like a runway model, that scrawny cat couldn't have been more welcome; he fought an urge to go and collect her up against his cheek.

Maria knelt on the grass cooing her hello and Doughnut sped up, trotting straight to her waggling fingers.

"Oh, she's beautiful." She rubbed the tiny, ginger-colored head with two fingertips. "Is she Joe's?" She looked up at Kyle, her dark eyes sparkling through a sheen of tears.

*Jesus, girl. You're beautiful.* Kyle tried to fix his gaze on Doughnut, saw the cat's boneless ecstasy under Maria's touch, and studied the barn instead.

"Yeah. She adopted him apparently."

"Doughnut, eh? What a perfect name for a sweet kitty." She bent lower and kissed the tip of an ear. "I wonder what happened to her poor little eye?"

"She's not saying."

Maria chuckled and stood. "Poor baby."

Doughnut snaked around Kyle's ankles. Not trusting his voice, he leaned down to rub her head and found the fur ruffed up. He wandered to the picnic table, acutely aware of Maria following him.

She stopped when he did. "I need to tell you something."

*Damn, now what?* Kyle turned and looked down into her face, trying to read those dark, wet eyes. He slotted himself onto the bench seat, hoping she wouldn't choose to sit beside him and was thrilled when she did.

"Remember the other morning in bed? When you started messing with my belly button and I shut you down?"

He studied her eyes. Was she was going to apologize, take it all back? Well, he sure wasn't ready to make it easy. "You got all uptight thinking you didn't have your cute innie anymore."

"And you flounced off like a diva on a film set." She smiled and nudged his shoulder. Kyle felt a frisson run down the side of his body, glad she'd sat next to his good shoulder. "Not that you flouncing off was such a unique occurrence."

"I never fl—"

"Anyway," she said, "so you remember when I mean—"

"Jesus, Maria. It was Saturday morning. You dumped me Sunday. I remember. I thought you actually had something new to—"

"Hang on! Hang on and let me talk. Please."

He bowed his head, swept a bandaged hand through the air, and heard her stifle a sigh.

"Kyle, I was worried I was pregnant."

His head snapped up and his stomach did a flip-flop. He stared at her, waiting.

"I didn't know … you know, innies, outies. I heard your belly button changes when you're pregnant." She laughed at herself and Kyle's heart leapt at the sound. "What do I know? None of my friends have had kids yet."

*What the hell? Did you freak out and dump me because you're pregnant?*

"So that morning, when you thought I was playing with my belly button, I was noticing I was getting kinda flabby. I like my flat stomach. And work hard to keep it."

His own seemed to be filling with Mexican jumping beans. He wanted to tell her no woman alive has a sexier stomach, but the words got crowded then lost behind a parade of intoxicating images.

"I started worrying. So that day I got a home test and …"

*Ma must already know!* he thought. *That'd be why she said she and Maria would be spending time together. The toy she stashed outta sight so fast tonight? That was for my baby? My baby? Jesus Christ!*

He could understand Maria being scared. They'd never talked about having kids, never gone near that kind of thing. They both loved kids, though. He was nuts about her. They both had work. Twenty-eight was a good age to become a dad.

Kyle turned on the bench, thinking, *as soon as she says it I'm going to hug her so hard. This is wild!*

"… I learned I wasn't."

"What?" He blinked once. "Wait." He shook his head. "Was? Was not? You're not?"

"No. I'm not." She had been picking at a wood splinter on the table's edge. She glanced at him. Her eyes filled with confusion, and she looked away fast. "Apparently I've just put on weight from too much Dairy Queen and so much time on the back of your Suzuki instead of my bicycle."

Kyle stood up, checked the level of the seed in the bird feeder at the edge of the yard. An image projected in his mind: her face full of joy as she gazed up at their laughing son held like an airplane above her.

"So this is the news you came to tell me?" His voice hardened with hurt; he kept his back to her. "That you're not pregnant. When I never thought you were?"

He just caught her whisper. "I wanted to explain why I broke up with you."

The child's face dimmed. The lingering joy bled out and flattened, the image faded and disappeared. His throat filled with a dull ache, as if he had swallowed the pain in her voice. He turned back to her. The dusk settling on the yard stole the details of her face. A firefly lit up near her shoulder.

He walked closer and, seeing her clearly, caught his breath. She was swallowing hard and blinking, her eyes fixed on the table. He'd hurt her again.

"Sorry, honey," he mumbled.

She raised her eyes, dark pools of mournfulness and surprise. "You know that might be the first time you ever apologized to me for … anything."

He felt a clutch of grief inside his stomach, followed by a rushing wave of hope. He wished he could see her face better, but the evening had grown very dim.

"So, Sunday … you kinda freaked out?" He sat back down beside her. Not too close. "And now you're … okay … does that mean we're … that we—"

In the shadows he could just make out her eyes opening even wider. It took too long for her to answer. His stomach clutched again.

"Ummm … what I'm saying is the … pregnancy scare showed me something. I want kids, for sure. So … if I wasn't thrilled to think of having a baby with you, then …" Her voice grew softer, he struggled to catch her words. "… we shouldn't really be together."

He sat up straight, cast a glance toward the barn, light and music now spilling from the doors. Where was Doughnut?

"I mean we …"

"Hey, no, this is great, Maria." Hearty, announcer voice. "Thanks for coming by to twist the knife. Everything's clear now."

He slapped a mosquito on his face, felt his injured hand protest, and felt her jump in the dark next to him. "Perfect. This is great. You're a gem." He quickly stood, stifling a groan at the sudden stabbing in his left hip..

Yellow light poured from the porch, carrying Vicky's cheerful voice across the yard to them. "Ice cream, you two? I stopped into House of Flavors today. So I have here some Blue Moon and some Michigan Pot hole. Woohoo."

Kyle froze, staring from the shadows into the glow.

Maria stirred first, bringing him to life. He spotted Doughnut stalking Vicky's trailing shoelace and, ignoring the pain, swooped forward to scoop the cat up to his good shoulder.

Vicky stopped several steps away, backlit by the porch light, and awkwardly presented a tray crowded with a couple of squatty jars and four sweating bowls of ice cream. "Umm, I read this all wrong, didn't I? This is—not a good time?"

"No, no! Great timing, Vick. Couldn't be better."

"Thanks, but no, Vicky." Maria came out of the gloom. "I'm off ice cream for a while. Time I headed home."

"Your work here is done, right?" Kyle kept his voice low and neutral. Still, Maria jolted and Vicky winced. *Direct hit.*

Then Joe was there, wiping his hands on a rag, enthusing over Vicky and the ice cream, Doughnut and the shoelaces, telling Maria how nice it was to see her. Filling the silence.

Maria strapped on her bike helmet and pulled on a reflective jacket.

"I can give you a lift, Maria. The bike will fit in back of something in there." Joe jerked his head toward the barn. "It'll be pitch black before you're home."

"No. I'm good." She kept her eyes averted from everyone and focused on clicking her headlamp on. Her words came in a rush then. "I need the exercise. There's never much traffic out here, you know, and I have my trusty—" her voice choked. She dipped her head and finished, barely audible. "Sorry. I've got to go."

She mounted her bike, started to push off then paused and rolled backwards to where Kyle stood. Lit now from the barn and the porch light, one foot resting on the pedal, she looked into his eyes. He glanced away and studied Doughnut's purring face, so close to his tight jaw.

"What I wanted most was to make amends. To say I'm sorry for how I went about it the other day." She was whispering again, the same voice he'd heard from his pillow only last week. "This didn't go how I'd hoped either. I just wanted to explain and to … to see that you're okay. Well, I know you aren't. You're all bandaged up, but … darn. Oh, man." Her voice choked again, and he turned toward the porch steps, holding Doughnut against his shoulder.

He let the screen door bang closed on Maria's shaky "I'm sorry, Kyle," and wondered if he only imagined the words.

A True Oldies song filled the cabin, this time some surfy song about California sun. His body throbbing with pain beneath his bandages, he felt the storm in him rising to meet the music, threatening to implode and destroy anything near him.

"So, Doughnut, for your own good …" Squinting against the light, he placed the cat on the worn, living room carpet and rubbed away the tear that had dripped from his jaw onto the crown of her head. "Get away from me; I'm a fucking loser!" He hurled the last word and a fat couch cushion toward the loft stairs.

Doughnut froze. Then, neck extended like a turtle, crept to the cushion and sniffed it with great care. She climbed into its soft middle and, kneading and purring, aimed a quizzical gaze straight up at Kyle.

Something between a sob and his barking laugh burst from deep within him.

Startled again, the cat's mouth dropped open, showing just the front edge of her curled pink tongue. Kyle laughed.

"Oh, my God. I can't believe you." He scooped her up again, whispering into her fur, "Poor pillow. Six-foot-two and I'm whaling on a defenseless pillow. Thank you, Doughnut."

Nuzzling the purring cat against his hastily dried cheek, he returned to Vicky and Joe at the picnic table. Looking sheepish with four half-empty bowls of ice cream in front of them, they seemed to be waiting for him.

"So I might try that Eagala thing tomorrow, Vick."

"Sounds good." Her voice was perfect, gentle without a hint of patronizing.

"Good night, you both." He turned back to the cabin, paused and glanced over his shoulder. "Don't dream."

Joe beamed at him. "Good night. Don't dream."

Vicky didn't reply.

# Chapter Eight
## June 28th

Joe toed open the interior door to the porch and glanced to his right. A slow smile spread across his face. Still in the camisole and girls' boxers she slept in, Vicky sat chuckling at the chipmunks and squirrels zig-zagging through the yard and hunting for breakfast or whatever they did. Cross-legged in a nest of sheets, she looked as rumpled as the oversized couch they'd been using for their bed since Kyle's arrival.

He offered her the red Formica tray he held. "Here ya go, hottie, 'breakfast in couch' … a mug of glug—one third hazelnut creamer, two thirds coffee—and toast that's hardly toasted with just a shadow of jam."

"Perfect. Thanks." She took the tray onto her lap and lifted her face for her kiss, eyes still twinkling, a crease from a sheet not yet faded from her cheek. "The chippies and such don't know what to make of that big, old car hauler in the driveway." She sipped her coffee. "Hey, Joe, I was thinking: when are you going to invest in your own hauler? You wouldn't need to keep making the trip home to rent one, then have to drive back to wherever you've bought cars from."

"Haulers are for the big guys. I've been lucky, but I can't just assume I'll keep finding clients and keep winning the bids on the cars they're looking for. Sorry, babe, I've got to head out now." Joe turned and went back inside the cabin, aware that Vicky was abandoning her breakfast to follow him in.

"No? Why not? You've been doing it for years now." Despite the teasing laugh, he knew her words were serious.

"I don't know, Vick. It's like tempting fate."

"Joe!" Her breath came out as a sigh, and the laughter was gone. "That's just nuts. What do you mean fate?"

Vicky stood inside the doorway as he moved around the cabin, pouring coffee into a Thermos, gathering paperwork from the roll-top desk, pocketing keys and wallet. She grabbed the hem of his T-shirt to stop him.

"You always do your homework, you know where to go, and what to bid on. You're doing well, Joe." She poked a finger into his stomach. "Trust that. Make it easier on yourself."

He kissed her full on the mouth. "Shh … Vick, that all sounds like dreaming."

"Right, your 'don't dream' mantra." She flung her arms up in the air and followed him onto the porch. "I really wish you and Kyle would quit with saying that. Act like the successful businessman you are."

Joe stared at her for a second, trying to read what was bugging her. "It's all good, hon. I don't mind. This is working fine. It means I can stop on my way through Muskegon and see Grandma again, too." He turned and let himself out of the cabin into the cool morning. In the yard, squirrels and chipmunks scattered and bounded into the woods. Wondering whether Kyle stood any chance of still sleeping, he held the edge of the screen door to keep it from banging.

Vicky slipped through and stopped on the top step beside him, bare arms hugging herself. "You *can* take a break from visiting Grandma today, you know. Don't you think three times a week is a lot to keep up for this long?"

Joe patted her on the backside, then jumped down the stairs in one leap.

"You're not hearing me, are you? You don't have to be a saint, Joe."

"Don't I?" He called over his shoulder, striding toward the car hauler Tommy and Jocko had picked up earlier from the garage on US 10.

"When did you become a smart ass?" Vicky's quiet question carried in the morning stillness.

"I didn't." He unlocked the transporter and swung up into the cab, then rolled the window down. "I thought I had to be."

"Had to be what?" He heard the impatience edging her words.

"A saint, Vicky." The engine roared into life. He raised his voice to carry, but kept his tone light—this was getting a little close to the bone. "Who would love me otherwise?"

He waved and eased down the narrow drive. She wasn't smiling, but she didn't look pissed off either.

*A saint?* he thought. *Damn. Let's get some tunes in here. Static today. What gives? So they brought the truck with the bum radio—grief from all directions. And I had to go and forget my iPod on top of it all.*

Joe stretched across to roll down the passenger window, turned onto Jebavy, and picked up speed, willing Rusty to still be tucked in bed with Ginny instead of aiming a speed camera at him. He'd learned as a teenager, when cranking tunes failed, fast driving and the wind from the open car windows kept his mind clear. All three together were best. But … not feeling a bit inclined to go back to the cabin and that conversation meant a tuneless trip to Grand Rapids today.

Just outside of Whitehall, he spotted signs announcing a slow zone for a road repair crew.

He dropped his speed and Vicky's voice floated over the rushing wind in his ears.

*You can take a break from visiting Grandma today, you know.*

*So,* he thought, *that topic's right up there—tied in fact—as the most disturbing.*

Searching his mindscape for somewhere safe to land, he fiddled with the radio dials again and remembered Kyle's remark about his loyalty to oldies, then saw Maria poised on her bike and whispering, Kyle charging into the cabin and Maria about to start bawling.

*Without a doubt, seeing Kyle so in love has to be a first,* Joe thought. *How rotten that Maria doesn't feel the same. After those works of art he created for her that she never even saw … and now probably never will.*

*Would the murals have done it for her? If she'd seen how much Kyle loved her, the amazing, full-color evidence all over his kitchen and bedroom, would she have stayed with him? Would Kyle have earned her love then?*

"Ok, maybe not such a good topic."

Pulling the hauler to a noisy stop at the temporary red light, he leaned over, stuck his right hand under the dash to feel for loose wires, and let his fingertips become his eyes. He concentrated on what they showed him, staring through the windshield without seeing, his cheek resting on the dash. The iconic gumball light atop the vehicle stopped in the oncoming lane broke through his spell as the light changed to green. He sat up fast.

*Uh-oh. Yes, hello. Not staring at you, Officer Friendly. Sitting up, two hands—I'm with it. I'm sane, for real.*

The policeman locked eyes with him, one brow raised as they passed each other. Joe put on his friendliest grin, making sure to take it steady and easy.

*A ticket's the last thing I need today,* he thought. *Okay, so …no tunes, no distractions. Go ahead—what the hell—think. How bad can it be?*

> *Grandma shuffled to the kitchen table with a smile of love on her face, rested her hand on his shoulder as she'd done hundreds of time before, and carefully poured a generous dollop of bleach into his coffee. She turned and made her way back across the floor.*
>
> *"Grandma! What are you doing?"*
>
> *Startled, she froze, hunched in front of the open refrigerator and hugged the jug of bleach to her chest.*

That was how bad thinking could get: remembering the day he'd lost his childhood champion, his rock. His memories kept running. With a vague awareness of still driving, he felt he'd been thrown onto autopilot, helpless to do anything but remember.

*He leapt from his chair and made an effort to gentle down his actions as he took the bleach from her and led her to the table. Her eyes were filled with fear and confusion, then, after he explained her mistake, she looked as if she were drowning in sadness. She moved to the door, wrapped an old wool shirt of Grandpa's around her shoulders and made her way out of the cabin. While she pulled weeds and planted pansies the rest of the morning, Joe had stayed inside, raging and swearing and crying.*

    *By the time she came in to sit across from him at the kitchen table again, she had made up her mind. "I'm a danger now, Joe. We need to make some changes."*

"Changes," Joe thought. *Such an innocuous word, it didn't sound so bad. It didn't sound like, say, "poison" or "toxic" or "abusive." But changes so often seemed to be portals to oceans of grief, to loss, and pain.*

Look at all the changes to his world since that day. The woman he'd loved since he first formed memories of the world had moved out of his daily life. First, a "geographic" to the assisted memory care home she had chosen. Then, worse—and little by little—to a place effectively beyond his, or anyone else's, reach. And he'd known it was going to happen, the second he'd seen—smelled—that bleach. Even before the specialists' tests had acknowledged her dementia was likely to be Alzheimer's, even before he knew anything about the disease, even while he was arguing with her that day, trying to convince her, as well as himself, that he could still look after her and keep her safe, he'd known everything was going to change irrevocably. They'd stepped onto a moving sidewalk. Whether they tried to run the other direction, or simply agreed to stand still and hang on, they were going to be steadily ferried away from what they'd known up until that day, inexorably, insidiously brought closer to today.

Today, two years later, his grandmother—more mother to him than his real mother—was living in room number 319 in Muskegon's finest memory care unit. With Grandpa taken by a massive heart attack four years ago, Joe was living full-time in the cabin where he'd spent most of his early life with the two of them. Where he'd been cuddled and cajoled and nurtured after having been left there—for reasons no one would divulge—by his mother on his first birthday, then just as strangely snatched back by his father three years later. Throughout all his school years, he'd gone—or tried to go—to the cabin and his grandparents first, to announce any news or prize or insult. With them, as reliably as finding the big, scarred desk in the corner of the living room and the worn carpet in the hallway, he'd known he'd find attentive, curious, warm interest, and joy, humor, and love.

His parents' words came to him, braided through the memories of those years, the caveats he'd always heard: *it was all his, as long as he was* good.

*If you're good, you can go to Grandma and Grandpa's.*

*How do you think Grandma and Grandpa would like to hear you talking like that ... see you scowling like that?*

*Your mother tells me you've been bad, I don't think Grandma and Grandpa are going to want a bad boy visiting.*

*With behavior like that, Mister, you can kiss your weekend working with Grandpa good-bye, right now.*

*Until and unless you shape up, you won't be seeing your grandparents at all. Do you think they'd want a lazy, selfish boy like you around?*

"Okay! Enough! Cork it!" Joe slammed his open hand against the steering wheel; the pain and noise broke him out of autopilot. Finding himself in a near empty parking lot, he gaped at the islands of well-groomed trees dotted around, the familiar yellow brick building in front of him. He searched out the second window on the third floor and leaned forward to anchor himself.

*Made it, Grandma, I don't know how I got here, but I'll be up as soon as I park this monster. It'll be good to see you.*

Inside her curtain-dark room, Joe crouched at her bedside and gently collected her right hand into both of his. He breathed in the powdery scent of her skin, held her fingers against his cheek.

"Ready to wake up yet, Grandma?" he whispered. "Want some lotion? That lemon one you like? Your favorite, summer one."

She lay still and small, sunken into her pillow; the sound of her sleeping breaths weaving through the trilling bird songs from just beside her window.

Joe stroked her forehead, talking low. "I forgot to bring our music this morning, but I'll remember next time. See I have bad days, too. Today's one of those. But we can put your radio on if you like, and I want to talk about you now, okay? I want to hear how you slept, what you're looking forward to doing today."

There! The pale blue eyes were now fastened to his. She lay just as she was, not smiling or moving.

"Well hello, gorgeous. Nice to see you. Do you have time to have breakfast with me or should I book you for lunch?" He stroked her cheek. "Is that a smile? Yes. You're thinking maybe both are a good idea?"

A movement beneath the covers at her shoulder caught his eye, he lifted the yellow quilt slightly to free her other hand. It approached his own cheek, rested there, then floated back to the quilt. He covered it lightly.

"Bobby," she whispered.

These days, she often asked for Grandpa.

"Yes, it's Bobby," he lied.

"Bobby." She closed her eyes, her thin lips moving for a moment. The soft sound of her breathing returned.

"Okay. So you and Bobby have a date. He'll be back at noon." Joe finished the sentence silently: *in case you happen to remember this plan, I'll be Grandpa for you. But I wish I knew how old Bobby is to you now … how old you both are now.*

He laid her hand on the quilt covering her chest and leaned back into the easy chair beside her bed. Faded, green, and welcoming, the chair's twin—he'd always think of it as Grandpa's chair—remained in the cabin, squatting beside the living room floor lamp. This one, hers, had always been tucked close to the fireplace until they'd moved it in here with her two years ago.

It felt too quiet in her room today. Without music to hang onto, his thoughts were on the verge of free falling again. He'd always been able to keep them in careful check and not just because the nursing staff advised him to now, for Grandma's sake. But, thanks to her, all through his childhood, he'd tried to pull up memories of banter and laughter.

Countless times she'd told him: *Think positive thoughts, Joey, cultivate an attitude of gratitude. 'Count your blessings' might sound old-fashioned, but it really can make you feel better.*

Without exception, his best times as a child had been with her and Grandpa, in the cabin, or anywhere. Now those times centered around Vicky.

Today, though, something kept niggling at him, and he couldn't get past it. He also couldn't quite put a finger on what it was—nor did he really want to.

*You don't have to be a saint, Joe.*

Where did that come from? That was Vicky, not Grandma.

*I thought I did. Who would love me otherwise?*

His hand shot to the dials on the bedside radio, then he stopped himself. It would be tuned to the oldies station, matched to the era she returned to. He knew she loved that music. In fact, she'd infected him with her love of it at a young age. Still, he couldn't very well blast it while she was lying there asleep. He wished he'd brought a photo album or a magazine like he often did. Brushing her hair while she slept was all he could think to do for her, but then he pictured hurling her hairbrush to the floor. He pushed up from her chair, fast.

"Sorry, Grandma," he whispered urgently, speaking against her forehead. "Bobby will be back for lunch. But Joe, who no longer exists in your world, has to get his mood far away from you before you feel it—definitely to somewhere with noise to fill his head."

He'd almost made it to Grand Rapids before he was pulled over for speeding. *At least*, he reasoned, *it wasn't the cop from Whitehall.*

# Chapter Nine
## June 28<sup>th</sup>

"Okay, ready Kyle? For now, just go introduce yourself to whichever horse—or horses—you want to. See how it goes."

Thinking he was alone at the edge of the arena, Kyle almost jumped at the sound of Mel's voice. While she was in the cabin grabbing a coffee and, he presumed, consulting with Vicky, he'd been standing cataloguing the colors and tones and shades around him. He needed his paints. And two hands that worked.

Although the sun had risen a couple hours ago, the light, the cool air, and the mood of the morning felt soft. Shadows stretched across the still dewy grass. Bird song and the occasional nickering of a horse brought color to the stillness. Kyle locked the scene in his mind and turned his attention to Mel. He wondered if she'd been born dressed in tiny boots and jeans, with her red hair in a ponytail. Beside her, also sipping coffee, stood the short-haired woman Mel had introduced earlier as Juliet, their "very welcome, summer intern." The woman looked so petite that, at first glance, he'd mistaken her for a child.

Now, Mel checked that Kyle had followed her instructions to wear sturdy boots in the arena. She nodded toward the appaloosa and the palomino grazing a little ways off in the paddock. He recognized the palomino from the demo; a third horse in the distance might have been the chestnut that had also been there.

"Spend as long as you like with whichever one—or all of them," Mel said. "Then come join us when you feel acquainted, and we'll explain the next step."

"So, I just … what? Wander out there and say, 'hay'?" He flashed his crooked grin.

Mel blew a strand of hair off her face and took a sip from the steaming mug cradled in her hands. Juliet didn't respond either.

Kyle turned away and rolled his eyes, more amused than annoyed.

*Not my best effort maybe, but not a bad joke for so early in the morning—especially right on the heels of my first solo scrubbing session.*

With Joe in Grand Rapids collecting yesterday's car purchases, Kyle had decided to take back his dignity and get used to showering without help. It had been a real prick and he'd probably not reached everywhere that needed ointment, but given the fresh bandages felt secure enough, he thought he hadn't done half bad. At least he wasn't trailing gauze like some molting mummy.

He'd also cut back on his pain meds as an experiment and felt good, not wired, but alert enough. He hoped he'd stay that way. Following Mel's suggestion and taking his time, he directed his steps toward the palomino mare. She'd wandered away from the appaloosa and had been staring at him since he'd clicked the gate of the arena behind him. He pictured her and the antics he'd seen the day before. Though it felt silly, he couldn't help wondering if this mare recognized him, too.

He heard Mel talking to the intern in low tones, reminding her it was important to never steer a client to any particular horse because the therapy started with that step. He slowed his pace to hear more. She said the client's choice usually meant something to them and fed into the metaphors that would develop throughout the session. Also, the horses that responded would be doing so for a reason—something in the client's energy would resonate with the horse and attract them to the client, or not.

Kyle decided he'd track Vicky down later and get to the bottom of how this stuff worked, wishing again she'd agreed to run this session. She'd flatly refused, saying it didn't fit Eagala's ethical standards for her to work with her boyfriend's brother. He admired her being such a stickler with the rules, but still … he felt pretty self-conscious walking across the paddock as Mel and Juliet's "client."

He pictured turning around and saying, "Hey, sorry, but let's forget it. I don't want to do this after all." But, as his thoughts churned, his feet kept moving forward, his dusty boots taking him farther from the women.

*I could blame Doughnut; say, "I don't need the horses, the cat got to me first." Ha. But I told Vicky I wanted a session. That's no reason I have to go through with this … whatever— voodoo? That pair at the demo, and that Gordy kid, what happened to them just wasn't natural. They went off the deep end. Besides, I'm fine.*

An image flashed through his mind: Maria, beside him at the picnic table in the gloomy dusk, distraught and stumbling through her words.

*No, I'm not fine! Maria wants kids, but not with me. In a year, more than a year, I never said "sorry" to her for anything—seriously? Joe's asking why I'm always angry at the world. I can't have a civil conversation with Ma—don't even last five minutes with her. And my dad seems happy to have nothing to do with me, even online.*

Something drew his gaze up from the scuffed grass, and he found a pair of dark, soulful eyes locked on his. *Maria!* He laughed at himself. *But this horse so has Maria's eyes,* he thought, … *and that silky, long forelock—that's Maria's blond hair.*

He shook his head, raked his fingers through his own hair, and stopped in his tracks. The mare shook her head exactly as long as he had, stopped, and resumed her steady gaze.

"Really?" he asked quietly. "Like this?" He shook his head again. Disappointed, he scoffed at himself when she stayed still. But she didn't break her gaze.

"No games then. Okay. What? Just: 'hello?'" With the halting pace of a bridesmaid, he walked closer, then stopped and admired the picture she made. As if holding her breath, she stood, a statue of calm against a background of pines that waved a quiet welcome to the day.

*What a morning.*

Kyle closed the space between them. Her nostrils flared as she tried to take in his scent. He presented the back of his hand just below her nose and grinned when whiskered velvet brushed his skin.

"You need a bit of a shave, darlin'. Just there and there—nothing major."

He glanced over his shoulder at Mel and Juliet. Despite the fact they were watching him intently, he felt reluctant to call out, to ask the mare's name. He turned back to her, putting his body between her face and the two women.

"So, beauty, what's your name?" He dropped his voice even lower. "You are just gorgeous, you know. You remind me of Maria." He reached up and gently stroked the heavy forelock covering the plane of bone between her tautly upright ears; it parted to reveal more of the stark white blaze that ran from her forehead all the way down to her muzzle. "Beautiful, gentle, and strong … So, are you going to make me love you and then leave me?"

He let his fingertips trail along the warm, twitching swell of the horse's face, to the muscle of her neck, resting them there. The world seemed to focus into that moment and that touch. She exuded innocence, strength, attentiveness. He breathed in her scent, a mix of sweet hay, dust and something like herbs, then took a deeper whiff to get more of it and stepped slightly closer.

"Wow."

Kyle directed his thoughts to her watching eyes: *Are you reading my mind? I can see why you pull us poor suckers in. Like Maria, right? No, sorry. You're no game player, are you? Sorry. And she wasn't either, was she? It was me right, Maria Horse? That's what you want to tell me. It was me?*

From the corner of his eye, he saw the chocolate and white appaloosa that had been watching from the far edge of the field, now hovering just a few yards to his left. Not moving from Maria Horse, he addressed the spotted horse out loud.

"And hello, who's this—Ma, maybe? Eavesdropping on a private conversation again? That's right, don't come too close, keep your distance. Keep your secrets.

Like about Dad." He squared his shoulders and felt his chin jerk higher. "So where is he, Ma? Eh? Ever going to tell us what happened on that ski trip and why we haven't seen or heard from him since?" Kyle followed Ma's gaze as she turned to the right and saw the chestnut horse, proud and powerfully built, staring into the distance.

"Ah, so is that Dad over there? Checking out greener pastures?" His stomach lurched. "Who left who, I wonder."

Kyle felt tears well up, then velvet prickles on his face as the palomino nuzzled his cheek. The gesture undid him. Tears flowing, he leaned his forehead against the solid expanse between her eyes and struggled not to sob. She stayed still.

The quiet warmth of her breath against his throat and chest calmed him. Gently raising his arms around her head, he clasped his hands up high between her ears. She simply stood, alert but relaxed. Like she was being as careful with him as he was with her; like she was tuned in to him.

*When we were small, Ma used to kneel down and do this with us,* he thought to her. *She'd call these head hugs.* He let his face roll to the side and his eyes grew wide. The appaloosa, Ma, stood tossing her head as if she were laughing. Kyle caught his breath. *Laughing?* His arms still around Maria Horse, his face against her shoulder, he stared at the other mare.

*We got so few of those hugs,* he thought. *But jeez, Ma, they did make us laugh.*

Distinct as a pebble dropped into his hand, he felt the word, *"Yummy."*

It was his turn to laugh, right from his belly. "Damned if I'd ever say that, but yes, you used to call those head hugs 'yummy'—told us we were delicious."

Under his shirt, he felt a shiver wash over him. *I am in the presence of …  something. Is this magic?* He looked into the palomino's eyes. She simply returned his gaze. *When did I stop being delicious, Maria?* In his mind he heard with utter clarity: *"Never."*

*Oh, I did,* he argued. *I got angry and stayed angry. I'm so sick of being angry, Maria … and Ma. What good has it ever done? Pretending to be so tough; it's hurting me. Screwing up my life. Us. Who's gonna say, "yay, anger? Bring it on—I'll have some of that." You were gentle, Maria. You were soft. No wonder it felt so good to be with you. And what soft woman is going to want an angry man to father her child?*

Forehead to forelock now, he continued to whisper, no longer caring what he said, only wanting to keep this connection flowing. Finally, he ran out of words, his mind emptied. He stayed in place until she shifted her weight, then she took the smallest step back, and another. The spotted mare waited as Maria Horse walked to her. The chestnut had moved deeper into the paddock, grazing alone.

Kyle stood in the middle of the arena and watched the two mares, shoulder to shoulder, hindquarters swaying, walk to the fence and begin to graze. For one long moment, Maria Horse paused and looked over her shoulder at him. Ears pricked forward, she dipped her head once.

Kyle nodded back, asking soundlessly, "*To what?*"

The mare broke eye contact and turned away to rip grass from beneath the lower rail of the fence.

Kyle just stood. He took a long, shaky breath, drinking in the beautiful animals who had just touched him so deeply.

Becoming aware of being watched as well, he turned and made his way back to Mel and Juliet. He felt both wiped out and awesome. Calm and happy.

When he reached them, Juliet spoke, her voice gentle and neutral.

"How was that, Kyle?"

Unable to force a word from his constricted throat, Kyle pressed his lips together hard and nodded. He looked over Juliet's shoulder to study the cabin.

"Okay," she said softly. "Mel and I noticed you pretty much spent the session with one horse."

His short laugh sounded out of place, but it woke his voice. "Yeah. Maria Horse."

"You called her 'Maria Horse'? Maria is someone you know?"

Kyle nodded.

"Why did Maria Horse remind you of her?"

"Maria is—was—my girlfriend, until recently. The horse has her eyes and same, you know, sort of hair."

"Any other ways Maria Horse reminded you of Maria?" Juliet asked.

"Yeah. Both woman and horse are gentle, kind, strong, and … gorgeous. We just had a talk."

"You talked?" Mel asked.

"Yeah. Get that. We did. Mostly me. Ha." He ran his hand through his hair. "But, yeah."

"What was that about?" Juliet asked quietly.

"Me." Kyle hesitated. This felt so personal, yet still okay, like he'd been cracked open somehow, and was still—he searched for the right word—*safe*. He went on, "Me being angry all the time; how crap that was for her, us. Me."

"Mm-hmm. And did it lead you anywhere?"

"Kind of, yeah. You know, the appaloosa, she acted like my mother, both good and bad, like eavesdropping on me and Maria Horse."

Juliet's eyes held no judgment, but hearing his own statement, Kyle stopped and stared a moment, hardly seeing her.

"You know, maybe it wasn't eavesdropping. Maybe that's just how I saw it? Maybe it was just … interest. Or concern." Juliet didn't reply and he couldn't read anything in her expression. He continued. "And I remembered stuff I hadn't thought of for years. Hugs between us when I was a kid. It was good to remember."

He scanned the field for the brown and white horse. There. She was still with the palomino, grazing near the river. "I think I'd like to see what she—the appaloosa—has to tell me."

"Sure." Mel checked her watch. "We have another appointment arriving in about twenty minutes. But we can set up a time in a couple days or just play it by ear if you like, try to catch us in a free hour. Whatever suits."

Staring out to the arena, he nodded, imagining the talk with Ma. He wanted that sooner rather than later. And he wanted to talk to Vicky.

He found her engrossed in paperwork at the big desk beneath the living room window but by noon they sat on the upstairs deck of the Blu Moon Bistro. His lousy luck Vicky had chosen that place, Maria's favorite; he saw the moment Vicky seemed to guess that.

She'd been enthusing over all the vegetarian options and how they served their meals in pie tins when "Margaritaville" started playing on the sound system. Before she'd even finished singing "nibbling," she broke off with a glance his way.

"I'm having the smoked turkey and avocado on sourdough—with deck fries!" she announced. "How about you?"

Kyle concentrated on the menu, shutting out the song and memories of Maria singing it. He'd have gone vegetarian for her if she'd asked; she hadn't though. And he hadn't offered. So today, he ordered the Tree Hugger sandwich.

He waited for Vicky to poke fun at him—like he'd always done with Maria, the name invited it. Instead, she launched into a story about Doughnut bulldozing their empty pizza box around the kitchen floor last night before leaping in to rip drips of melted cheese from the cardboard.

They shared an order of onion rings and more Doughnut antics until their meals arrived.

"Gotta support local," Kyle said, raising his Black Cherry Cola to Vicky, glad he could safely hold a glass again despite still being bandaged. He took a swig, smacked his lips, and leaned in. "Okay, so Vick, tell me how this Eagala stuff works."

Vicky smiled and decorated her fries with ketchup. "What do you mean? How?"

"I mean 'how?' Like … I don't know … are horses mind-readers or do they plant thoughts in our brains?"

Vicky chuckled and bit a French fry in half. "So, clearly it worked for you this morning?"

"Yeah, but don't change the subject. Answer my question." He pulled a "yikes" face and tacked on: "Please."

"Okay. It's weird, though, since you're in the midst of the therapy—well, I should ask, not assume. Are you planning to go again?" He gave a quick nod and she carried on. "It's like explaining the special effects in a movie you're about to watch."

"So, it's all contrived then?"

"No. That's not at all what I mean. Sorry. Bad analogy. Okay, I'll try to explain and, as an informed friend, not as a therapist." She took a long drink of raspberry iced tea. "Horses are prey animals, okay? And they have been forever. In the wild they're the hunted, not the hunters. They have to be really tuned in to their environment, really sensitive to what might be a risk or pose a threat. That innate wiring doesn't go away just because they're domesticated. When a person approaches them, they zero right in on our basic energy, any posturing, and, essentially, our bullshit."

Kyle nodded and kept eating, hoping she'd keep talking. After a small bite of her sandwich, she did.

"Horses are one hundred percent who they are, no faking or pretending. They respond to us as we really are underneath, not the act we put on. And if we want them to respond to us in a particular way, to do something we need them to do, we have to be totally authentic or they're going to resist. They don't respond well to split messages or negativity. So, in that way we learn to drop our own façade when we're with them, own up to our truth, and listen to our own inner wisdom. Their sheer size comes into it all, too. It's not like you can bodily shove them into a position or make them do whatever task you set."

"What do you mean, 'task'?"

"Didn't Mel and Juliet work with you to set goals for your session?" With a mouth full of fries, Kyle nodded. "And then invite you to set a task that would let you play out that goal in the arena?"

Kyle shook his head. He realized she'd hardly begun eating while he was halfway through his sandwich; he set it in his pie tin and took a drink. *Selfish again,* he thought. "No. I don't remember anything about a task. We did talk goals, right after they arrived. I said I wanted to understand what went wrong with a particular relationship. Juliet asked me to boil that intention down to a word. I think maybe I said 'self-awareness.'" He dipped his head toward his shoulder with a little shrug.

Vicky tipped her head in reply, a warm smile lighting her face. She peeled some Gouda off her sandwich and popped it in her mouth.

"I think initially I was just supposed to go say 'hay' to the horses." Kyle waited a beat and Vicky laughed, her hand covering her mouth. "But I ended up staying out there the whole time and didn't come back to them. I went and used up my whole session on the intro."

"That's fine. There aren't many hard and fast rules in Eagala; the client is in charge. There is a distinct structure though and, within that, a few strict no-nos."

He asked around another bite of his sandwich, "Like?"

"Like, it's strictly ground-based, no riding involved. It's not about riding skills or horsemanship—"

"Yep, Mel made that clear."

"—and the horse has to be an integral part of the therapy. For example, if the session could just as easily have been done in an office, if it becomes 'talk therapy,' then it's not really Eagala. The interaction with the horses and what the client makes of it, that's what fundamental."

"Okay, but why? Why did it feel so powerful?" Kyle stabbed a French fry in the air between them. "Keep talking."

Vicky took a sip of her tea. "Well, because as people we always put meaning to things, our own perspective colors what we make of everything that happens to us and the stories we tell ourselves—and therefore how we relate to the world and to other people. The metaphors that clients develop in the arena are revelatory. Eagala recognizes that."

"Revelatory? Revealing what? Our inner selves? Our way of looking at the world?"

She saluted him with a French fry, then ate it. "You got it. The therapy team can point out factual observation, what we saw the client doing, and note the horses' behavior—you know patterns we observe or discrepancies from the norm—but we have to leave it to the client to make their own interpretations and metaphors. The people in the team absolutely must not guide or unduly influence the interpreting. We carefully help the client to verbalize it, maybe, or probe and encourage—up to a point—but that's it. Taking care to do *only that* takes a lot of skill: clean language—meaning *no* implied judgments, interpretations or assumptions—that's key. If the human part of the therapy team slips up with our language and puts our spin on what happened in the arena between the client and the horse or horses, we can totally blow it. We might see it utterly differently than the client did and that can undo the work or even set some people backwards. At the very least it's disrespectful and not empowering."

Kyle swiped his fingertips against his napkin and raised his right hand to offer a careful high five.

Eyebrows raised in question, Vicky gently tapped his fingertips with hers, then turned her attention to the last of her fries.

Kyle shrugged. "Just 'cause it's really cool—I had no idea how *fast* stuff would happen. And I get now what you 'do' and I'm impressed."

"Well, thanks." Vicky looked genuinely pleased. "It's nice to see a softer side of you, Kyle."

"I don't show it heaps, do I?" He looked around at the other diners, picking out the tourists by the degree of sunburn they had.

"No."

Kyle heard the affection in her voice. Still avoiding her eyes, he dragged his hand through his hair. "Is this going to last?"

"What you got out of today, you mean?"

He nodded. "It happened so fast. That's the weirdest part. It's hard to trust."

"You can trust it. Eagala isn't magic. It feels like that to lots of people—"

"It *does*. I felt cracked open, Vick."

She nodded. "Because it usually works so fast and goes so deep. That's the beauty of it. But that's also why people just hearing about it tend to be skeptical. It's hard to get just how quickly it *can* bring about change … until they try it themselves." She took a long drink of tea, and he waited. "Will what you got from today 'last'? That part's up to you. For some people it gets them over a hurdle; maybe breaking an emotional stalemate was the only nudge they needed to move on a healthier path. For others, it's a crucial starting point—opening up the tough nuts."

With a sideways glance at her, Kyle downed the last of his drink. *Do you put me in the tough nut category?*

She finished, "It gets people ready to delve deeper with other therapy." Her face gave nothing away.

He nodded. "Okay, I know my next question should be 'Like what? What's next for me?' But I can't go there yet." He paused, studying his hummus-smeared pie-tin then looked up and shook his head. "Nope."

Vicky nodded. "Not a problem. It's your pace, your deal. Don't even feel obliged to share any of what comes up for you. It usually helps—we're social creatures. So, some people use talk therapy, and some use journals to put down what they learned and kinda explore what they're feeling. Others use art. That might be perfect for you, Kyle."

"Yeah?" Feeling his intimacy quotient maxed out, he drummed his fingertips on the table. "How're you doing? I'm ready to go." He stopped just short of pushing back from the table and tacked on a polite: "Okay?"

"Ha! There's progress. Thanks, Kyle." She reached for the bill as their server approached. "I want to get this."

*What a long way I have to go.* Kyle stood and stretched, then smiled as a familiar voice piped up.

*"One day at a time."*

*One of Grandma's favorite sayings.* He almost laughed at the memory. *I hear you, Grandma. Pretty much everyone has weighed in today, it seems. And that Tree Hugger? What a seriously good sandwich.*

# Chapter Ten
## June 28th

Joe took in the colorful marina view through P.M. Steamers' wall of windows, admired the brass fittings, and soft lights inside the restaurant, then leaned back to appreciate Vicky for a long minute.

Her gray eyes twinkled at him over the rim of her wine glass and she bobbed her eyebrows at him. He bobbed his back at her and leaned in as if confiding a precious state secret. "You look seriously amazing, lady—so sexy. Red suits you."

"Thank you, sir." She reached across the table and squeezed his hand. "I think it's the first chance I've had to wear this dress."

As she surveyed the high-ceilinged room and the diners around them, he caught himself chewing the inside of his cheek and stopped. *So far, so good,* he decided. It seemed their surprise dinner-out might smooth whatever had ruffled her feathers that morning.

"Isn't that beautiful?" Vicky pointed, peering far above their table. A wooden rowboat hung displayed among the dark wooden rafters. "I don't know the last time we ate in a place like this."

"You could probably count them on one hand."

He listened to her describe her day, watching a parade of expressions cross her face, and realized how easy it had always been to be with her. More than anything he wanted it to stay that way. Easy. She offered him a bite of her risotto.

"Today's my lucky day," she said. "This is the second time a Carson man took me out to eat."

"Kyle got you lunch?" Joe rubbed his thumb over water drops on his bottle of beer. "Why's that?"

"Actually, I treated him." Vicky redirected a forkful of his wild mushroom meatloaf her way. "I had to celebrate the new Kyle I saw today."

"So, his session went well?"

"Seems so … but that's as much as I'll say." She mimed locking her lips closed and dropped the invisible key into Joe's water glass.

"I know: 'confidentiality.'" Joe peered wistfully into his glass, wishing the key was real and he could use it, a wish he'd made countless times since she'd started working as a therapist three years ago and stopped being the open book she'd been in high school. But while he often thought that, he'd never say it.

"It sucks about him and Maria splitting up; first Ma and Dad, now them." He paused and added, "Too bad Maria didn't see those masterpieces Kyle painted for her."

"Why? You're thinking his murals would've made everything okay?"

"Well. Yeah." Chewing, he studied Vicky's expression. "Maybe," he tried. "No?"

Vicky gave her head a soft shake; her hair tumbled then settled around her shoulders. "Kyle would've had to have done a lot more to hang onto that one."

"She told you stuff?"

"No. I liked her, but we never really hung out." Vicky thought for a second. "She and Kyle were hardly ever apart, were they?"

"So why do you say he needed to do more?" An uneasy feeling had started in Joe's stomach; he finished his second beer and hoped their server would come soon to offer another.

"As in be different with her. I know we only saw them a few times, but it was enough. At least twice I heard him say 'buzz kill!' and shut down something she was saying." She ate her last morsel of risotto and made a wide-eyed, yum face at her plate.

"But he would have been joking." Joe almost added, *I hope.*

"You didn't see Maria's face when he said it."

"I don't remember the time."

Vicky shook her head and he recognized her "of course you don't, you goof" look.

"Anyway, I don't like talking about people behind their backs." She poked his hand. "What about *your* day? Did you get a hauler?"

His stomach sank. He leaned into the path of a passing server and, with a grin that bordered on a grimace, held up his empty beer bottle. "Another of the same, please?"

A strange look clouded Vicky's face for a moment. As she started to say something, he hurried to answer her question, "'No' to the hauler, but I did get all the cars and had lunch with Grandma. It's great that she's right on the way to the auction house."

"Say again, Joe, why'd your family choose a place for her so far from here? I never understood; why not in Ludington?"

"Pure Grandma. You remember when she first went in she was still able to be part of decisions?"

"I do. And I remember it never being like her to make things difficult for people."

"No, you're right. That's why she insisted on going somewhere well outside of Ludington. She didn't want to be right under people's feet, so close they felt they had to stop in to visit all the time. It was her pick."

"Hmm, interesting reasoning. She's such a darling ... she purposely created an excuse for people to start letting go and moving on with their lives."

*Uh-oh,* Joe thought, *don't take it there. I'd love for you to let go of this subject.* His brain clicked from one topic to another, searching for a safer conversation.

As their server approached to deliver his beer and whisk away their plates, he felt his face light up. *Saved by the beer.*

"By all means, please." He welcomed the man's invitation to bring them the dessert tray to see—Vicky loved dessert. But she kept on topic.

"Joe, don't you think it's time to follow Grandma's wishes?"

Joe stifled a groan. *Okay. Here we go.* He picked at the label on his beer bottle till he knew he could keep his voice light.

"I'm not going to abandon her, babe." He laughed a little.

"That's not what I'm saying. You know that." Joe kept his attention on tearing the label to shreds and Vicky softened her voice. "Does she even know you?"

"That doesn't matter—I'm someone she loves. She needs to have someone." He paused, chewing the inside of his cheek again. "Today, according to her, I was Bobby. Grandpa." He frowned at his beer, pinching off damp scraps of paper.

Vicky took his hand in both of hers. So much love shone in her eyes that he had to move his gaze. Focusing on the brass light at the edge of their table, he rushed on. "She scolded me, you know 'her husband,' for drinking. Then complained about my dad's drinking, saying 'what kind of life will that little boy have, now?' What little boy, Vick?" He looked at her, his eyes swimming with tears, but didn't wait for an answer. "Her boy—meaning Dad? Or Kyle? Me? The kid we caught Ma wrapping some present for? I didn't know what year she's in and kept trying to get her to change the subject because she was getting all agitated. Like me now. Sorry." He swiped at his eyes with his napkin and caught sight of the waiter approaching.

"Oh, Joe, you're such a sweetie, you know. No wonder I love you." Vicky let go of his hand and looked up at the man standing beside their table, holding a tray laden with desserts but poised as if to leap a gap, clearly noticing the tension at the table.

"I can come back in a minute," he suggested. Vicky nodded.

Joe concentrated on tidying tiny paper shreds into a squishy ball. Finally, he asked, "So, I'm not in the shit?"

"In the shit? What?"

"After this morning, you know when I was leaving …" He tried to sound teasing, but couldn't bring himself to look up. "All day I thought I was in trouble."

"You're one in a million, Joe." He found her eyes warm on his, her head tipped to the side. "So many of the guys my friends go out with barely notice even if the woman is seriously pissed off. It usually takes a verbal club between the eyes to get them to pay attention. You pick up on it when I'm only frustrated."

"So …" Joe hesitated, smashing his label ball flat. "But, why are you frustrated?"

Vicky toyed with a pair of spoons the waiter had forgotten to collect, holding them like horse's reins between her fingers. "Mmmm—"

A loud clanging bell stopped conversation in the restaurant and all around them diners turned to the wall of windows, unnecessarily telling each other, "The Badger's coming in."

Vicky watched the enormous car ferry steaming across their view and Joe watched her. Her eyes followed the movement of the stately ship then seemed to lose focus. She let the spoons dangle from her fingertips. Laying them on the table, she looked back at him.

"I think it's all this 'don't dream' stuff with you and Kyle lately. It's getting old and it's made me see how, over the years, both of you kind of … sorry, but you both pretty much … rest on your butts."

"What?" Joe quickly erased the deep furrow that sprouted between his eyebrows. "It's not exactly like either of us are losers." He wiped his mouth with a little laugh.

"No, not at all, no. It's just … you know. You both seem perfectly content with the status quo. Keep on doing what you do because that's what you've always done."

*That's because change sucks*, he thought. *But you sure don't want to hear that.*

He blinked at the waiter who had returned and now stood flicking exaggerated and meaningful glances between the desserts on his tray and the two of them.

"No dessert for us, thanks. Maybe next time. Just the check would be great." Joe reached in his trousers for his wallet and quelled a twinge of guilt as Vicky dragged her eyes from a generous hunk of carrot cake moving back toward the kitchen with the departing waiter.

"I happen to think my status quo is perfect, Vick. Since you're in it." He leaned across to kiss her with a gusto he didn't feel, folded his napkin, and looked around the room. "And so's this place. Did you like it?"

Not waiting for her answer, he looked at his watch and sat bolt upright. "We'd better go, babe." Throughout the waiter's return and departure, he talked non-stop, handing over his credit card without checking the bill and pretending not to see Vicky's confused expression at the hustle as she downed the last of her wine.

"The rest of tonight's surprise package is a movie. Your pick," he said. "But they all start soon. So, we don't really have time for dessert, sorry. I guess I should have made this reservation for earlier."

Standing to help move her chair over the carpeted floor, he peeled her little sweater from the chair back and held it out with a small bow, murmuring, "Your flimsy thingy for your sexy shoulders," then took her hand and steered her toward the foyer.

Head bent low with his mouth against her hair, he spoke into her ear, "I have a confession, hon. I got a speeding ticket today. Sorry."

*That should get us off "status quo" and onto safer ground,* he thought as they wound their way out of the sun-drenched dining room.

# Chapter Eleven
## July 3rd

Kyle studied the sunrise he'd painted on the east wall of his bedroom. Head tipped back, he turned in a slow half-circle and followed the designs that spread up to the ceiling above the bed then bled into the edges of a wide swath of stars—hundreds of daubs of reflective silver paint. He'd imagined countless nights of making love with Maria beneath their faint glow.

Remembering lying with her under the stars in the October-cold sand of Buttersville beach, his throat tightened. With a deep breath, he dropped his gaze to the west wall's blazing sunset. He'd gotten the effect he wanted: highlights within his brush strokes mimicked real light. It looked lit from within.

Minutes ago, Joe had dropped him off on the way into town and dug a promise from him to not try painting out either of the kitchen or bedroom "masterpieces." Even as he'd yelled "yes, boss" over his shoulder, he'd known he'd decide that once he got inside, once he knew how it felt to have full-color reminders of Maria all around.

As he walked around his room, the emptiness of the house, the new emptiness of his life, wafted in the echoes of his flip flops and the still faint smell of paint. He sank onto the bed, laying back to scrutinize the constellations above him. Letting his head roll toward the soft colors of sunrise, he felt the coolness of his first morning with the horses, remembered how he'd opened up to Maria Horse, her breath warm on his throat, how looking into her eyes he'd somehow felt connected to Maria the woman.

He let his gaze roam over his mural and the stillness of that morning spread through him, bringing with it a curious sense of clarity and purpose.

*The art would stay.*

The critical, professional part of his mind knew it was damned good. But more than that, he'd done the paintings for Maria; somehow they felt like another sort of a connection, like maybe she was still a little bit with him. Living with reminders of her every day would probably hurt, he realized, but it would hurt more not to. Maybe he needed that hurt to keep on his new track.

*On the subject of hurting* ... he thought and pushed up off the bed. The time had come to do what he'd come home to do, to test how much he'd healed and how soon he might be ready to move out of the cabin. As cool as Joe and Vicky had been, he felt more than ready to be back in his own place.

Twenty minutes later, he sat on his front porch chair waiting for Joe to pick him up. He avoided looking at the satin bathrobe across the chair's arm, or holding it to his face again. The scent of Maria's shampoo—coconut—and her shower gel—mango—already seemed caught in his nostrils. He scanned his unkempt lawn and drew the back of his fingers across the slinky white fabric, feeling the smoothness of her neck.

"I'm keeping this." He announced to the yard. He stood up fast, about to unlock his door, just as a hot orange Chevelle careened to a stop in his drive. He turned back to the driveway. "Okay, then I won't."

"Hey! Nice little dress," Joe shouted over the lyrics from "Help Me Rhonda," then reached to turn down the radio. "Doubt it'll cover your tush, though."

Kyle tossed the robe through the car's passenger window. "Good thing it's such a great tush then." He climbed in, collecting the robe into a wad on his lap. "Stop at Ma's as we go by. She can give this back to Maria. It was hanging on my bathroom door."

"Good decision." Joe nodded, squinting over his shoulder as he backed the car out of Kyle's narrow drive. "White's not really your color. Too, I don't know, virginal."

"Virginal, hell. It'd drive me nuts having this thing around."

"Smells like her?"

"Arrrgh!" Kyle buried his face in the fabric one last time. "Flipping excellent."

"You'd only have to wear it once to take care of that." Throwing him a sly grin, Joe stomped the accelerator.

"You're one to talk. I'm gonna make you an air freshener necklace for your birthday." Kyle waggled the seatbelt latch at Joe before clicking it closed.

"This is a '67. Anything newer than Jan '65 has to have them."

As Joe sped along Jebavy Road, Kyle leaned into the car's turbo power.

"You and Vick are lucky," he said. "You got me for another week or so. I've got too much economy-sized crap at home." He flexed his bandaged hands, stretching his fingers. "Even if I could open packages or use knives to cook, I'd be dropping jumbo laundry soap containers trying to do the wash one-handed."

"That's fine." Joe seemed to hesitate a long time before he added, "Let's lay off the 'don't dream' thing, though. Apparently, it's getting to Vicky."

Kyle quirked an eyebrow. "I didn't think much got up Vick's nose. Why's that bugging her?"

"She figures we're holding ourselves back." Joe slowed and turned into their mother's driveway. "That we're stuck in a rut." He drove all the way down the drive and parked by the gate to the back yard.

Kyle laughed and slung Maria's robe over his shoulder as they climbed out of the car. "Yeah, well, she's probably onto us." He shrugged his good shoulder in response to Joe's puzzled look.

Joe shrugged back. "I'm going to check Ma's garden, see if the rabbits are leaving her anything." Pausing halfway through the gate in the chain-link fence, he added, "Try not to strangle her in there, okay?"

Kyle grinned down from the crowded little step at the kitchen door. "Hell, I'm still feeling pretty chilled from that thing with the horses last week. I'm not promising anything though once she finally confesses where she's buried Dad."

Joe rolled his eyes and disappeared into the backyard.

Kyle called after him, "Look for any freshly turned earth."

He rapped on the kitchen door with his fingertips. Waiting for his mother to respond, he realized, despite the crash and Maria and all, he did feel pretty okay. *There'd be plenty of pharmaceutical companies out of business if Eagala could bottle that horse therapy,* he thought, raising his hand to knock again, then dropping it. *Idiot, no one could hear a thing over that stupid air conditioner.*

The noise of it drowned out the squeak of the door as let himself into the kitchen. The room smelled like lemons, and a bucket of gray water and a squeeze mop stood abandoned in the middle of the still-wet floor. Music, dragging and mournful, filled the air.

"Within my heart I know I will never start to smile again until I smile at you."

Registering the voice as unmistakably Frank Sinatra's, Kyle toed off his flip flops, thinking it'd be fun to skid barefoot over the floor, until he remembered where he was at with his road rash. He picked his way around the edge of the room to the open door of the TV den, then stopped.

The scene before him washed over and sank his buoyant mood. He swallowed the "hello" on his lips.

On the edge of his father's worn recliner chair, his mother sat beside the desk radio, her eyes wide and wet with tears. A wash rag dangled from her limp hand, dripping water onto the thin carpet between her slim, bare feet; she stared at the spreading gray dampness without seeming to see it.

An old memory slammed into Kyle. He saw her face, much younger, but slack and unfocused like this, while he sat staring at her from across the homework-cluttered dining table, gulping down his fear.

He stepped backwards onto the wet kitchen floor then froze. His younger self wanted him to run and to keep running, but something stopped him. Pressing his fingertips to the door jamb to keep his balance, he stayed just out of view and listened as the song slid to a close.

National Radio's announcer spoke: "While many of you know 'I'll Never Smile Again' jumpstarted Sinatra's career, few might realize the words were written by Canadian Ruth Lowe after the unexpected death of her husband. Lowe's lyrics have earned praise for expressing both her desolate loneliness and her intent to remain true to the man she lost. I'd agree—"

Kyle heard a soft thump and the rest of the announcer's words were lost to the sound of his mother's sobbing. He leaned through the doorway, and seeing her now on the floor slumped against his father's chair, crossed the kitchen fast, grabbed his shoes, and was outside.

Pulling the door closed behind him, Maria's robe still across his shoulder, he sank down amongst the collection of flowerpots to sit with the drone of the air conditioner, a background hum that couldn't drown out his mind's louder soundtrack, sounds of his mother and his own younger self. Crying mixed with words of grief and loss.

# Chapter Twelve
## July 4th

Joe's involuntary gasp joined the cries of countless delighted Ludington locals and visitors as shimmering fingers of lime, lavender, orange, and yellow melted from the dome of the night sky. Sherbet light dripped into its own reflection in the waters and sandy shores of Lake Michigan, bathing Stearns Park in a surreal twilight. For the length of a breath, the sublime gave way to ordinary as the sky rested into black before being split again. A shivering tracer raced up, hovered, and bloomed into a cascade of white and gold fire. As it rained down, shushing and fizzing into dozens of swirling bouquets, the delayed "boom" tripped Joe's heart in the same instant as Vicky's belly laugh. Shouts rose up from the families and couples reclining in the sand around them, the sound of cheering mixed with laughter and distant car horns honking.

"Those are your favorites, aren't they?"

They lay together in the two-person sized hole they, like dozens of locals, had dug in the sand. The Ludington tradition went as far back as he could remember and made anyone watching fireworks from atop the sand—rather than dug a foot or two into it—stand out as an uninitiated tourist. He leaned against their towel-lined backrest of packed sand and held Vicky's body against the length of his, her back pressed to his chest.

"Oh, yeah," she breathed.

Joe squeezed her around the middle, smiling at the reverence in her voice. Her face turned toward the ribbons of red, white, and blue spreading like crazed ivy across the indigo sky. He rested his chin on her head, catching strands of her hair on his unshaven jaw, and felt her body strain to take in the sight overhead as the ribbons formed an enormous patriotic heart. The crowd went crazy.

Vicky tipped her head back to a comic angle, blew him an upside-down kiss, then twisted around in the circle of his arms to face him.

"Look at you." She wrapped both arms around his waist, snuggling deeper into their hole. He smelled coconut-scented suntan lotion. "Look at that grin. I love that grin." Her voice bordered on a low growl.

"You love it?"

"And then some." She curled one leg over his thigh, her head on his chest, face tipped again to the sky.

Her parted lips and wide eyes told him he'd lost her to the carnival of gumballs bouncing hundreds of feet above the lake.

"Why doncha marry it, then?" Joe spoke above her ear and heard her catch her breath.

"What?" She struggled to rise up onto her elbow, twisting toward him again and grabbing a fistful of his T-shirt. Her wide eyes reflected a kaleidoscope of purple, green, and red. "*Marry it?*"

"Me. How about you marry me, then?" Joe grinned down into her face, willing all the love he felt in that moment, and over the past ten years, to pour into her through his gaze.

She stared up at him, tears blurring the dancing spirals in her eyes. "Joe?" she breathed.

"You get the grin for good. And everything north and south of it." He struggled to dig in his front jeans' pocket, gently unlatching the fist that still clutched his shirt. Vicky's smile started to tremble.

"Oh, Joe, oh my God—finally." Something between a laugh and a sob broke from her.

He extracted a tiny velvet pouch, opened the drawstring and sat up, pulling her into his lap. As he took her hand, he felt her warm tears, one then another, fall against his wrist. Vaguely aware that while Vicky held her breath in their little sand pit, the noise of the crowd around them had begun swelling ever louder, he twisted and turned the ring till it slid into place on her finger. In his mind he voiced a plea, "*Let this be forever*," as he brought her hand to his lips and kissed it.

Without a glance at the ring, Vicky pressed both hands to his face and pulled him into a long, deep kiss.

Joe finally drew back and leaned his forehead against hers for a heartbeat, his breath mingling with hers. "Don't go trying to wiggle out of this, woman. Saying 'finally' isn't the same as saying 'yes'. And I'm not taking 'no' for an answer."

Vicky swiped both hands across her wet cheeks. "Oh, the answer's yes, Joe!" She finally stared at the ring, laughing. "I'm certainly *not* saying no."

"Ever again," Joe stated.

"Hey, wait! Hang on now!"

They hugged and laughed as if they'd invented cleverness, while the din of the crowd rose to a roar of sustained shouting, laughter, and honking.

They turned together to see the finale bursting across the sky. Vicky rubbed her wet face against Joe's T-shirt then kept it pressed to his chest.

Ground displays burst into life, spurting geysers of brilliance skyward as a repeating Niagara of jewel-bright color arced down to meet them.

***

"Hey, it's you!" Kyle shouted over the cacophony. "I thought I'd managed to lose ya." He squatted at the edge of their sand pit and peered at their faces, stark in the intense light. "Whoa. Check out you two! What's with those shit-eatin' grins?"

He leaned closer, glancing between their faces and the show overhead until Vicky brought her ring finger to dangle within inches of his face and he forgot about the fireworks.

"Is that what I think it is? Or is this a prank?" Kyle grabbed Vicky's wrist and made as if he was going to bite-test the diamond.

Vicky yanked her hand back with a chuckle and raised the ring close to her eyes, staring at it, then at Joe with the biggest grin Kyle had ever seen on anyone. She seemed to be laughing, but the chaos just starting to subside around them obscured the sound.

"I figured it was best to get in and clinch this deal while she was on a fireworks' high!" Joe yelled.

Kyle nodded, then stood to stretch, wondering why he could find nothing to say, watching the last fireworks' spidery ghosts backing away and creeping into the black hole of the lake. The sky had lost the crowd's attention; the shouting and laughing had faded to a still-excited hustle of packing-up noises and strangers surreptitiously racing each other to be first in the line of cars going nowhere. Joe and Vicky abandoned their sand pit, dragging a beach towel out with them.

As Joe shook sand from the towel, Vicky crowed, "You guys, I've been ready for this since the first day Joe carried my lunch tray in the school cafeteria."

Kyle stood wordless while she beamed up into his face. With a flick to his good shoulder, she grabbed his fingertips and started dragging him and Joe through the swirling crowd.

The physical dragging mirrored something deeper rising within him. As if acting out a behind-the-scenes role in a play he was closely invested in, he observed each action before him, dissected every line spoken.

He felt the strength and warmth of Vicky's hand as she towed them along, stopping and starting as strangers blocked their path. Then they were in the picnic area where Ma stood guard over their clutch of lawn chairs, Vicky let go of his fingers, and the emptiness felt cold where her hand had been. Joe was dashing away glittering tears and grabbing for her hand again to hold it up in front of Ma's face and Ma made a little squeak he'd never heard from her before. She and Vicky were doing some kind of hug dance on their tiptoes, then Ma was hugging Joe, and Vicky again, and Joe and Vicky together.

Now Kyle felt an arm hook around his own neck and the hug included him. He smelled the sweetness of a woman's hair—Vicky's? Ma's?—and felt the stubble of Joe's chin against his own jaw. His stomach started cartwheeling and he couldn't tell if he was about to laugh or … *God, what's this about?* Was that a cry in his throat? He forced it to emerge as a barking laugh, and it shattered the bubble encasing him.

Grateful, he went with it, roughing up Joe's hair and planting a hearty kiss on Vicky's forehead, tasting suntan lotion and smelling sweetness again.

"So, I'm finally going to have a little sister!" he said. "You're off the hook, Ma. Now I have someone to torment and protect. Plus, I can sneak around trying to read her diary."

Joe leaned in to nudge Kyle's good shoulder. "I doubt there's any protecting required with this one, but I'll be on call for that."

"I do keep a diary, though." Vicky laughed. "So, thanks for the warning, and good luck ever finding it now."

Ma pulled her into another hug. Then Vicky and Joe were hugging again and Kyle heard her whisper, "I'm going to remember this night forever, Joe."

Inclining his head toward the pair, Kyle stepped close to Ma and put his mouth to her ear. "Okay if I stay at your place tonight?"

Ma grinned at him, nodding. She laid her hand against his cheek, then turned and started loading picnic supplies into her trundler. Kyle saw the next few moments through a sudden blur. Frantic to blink away unwelcome tears, he dropped his head back. The familiar stars of a Michigan night sky had resumed their quiet roles.

When had she last touched him? He turned and began folding a lawn chair, trying to concentrate on the cold aluminum in his clumsy grip, to resist the urge to touch his cheek, to see if he could still feel the brief warmth of his mother's hand. That moment had been a first, the touch mixed with a look of pure approval and affection.

Had she been affected as well? He glanced her way. She ran a flashlight's beam across the grass in front of their space, stooping to dig out a bottle cap that had been pressed into the ground probably months ago. Had the mundane returned just like that?

As Ma looped the strap of a jute carry-bag over her shoulder, the flashlight in her hand lit the leaves of the oak tree behind her and shone onto her face.

Kyle glimpsed her private smile, her eyes soft with contentment, and wished he knew if her smile was just for Joe and Vicky—*or maybe for him, too? Or is she thinking of Dad?* Hoisting two of the lightweight chairs onto his right shoulder, he tried to wedge into place beside her.

The crowd moved around them, surging as one toward the parking lot and real life. A rail-thin young woman hidden inside a hot pink hoodie pushed in front of him and set a whimpering toddler down beside her. She clamped her hand onto the child's head like a skull cap and steered him along the lumpy grass, forcing Kyle to walk with baby steps to avoid stepping on the small boy's heels.

Over and over, the young mother mumbled, "Josh, we gotta find Grandpa. We gotta find Grandpa."

Several paces ahead, Joe's voice came back to Kyle in the dark, "I know it's totally different, but I think tonight's fireworks rivaled the Northern Lights we get up here. Ludington's displays just get better every year."

Kyle picked out Ma's answering voice, "They ought to. They have a bigger pot of tax money to spend every year."

Vicky chimed in, "Well, tonight's were amazing! And Joe, now you've got me thinking more than ever about seeing Alaska's Northern Lights; maybe for our honeymoon?"

Some family moments were worth being part of and thanks to this skinny, knocked-up … Trying to twist past the pair, he almost toppled over the boy who jolted and froze in place when the young woman shrieked.

"Grandpa!"

Kyle clapped his free hand over his ear. In six years of teaching, he'd never gotten used to how shrill female voices could be.

She launched herself at a bear of a man suddenly in their path.

"Tabby! Tabby! How did we lose you and your brother?" The bear nuzzled her hair and squeezed her close while swinging the boy across his shoulder in a fireman's carry. "One minute you're there and the next, you're both gone!" The big man's voice choked.

The light of a street lamp at the edge of the thronged parking lot showed the girl to be no more than ten or eleven, her face covered in freckles, her huge green eyes streaming tears.

*"Jesus!"* Kyle silently ripped into himself, *"you can be an impatient, judgmental, selfish jerk."*

"Kyle!" Joe charged to a stop at the edge of the path, beaming. "Hey, best man, gimme those chairs and haul ass. We're going to join a jillion or so other people and go for ice cream. Ma's treat."

"What?" Kyle faked confusion as he handed off the chairs and fell into step beside Joe who strode, oblivious, past the happy reunion underway beside Kyle. "Are we celebrating or something?"

Looking over his shoulder, Kyle sent a mental apology to the two children now attached like barnacles to the burly man. The man stood before an open SUV, alternating planting kisses on the tops of their heads, and trying to gently disengage their twined limbs to transfer them to the eager arms of a white-haired woman waiting inside.

Joe poked a swift punch skyward. "You betcha, man! Best man!"

"Hang on." Kyle sped up to match Joe's pace as they left the snarl of beach traffic behind, heading to the quiet street they'd parked on. "What'd you say?"

"Are you kidding?" Weaving past slower-moving families, they'd caught up with Vicky and Ma at the car, unloading and folding Ma's trundler. "Who the hell else would I ask to be my best man?"

"Not ask, Joe. Tell!" Vicky laughed. "You *tell* him he's going to be your best man." She reached to ruffle Kyle's hair and he ducked away.

"You heard the woman." Joe jammed the chairs and picnic things in the trunk, opened doors for Vicky and Ma, then jogged around to the driver's seat. Vicky climbed in front, leaving Kyle to join Ma in the back.

He shook his head in mock despair. "Look at that—the orders start now—before the ring is even on her finger!"

Joe eased into the flow of traffic, waving thanks to the driver behind them.

"Oh, the ring's on my finger all right." Vicky held her right hand near the windshield, angling it this way and that with every street lamp they drove beneath; reflections glittered across the car's ceiling above Kyle's head. "Can't you see it shining up here?" she asked.

"Is *that* what that is?" Ma joined in. "I thought you'd left the interior light on."

"Oh, yeah!" Vicky crowed. "And this baby's not coming off till the next one goes on."

"Hey!" Joe squawked. "What's that supposed to mean?"

"The *wedding* band, goof." Vicky laughed. "Even *I* know it goes *under* the engagement ring."

"As long as you're not planning husband number two." Joe slapped his forehead. "Wait! You mean I'm buying another ring?"

Beside Kyle, Ma peered out from her window. "Okay, you clown. You've just missed all the best side roads off Lake Shore." She leaned across him to look from his window; he pressed himself back into the seat. "You know Ludington

Avenue's always a zoo after the fireworks. You wanted to head out to 31 for the Dairy Queen. They'll be mobbed in a minute."

"Ma, I did it on purpose. But I should have checked—you okay if we go to House of Flavors, instead of DQ?" Joe asked. Kyle darted a glance at the rearview mirror and just caught Joe's wink. "Can your wallet handle getting a pint or two of that Moosetracks ice cream we used to have at Grandpa's?"

Kyle turned away to hide another welling of tears. *What a crybaby I've become. How in the hell did Joe remember—or even know—that DQ means Maria?* Had he talked about how Maria had first kissed him there or about all the other evenings they'd spent laughing under those fluorescent lights and slapping mosquitoes? Or when they'd lined up on opening day last March, despite freezing their butts off.

"I don't know." Ma leaned forward and squeezed Joe's, then Vicky's, shoulder. "That might just have to be your wedding gift, then."

*Did Ma just giggle? This night's one for the books,* Kyle thought. He turned to the window again, swiping at the annoying tears.

"I propose …" the smile in Joe's voice couldn't be missed.

Vicky took her cue, "Yes, you did! And there's no backing out now."

"I propose," Joe continued, "we avoid that mob at H.O.F. Check it out!" He slowed to a crawl as they passed the ice cream store then turned onto South William to circle the block. "Let's take it back to your place, Ma. We'll set up the lawn chairs in the back yard like we used to as kids."

"To watch the stars and look for fireflies—that was years ago." Ma leaned forward again. "Do you two still remember that?"

Kyle knew he should be joining in. He felt his mother looking at him and pictured leaping in with some quick remark, but something stopped him. In part, fear that his voice might quiver or his eyes well again. But more that this night just didn't feel real; he couldn't trust it. With all the motherly affection and teasing, it all felt too foreign.

"Sure we do—right, Kyle?" Joe went on without waiting for him to answer; the skills of a diplomat, his little brother. "Of course, it was uncool to keep it up as teenagers, but those nights we hunted for nightcrawlers before going fishing with Grandpa, we'd be on the lookout for lightning bugs, too. The only difference, we didn't stuff 'em in a jar with a handful of grass and holes in the lid."

Kyle tried to let the banter seep into him. But one evening, one touch didn't come close to breaking down the wall that had grown between Ma and him. He sent himself back to the moment of his mother's hand curving against his face. The feeling he'd experienced didn't return; he had closed to her again.

He shut his eyes, trying to conjure the dark eyes of Maria Horse. There they were, vivid in his mind. No sounds, just the deep, silent gaze of a horse. Her breath on his face. She sniffed his eyes, his nose, his chin. He held still, feeling the softness and the prickliness of her muzzle grazing his skin. He didn't want to move. Like holding your breath when a butterfly lands on your arm. Like wanting your mother's touch for an hour or a lifetime as a child, not for a mere instant as a man, two decades later.

"Kyle, come with me," Ma ordered. "Joe, you keep circling till you see us at the curb."

Kyle heard his mother's car door open and close and then she stood holding his, offering her hand to help him step into a sensory overload: the crowd, the lights, and the happy bedlam of a Ludington landmark on a summer holiday.

Still awkward in cars, he pulled himself out, ignoring her hand then paused, feeling naked and young, and not liking it in the least. Maria Horse, and maybe Maria herself, had left him with cracks in his protective shell. Now here he stood about to go alone with Ma into a loud crowd of strangers to buy ice cream.

"Kyle! We're double parked with a line of cars behind us. Shut the door!" Joe called.

Kyle poked his hand back into the car, delivered the best bird he could offer with a bandaged hand, then stepped away and slammed the door with a wince.

Ma winced, too. "Did you use the wrong hand?"

That threw him—*sympathy now, too?* Before he found an answer, she started moving ahead, sidestepping between oblivious couples, kids with earphones, and adults on cell phones. They managed to get into the shop and met twice the chaos inside.

"Oh, this was a bad idea," Kyle raised his voice over the racket.

Ma either ignored or didn't hear him. Holding her purse against her chest, she kept weaving, pausing, and walking—making her way through the clots of people, not stopping until she was in line, two customers away from the jangling cash register.

Following close behind, Kyle looked over his shoulder at the mountain of a crowd she'd just reduced to a molehill.

"Most of them have ordered already and don't know enough to move on." Ma smiled at him. "You still don't like crowds?"

Kyle shrugged one shoulder. "I don't know. Did I not use to?" He pretended to read a list of ice cream flavors offered. "I just couldn't tell they weren't all still in line."

As they moved closer to the counter, she started rummaging through her purse. "Don't assume failure or you guarantee it."

Despite the smile on her face, her words felt like a slap on the wrist. In the midst of formulating a cutting reply that didn't include any four-letter words, he found her waiting to catch his eye.

"I'm sorry about you and Maria, Kyle. I really like her."

The fight drained out of him. "You like her? You said that the other day, too … but in present tense. We're past tense."

"Still," she insisted. "I'm sorry and I like her."

"Next! How can I help you, ma'am?"

"I'll have two pints of Moosetracks, one of Blue Moon, and one of Praline Pecan. Please." She pulled her wallet from her bag, smiling at the earnest-looking counter worker.

The teenager released her pink-glossed lower lip from between tiny teeth, shot Ma, then Kyle, a big grin and a bright: "Right away!" With that she became a real person, not a stranger to be forgotten as he'd done with hundreds before her—someone to serve him or sell him ice cream or shoes or gas, then disappear when he'd gotten what he needed. He looked for her name tag: Cassie.

With grace and speed, Cassie hand-packed their pints from the canisters displayed in the glass case between them. "Here you go. Would you like a sample of anything new? You don't have to buy it to try it."

"What a great saleswoman you are! But no, thank you, Cassie." Ma paid and dropped a tip in the jar beside the cash register. "My other son is circling the block; we're racing home to celebrate him just getting engaged an hour ago."

"That's cool. Congratulations!" Her smile included them both again.

Kyle noticed her tongue's venom piercing and the single deep dimple in her left check.

"I hope the wedding is wonderful," she said. "When you're planning, maybe think Grandma Kay's award-winning apple crisp instead of cake."

Ma laughed. "You'll go far, young lady." Kyle felt her touch his elbow as she started to move away. "You have a good night! I hope you can finish soon and get out to enjoy it."

"Not long now, thanks! Next?"

Kyle wondered if he imagined it or if the girl's voice somehow sounded happier, more real. He called ahead to Ma's back, "Was that working the room, Ma?"

She continued to wade through the thinning crowd, but threw a puzzled look over her shoulder.

Grateful for the chance to change tack, he asked, "I mean, did you know her?"

"No. But why shouldn't we treat each other like human beings?" Ma pulled the restaurant door open and the summer night rushed in with an onslaught of conversations. She raised her voice. "She seemed lovely. Oh, there's your brother! Joe! We're here! Run, stop him, Kyle!"

Like a ten-year-old at his mother's bidding, Kyle ran, swerving around couples and families, then an empty double stroller. He narrowly missed plowing down the stroller's recent, knee-high occupants standing unsteadily in front of it. Looking straight down, Kyle saw a curly-headed, round-bellied boy holding onto his twin brother's shoulder for balance while smashing a miniature vanilla cone into his identical laughing face.

Startled, Kyle barked out a laugh as a female shriek sounded behind him, he presumed from the children's mother. As he shouted for Joe, he braced for the earsplitting wail he expected, but instead, wild giggling tumbled from both the attacker and the attacked.

Back in the car, Kyle shared the story of the two small boys as Joe maneuvered the traffic to leave town.

Amidst the ensuing laughter, Joe asked Vicky, "And you're sure you want kids, Vick?"

"Absa-frickin-lutely! Sorry, Ma!" More laughter. "And those are the kinda kids I want. What good sports—and spirited!"

"Like a good horse," Joe suggested.

"But just a little smaller," Kyle said. "Especially at birth."

"Ow. Ow. Ow." Vicky squirmed and winced. "Don't remind me of that part!"

Ma laughed. "Oh, you'll forget that part."

"Yeah, that's what they all say." Vicky hunched her shoulders around her ears and disappeared into them. "I find that hard to believe."

"Truly. Trust me." Ma touched Vicky's shoulder and Kyle glanced away, swallowing a twinge of jealousy. "You'll forget as soon as they lay that baby on your stomach screaming his lungs out."

He turned back to gape at Ma as she finished. "You'll be so flooded with love you won't have room for a thought of anything else."

Kyle and Joe spoke over top of each other.

"Except a thought for your ecstatic and loving husband," Joe insisted.

Kyle managed to blurt a single, "Awwww …" before shrinking against his car door overcome by an urgent need to escape a rising claustrophobia.

No doubt Ma had brought on this weird funk. She'd had been a different person for most of the evening, but he'd really noticed it in the ice cream shop: in the moment and in charge, but less bossy than he knew her to be. She'd seemed more relaxed, confident, and friendly than any memory he had of her. He decided to test that thought and, minutes later, still hadn't come up with anything other than Ma in her head and in the future, or in other people's lives, giving orders, scolding and cautioning. Always worried, she forever tried to control every single little thing—pissing him off to the point of wanting to explode, nothing ever good enough for her. During his early grade school years, she'd looked dopey and half out of it most of the time, the way she'd looked in front of the radio last week when he walked in on her crying.

*No, that looked like pure grief.* His stomach clutched a little. *Dad should be here,* he thought, *part of all this. We should know what's happened to our father. I'll give Joe and Vicky their night tonight, but tomorrow morning, when Ma and I are on our own, I'm getting to the bottom of this.*

"Earth to Kyle!"

Kyle blinked and looked, first at Joe leaning into the back seat, then around the car where he now sat alone. He mustered a half smile.

"Hey, you coming in with us any time soon?" Joe poked a finger into his good shoulder. "Or do you plan to sit here and let your ice cream melt to brown slop then blow bubbles in it like we used to?" Stretching farther into the car, Joe offered a forearm for support.

Kyle took it.

# Chapter Thirteen
## July 4th

*Sex and champagne, the perfect sleeping pill*, Joe thought. He pulled Vicky closer to his chest so she wouldn't see him stifle a yawn. *A cruel joke of nature that the combination doesn't work for women like it does for men.*

*Me. What do I know?* He checked himself. *Only that it doesn't work for my woman. My fiancée.* The words still sounded awkward, even to think. But he'd get used to it.

*Right?* He wondered. *People do. It doesn't have to happen all at once, anyhow. One thing for sure, proposing sure made Vicky happy; that always feels good. And no guy can be accused of sitting on his butt when he's just proposed.*

He looked down the length of their bodies as he and Vicky lay together on the porch couch; a pretzel of toned and naked limbs, lit only by a single strand of white twinkle lights they rarely remembered to plug in. Crumpled behind them, a sky-blue and fire-red Indian blanket waited for the breezes that would soon blow in from the river.

Earlier, they'd charged up to the loft bed for a private celebration of the big proposal, one that, this time at least, had nothing to do with Moosetracks ice cream. He smiled and kissed the top of Vicky's head, remembering times they'd done unusual and erotic things with Moosetracks, feeling especially lucky there weren't any neighbors within earshot of the cabin. He peered through the screen before them into the fresh-smelling midnight.

He'd have been fine staying put and falling asleep in the loft, but here they were, on Vicky's request, back amongst the breezes and the night noises of the porch, staring at the starlit yard and sipping more champagne. At least, he was having more.

Each day since what he thought of as "the status quo dinner" at P.M. Steamers, he'd turned to a drink or two—maybe more, if he was honest about it—while he mentally geared up for the proposal. Not too many drinks to worry about, just enough to soothe his jitters and take the edge off the sting he'd felt since hearing Vicky's assessment of him. Just now, though, it seemed the natural high that had carried him through the evening needed a little boost. Moët Chandon would be that boost, and a nice one at that.

Vicky, however, had more talk than sleep in her. He hovered the neck of the bottle over her glass, and she inserted her hand in between, starting a new topic without missing a beat.

"From all reports, and from what I've seen, Juliet is doing great."

Joe refilled his glass to the rim and listened to Vicky's voice, a nice sound with the quiet gurgle of the river beneath it.

"I'm planning to hire her and, if all goes well, another Equine Specialist I'm meeting next month at the conference. She has all the experience hours she needs, but no barn or team yet. She wants to come see this place."

Joe hoped he'd caught the gist of what she'd been saying. "You want to hire two more onto your team?" He gave himself points for forming and expressing a coherent sentence.

"Yep, it'll give me more time for marketing and building the business, getting more contracts."

"Sounds like a lot to take on. You just got the contract with those schools and um … that other place."

"The park district. No prob, we can handle more." She turned her head and bit his shoulder lightly, then kissed away the teeth marks. "*And* still plan the perfect autumn wedding. My sisters are itching to help, of course."

"Wow. You called them already?"

She squeezed his thigh.

"Of course, you did." He hugged her. "I need some of what you're on." Somehow the Moët didn't seem to be having any effect. Vicky's words brought the familiar uneasiness that wound round his stomach when her ambitions loomed large. He was starting to wake up.

"I'm not on anything, except a big dose of tonight. It's got me high. It's been amazing." She twisted round and looked at him in the low light. "Thank you, Joe."

"Any time."

"Don't you think it was perfect? This!" She held up her left hand, moving it just so to catch a glint of light. "The fireworks, the ice cream, joking around in the car and your Mom's yard, then … wow, upstairs together just now? It's been perfect."

Joe moved a little deeper into the couch, trying to stretch. His right leg had managed to fall sleep even if he couldn't.

"Yeah, it was all good. Great. I guess I just wish—" he chewed the inside of his cheek, considering whether he should go down this track. Vicky gave his jaw a gentle poke and he went on, "I just kind of wish Grandma and my dad had been part of the family thing."

"Mm, I can see you wishing Grandma was there, but," Vicky seemed to hesitate, "you think having your dad around would have improved on tonight?"

"Well … no, actually, you're right. It probably wouldn't have been as nice." He felt a cramp starting in his left leg and tried to stretch it. "Okay, then, I wish he, or they'd *both*, been there and in the condition for it to be good."

"It's hard, eh, baby? I can't even count how many clients have come to Eagala hurting from the damage caused by alcoholism." She caressed his cheek. "It's really lucky at least you missed out on a few years with your parents. I feel for Kyle."

"Where do you think he's been all this time?"

"Your dad? He could be anywhere, really. A free man. I'd say that ski trip was the final turning point for your mom and him. The death knell." She thought for a second. "Only your mom knows the how and why, I guess. And she may or may not tell us. But if she does, it'll be in her own time—unless Kyle manages to wring it out of her. And somehow I don't see that happening."

"It's weird to not even be able to tell Dad we're engaged." Joe couldn't feel his leg at all now.

"You're right. It is. Your mom seems better off with him out of the picture though … especially the past few months, don't you think? Tonight she was even *fun*."

"Yeah. She's way easier to be around lately, more chilled."

"The life she had with your dad would damage anyone … how *not* to do a marriage. I'm so glad you're not big into drinking." She squeezed his thigh again, then leaned forward, her eyes fixed on something outside and mumbled, "Though you do seem to have done a number on that champagne."

"It's a special occasion. Besides, it doesn't really keep well once you've opened it." He reached to tuck the bottle out of view.

"Is that our little Doughnut out there?" Vicky sat up a little more.

Joe held his glass away as she extracted herself from their twining. Pins and needles engulfed his right leg. Massaging it with his free hand, he took a long drink and watched her slip through the screen door to stand, naked, on the top stair.

"Much too big for our Doughnut," she spoke in a hushed voice. "That's our resident raccoon."

Joe sat up in time to see a fat, dark shape trundle through the starlight and shadows toward the river. Vicky sighed as she leaned against the door jamb.

"Is that a happy sound?"

"It's just so beautiful here." She held the door ajar and glanced back at him.

"Oh, right, an invitation." Joe ducked his head as he swallowed another yawn and the rest of his champagne. He dragged himself off the couch, testing the reaction of his dead leg, and limped out beside her. "I'm thinking of mosquitoes and all the places I really don't want to be bitten."

"Ha, I'll protect you. You know they always go for me first."

Joe moved into the space she created for him, closed the door behind them, and wrapped his arms around her middle.

Taking in a lungful of air, and closing his eyes, he focused on the scent of pine and moist earth. It tied with old leather for his favorite smell in the whole world.

"Feel that," Vicky whispered, resting against him.

"Sorry, honey, the champagne's kinda stung my stinger if ya know what I mean."

"No, I mean, feel the breeze on your skin. I love that."

"I know. Me, too. And that smell." Joe took in another deep breath.

"I'm going to miss this place," Vicky said as she stepped out of his arms and stretched her own high in the air. "Being naked outdoors; is there anything more erotic?"

"Did you just say you're going to miss this place? Where are you going?"

"Whisper," she urged him. "I mean when we move."

"We're getting married. We never talked about moving." His attempt to whisper failed.

She turned to face him, but Joe couldn't see her features in the dark. He only heard her incredulous undertone.

"Seriously?"

"What?"

"You're thinking we'll always live here?" She talked in a normal voice.

"Well … yeah. Why wouldn't we?" Joe felt a strong need for some space. Sliding sideways till he could open the door, he went inside, hearing her follow him in. He switched on a small lamp, spotted a pair of shorts poking out from under the couch, and stepped into them, feeling Vicky's eyes on him as he dressed.

"In your grandparents' cabin?" She turned in a circle as if surveying the porch and beyond, through the paned window into the silent darkness of the living room.

Speechless, Joe sank onto the couch, staring at her bare back in the soft lamplight then dropped his eyes when she came to stand naked in front of him.

She lifted his chin with a fingertip. "Why do you look as if I just suggested we roast Doughnut for Sunday dinner?"

"Well," he struggled for a casual tone despite the churning in his stomach. "I guess I always thought you loved it here."

"I have. I do." Vicky peeled a rumpled T-shirt off the Indian blanket and dove into it. Emerging, she asked, "But we *are* going to have kids, Joe. Right?"

"Well, yeah. Of course …" He retrieved the bottle and glasses from the floor and, gauging his pace so he didn't appear rude, moved toward the kitchen. "What's that got to do with it? I lived here as a kid." Once in the hall and out of sight, he tipped up the bottle and drained the last of the champagne straight into his mouth.

"Till you were four. That's no reason to squeeze our kids' lives into this space." Her voice came from the loft. "Heck, who's to say we'll even be in Ludington?"

At the kitchen sink, Joe froze. "Where else would we be?"

"I don't know, Joe. We're young." He could tell she was leaning over the loft railing to be sure he heard her. "Time's not gonna stand still, you know."

*What would be so wrong with that?* Staring at his reflection in the kitchen window, he saw a very glum face looking back at him. A happier face appeared beside it and he felt a pinch on his backside.

"Right, honey?" Happy reflection laid her head on Glum reflection's shoulder and spoke to the glass. "The world's our oyster."

"Is this about your business?"

Vicky turned to look at him and he lowered his eyes to hers, hoping his face didn't betray the sadness he'd seen in the window.

"Business? Sure, both mine and yours. But mostly our future." Vicky twined around him, dressed now in the skinny little sleeping outfit he was used to seeing on her. She held her left hand up and Joe watched her admire the diamond sparkling in the light from a bulb above the sink. "We've got wings now."

She sounded so happy. *What is it about a diamond?* he wondered. *Aren't we the same couple we were this afternoon?*

Joe attempted his best Groucho Marx imitation: "It's a ring baby, not a wing." He tried the imaginary cigar tap then gave it up. *It was a crap imitation anyway.* He kissed Vicky on the nose and turned toward the bathroom. "We've always had wings."

Before she could contradict him, he hurried to ask, "Porch or loft for sleeping?" He closed the bathroom door on her reply. She'd know the question was rhetorical; he'd sleep wherever he found her.

Or try to. All night he heard her words repeating in a loop, too loud to be drowned by the river's murmuring beyond the porch or Doughnut's ragged purring beneath his ear. He watched as a gray then rose-colored wash moved up the sky, searching his mind for positive thoughts. An image of a moving sidewalk—that he had put in motion—took the place of all the sayings he used to keep his balance.

# Chapter Fourteen
## July 5th

Kyle burst out of his mother's house and strode down the stairs, smacking the heads off several pansies on the way. Pacing the driveway that ran along the backyard fence, he glared at the cracked cement, both hands jammed deep into his hair. Joe pulled up in a yellow convertible, radio blaring the command to twist again, like last summer, and gave Kyle's venom a new target.

Thrusting his bandaged palms at Joe, as if to push the car back into the street, he shouted over the music, "I don't want to hear about your frickin' awesome night or play nicey-nice because you just got engaged. I'm pissed off and you're going to hear about it." He paced the fence long enough for Joe to turn off the ignition, then turned up his rant.

"Last night, everyone in our so-called family went all googley-eyed over our resident lovebirds. But no one even mentioned the absence of the man who is supposed to be, or arguably, once was, the head of it. Not you, the golden son. Not the mental health professional you're marrying. And not the man's darling wife, our mother."

"Or you. And I did miss—"

Kyle shoved the air between them hard and raised his voice. "So, okay, I decided I'd give you the night. I planned to get our dear old mother alone this morning. Finally pry out—what the hell is that noise?" He stopped pacing long enough to laser a look down the length of the drive to the road but saw nothing. "Finally pry some long overdue answers out of her. Well! Whaddya know?" He took on a mocking tone, "I hear the front door at frickin' six-forty-five on a Friday frickin' morning—and look out my window and there's dear ol' Ma, happily tripping along the front path—de, de, dee," he mimicked a woman's hip-swaying walk, "to the car waiting on the road for her. The car driven by—get *this*—my former darling!"

He drew himself up, feet planted far apart, and directed his frown to the noise that was growing ever louder just out of sight, then scowled at Joe who didn't look a bit pissed off. Instead, he looked as if he'd just spotted Santa's sleigh approaching Ma's drive. Shooting Kyle a grin, Joe scrambled from the car and headed to the street.

Kyle stalked after him, a roiling mix of anger and growing curiosity. An enormous grass green tractor driven by his parents' nearest neighbor rolled into view. Gillian watched them from inside the open cab, slowed, then stopped directly across from where they stood.

As the huge machine ramped down from full throttle to idling to silence, Kyle felt the descending noise diffuse his anger. It was either that or the old man himself, still peering down at him and Joe.

They stood waiting, hands raised to greet him as Gillian climbed from his high seat, stiff and slow, then made his way across the road with his soft canvas hat in his hand, his weathered face unsmiling.

"Good morning, Mr. Gillian," Kyle said in unison with Joe.

Waiting as Joe pumped their former neighbor's hand, Kyle thought time had not been good to Gillian. Though his eyes were still an intense blue, the worry and smile lines that used to fascinate Kyle's artistic eye seemed to have multiplied and carved considerably deeper. The old man kept his canvas hat squashed in arthritic-looking fingers and pressed to his back in a gesture of chronic pain. There was no trace of the generous smile that had reassured Kyle as a child this otherwise gruff and intimidating figure was a kindhearted man—with reliably the best Halloween treats in all of Ludington.

"Taking her over to Scottville for the Show, end of the month?" Joe waved toward the tractor hulking across the road.

Gillian looked over his shoulder. "This one?" His sunburned cheekbones raised in a grimace. "She may not look it, but she's too new for that show. And me, after not missing a one in near forty years, I might be too old for it, finally." Though he answered Joe, Kyle noticed Gillian's eyes had moved to his, a deep furrow marking his brow.

Kyle stepped up to extend his hand and Gillian took hold of the fingertips, awkward but careful, the grip firm.

"Morning, Kyle."

The strong voice Kyle remembered hadn't changed. He submitted to Gillian's quiet inspection as the blue eyes roved over any bandages not covered by his T-shirt and shorts.

"Good morning, Mr. Gillian," he said again and squelched a grin at his automatic word choice. Would his own middle school students ever have called him 'Mister', much less when they were well on their way to thirty? Did he even know Gillian's first name?

"Mighty sorry to see you so banged up, young man."

"Getting better every day; should be pretty soon now, maybe next week I can stop wrapping up in these." Marionette-style he raised then dropped a bandaged arm and leg. "Or at least use fewer bandages. It was a pretty mild road rash, I'm told."

"Road rash, they call it?" Gillian squinted at him, his head tilted down and to the side as if studying Kyle's voice.

"Euphemisms, huh?" Kyle grinned.

A ghost of a smile crossed Gillian's face and his shaggy, gray eyebrows tweaked. He shook his head once. "Euphemisms? There you go reminding me how grown up you both are." His gaze shifted to include Joe. "No matter how tall you two get, I see the scrawny, scratched-up pair of you sneaking around Ruth's apple trees in the fall. You on the ground with a catcher's mitt," he nodded at Joe, "and you, Kyle, up in the highest branches lobbing down the reddest ones you could find."

"Just for the challenge." Kyle grinned.

"We had to rake a lot of leaves to get back in Mrs. Gillian's good graces after getting caught at that," Joe remembered.

"Every year!" A low rumble, Gillian's distinctive chuckle, unrolled beneath the words. "Ruth knew what she was doing."

"You mean she wasn't pis—um … mad?" Kyle asked.

"You mean she wasn't mad?" Joe asked in unison.

"Are you kidding? She thought the sun rose and set with you boys." The deep rumble sounded again. "It was just a good way to get the leaves done."

"No way." Kyle faked outrage while Joe shook his head, grinning.

Gillian tipped his head to the side, his expression solemn but his eyes twinkling. "Way."

This time it was Kyle who chuckled, thinking you just didn't expect slang from Gillian; it didn't seem somehow to fit in his mouth. Still, many times the old man and his wife had surprised him and his family in much bigger ways. Like the time their dad had taken them away on a rare, family-camping weekend and Gillian had apparently sent his fencing crew across the street to repair their sagging backyard fence. The couple had never taken credit for the gesture nor caved and confessed despite repeated grilling. Ma, though, had once told of bringing up the old mystery over coffee many years later and catching a twinkle in Ruth's eyes. That was the closest anyone had come to confirming the favored theory in town that the event bore the stamp of Gillian generosity. The Maytag washer and dryer combo Mrs. Gillian won in a sweepstakes but had delivered instead to his parents was no secret, though Kyle was sure it would have been if she'd had her way. As it happened, if Mrs. Gillian hadn't intervened and owned up, his mother would have succeeded in ordering the delivery men to turn their truck right around and go away, explaining later she'd anticipated a nightmare when the company learned she'd never ordered the appliances, despite sorely wishing she could afford something so reliable.

The memory of Kyle's favorite surprise was as vivid as the sun shining down on the three of them as they stood in his mother's driveway. The Gillians had organized an overnight hotel stay for his parents' wedding anniversary. Presented as a package deal, it meant he and Joe were invited to camp in the Gillians' oversized backyard where they roasted hotdogs and marshmallows under the stars and listened to the couple take turns telling the best ghost stories any adult had ever dreamed up. So good, in fact, within minutes of the pair saying goodnight and leaving him and seven-year-old Joe alone beside their little tent, the boys had agreed—without a word—to haul their sleeping bags onto the couple's cluttered back porch to sleep there instead.

"How is Mrs. Gillian?" Joe asked.

"Beautiful." The old man nodded, his eyes crinkling with warmth. "A box of fluffy ducks."

Kyle bit back a laugh. "And you?" he asked.

"Well, Kyle," Gillian started, "my heart's been troubling me." He cleared his throat.

"Oh, no," Joe jumped in. "Have you had tests?"

Gillian raised a hand, then squeezed his mangled hat. "Not like that. Not like that. But seeing you like this." He waved his hat up and down in front of Kyle. "And—I'm so sorry—the awful news of your dad, and ... the rest of it ..."

"Our dad?" Kyle demanded. "The rest of it? What do you mean?"

Gillian flinched, his voice faltering, "Your dad ... and ... that little guy?"

Seeing tears well in the blue eyes, Kyle felt his stomach clutch. He stepped closer, "Mr. Gillian. What have you heard?"

"Hang on." Those eyes, flooded with confusion, latched onto his, then moved to search Joe's face. "You fellows ... don't know?"

"No. And it's driving us nuts," Kyle said. "You know what's happened to our dad? How?" A shiver ran up his spine.

"A cop came to our door—before your mom got home from that trip. Ruth thought he was confused, that he was looking for your mom ..." the strong voice wavered.

"A cop from where? Tell us what he told you." Kyle could see his intensity was disturbing the old man, making him unsure, but hell, this was the first real chance he'd had to get answers.

"Please, Mr. Gillian," Joe urged him, his voice gentle. "Ma won't talk about it."

"She won't?" The blue eyes swept the driveway as if he'd lost something. "You boys don't know about your dad? Or the—" he stopped short and took a step back, shaking his head.

"What about our dad? Is he okay? 'The what'—little boy? Does he … have a little boy somewhere?" Kyle felt Joe watching him, willing him to back off.

"Kyle, Joe, I'm sorry." Gillian seemed to age in front of them. He stepped away as if to leave, then paused. His brows met and his mouth puckered, turning his face into a mass of wrinkles. "I can't. This is for your mother to tell you. I'm so sorry." He turned fully and walked rapidly back to the massive tractor, lifting his crumpled hat over his shoulder in an apologetic farewell.

Kyle moved to follow him, and Joe grabbed his arm, pulling him back. "Don't, Kyle! Let him—"

"Ow! Jeez, man!" Kyle shook the hand off and cradled his forearm against his body, glaring at Joe.

"Sorry, I forgot for a second. Just, you know, don't chase him," Joe shouted over the noise of the departing tractor.

"What the hell! He knows, man!" Kyle hissed. "And you're fine with him just keeping us in the dark?"

"Like he said, it's for Ma to tell us. It must be big."

The flicker of fear on Joe's face became a match to the fuel Gillian had just poured all around them.

"Hell *yeah*, it's big! And our mother's *not* telling us, in case you hadn't noticed!" Kyle stepped within inches of Joe. "But I don't think you really want to know, do you, Joe?"

"Chill, man." Joe raised his chin and glared back at him.

Kyle shoved him in the chest. "Chill? Is that your answer to everything? Chill? Stick your head in the sand. Keep things all nice and same-same. Don't rock the boat? Make peace."

"Shut up." Joe turned and marched to the car. Kyle kept close on his heels, repeatedly jabbing him in the shoulder.

"Listen, you idiot! We don't even know if our dad's alive!" He swerved to his side of the car, yanked his door closed, and turned to deliver an order. "Take us into town, Joe. We're driving around till we find our mother and get some answers. Better yet, let's go talk to Rusty. He should know."

Joe slammed the car into reverse and backed onto the road, facing in the direction of the cabin. "We can't now, Vicky's waiting."

Enraged, Kyle spat out, "What the hell?! Call her! Go into town!"

"No. Leave it alone." Joe didn't look at him. "Today's supposed to be … nice."

"Nice? Did you say *nice*?" Kyle bit the words. "Get your head outta the sand, Joe! It's not *nice* when our dad's probably dead and our mother isn't telling us." His head snapped against the headrest as Joe punched the gas and sped down the straight section of Jebavy Road.

"You're messed up to think she's that bad." Joe snapped the radio on full volume.

"And you're so …" Kyle jammed his feet against the floorboards as Joe took a corner fast. The car rose onto two wheels; he gripped the edge of the door then dug around for a seatbelt with his other hand but found nothing.

Squinting against the rushing wind, he glanced at Joe's clenched jaw and made an effort to rein in his own temper. He flicked the radio off.

"Look, I saw Ma bawling her eyes out last week, listening to that Sinatra song that some woman wrote for her dead husband." Kyle gaped at Joe. "You know the song, don't you? You've just gone all white."

Joe stared at the road ahead. "Yeah, I know the song: 'I'll Never Smile Again.'"

Silent, Kyle sat grinding his teeth, one hand jammed into his hair. He watched Joe, waiting for him to reach the same conclusions he had.

"It doesn't mean anything," Joe said.

Kyle growled and threw his arms up.

"So, Dad didn't come home from skiing with Ma, and she doesn't think we need to know why." Joe still wouldn't look at him, but at least he'd slowed down some.

Kyle leaned over and enunciated in his ear, "For. Months. Joe."

Joe jerked away from him and kept talking. "So, she's living alone and gets choked up over some sad song about a lonely woman."

Kyle pressed his hands to the top of his head. "And bawls her guts out? Then our old neighbor tears up while spilling the beans about some news he assumes we'd know, but thinks is too big to tell us when we don't?"

The convertible slowed to turn onto the grass driveway to the cabin. Kyle knew in a minute they'd be out of the car and he'd have lost this chance to turn Joe into an ally. They bumped through the unkempt tunnel of trees.

"And who's the little boy, Joe?" He automatically ducked away from branch after branch. "Remember Ma went all weird and hid away some kid's present when we came in? So, okay, probably—*hopefully*—Dad's alive. Maybe he's got another family somewhere."

"Pfft. Like Ma would be sending a present to Dad's—"

"Yeah, okay, but don't you want to know, Joe?"

"No, Kyle! I don't! I want to leave it alone." Joe stopped the car with a jolt and twisted off the ignition. "I want to get Vicky and drive to Muskegon and tell our grandmother about the engagement and … have a good day."

Kyle dropped his voice and leaned closer. "Still believe in Santa, Joe? The world's all sweetness and light, right? And the tooth fairy would come if you lost a tooth?"

"Screw you."

Kyle saw Joe's fists clench as he reached for the driver's door handle. "Go for it, Joe. You want to hit me? Show some balls. Right here." He turned his jaw to his brother, tapping it with his fingertips. "Right here."

"You're a prick." Joe pushed the door open.

"Maybe I am. But at least a prick has balls, Joe. Have you even got any?"

Joe climbed from the car and, without looking, reached behind to close his door.

Kyle snorted, shaking his head in disbelief, but stayed in his seat. Ahead of him the barn door filled his view. Breathing hard, he stared at its peeling paint, then threw a look over his shoulder to see Joe disappear into the cabin. The little brother whose trusting face he'd aimed apples at from high within the maze of Gillian's trees and slept close beside on the hard porch floor. He leaned his head against the headrest, his fingers jammed into his hair, and replayed the last few minutes in his head: Gillian's words, Joe's face as he sped—white as flour and looking as if he'd be sick—and his own taunting. But over and over, Joe's face.

He heard a horse neigh from inside the barn. An answering nicker came from the pasture.

"Yeah," Kyle muttered. "We all want our old buddies."

Cicadas buzzed in the trees beside the drive. Feeling as old as Mr. Gillian, he let himself out of the car and trudged into the barn.

"Okay, Eagala team. Today's goal: to discover why I've always been such a prick."

# Chapter Fifteen
## July 5th

Joe grabbed Vicky's hand and turned sideways to slide between the elevator doors. They sprinted toward the animal sounds coming from down the hallway, running past his grandmother's open door and on to the next door down. He skidded to a stop beside her abandoned walker, covered in goose bumps before he even saw her—a picture of aged fury— inside her neighbor's room.

Crouched and growling, Grandma hung onto the empty sleeve of a navy blue cardigan, pulling with both fists and all her meager weight. Inside the rest of the sweater, her breathless neighbor, Margaret, panted. Standing hunched at the foot of her bed, Margaret gripped the edge of the garment against her chest with one gnarled hand, and clung to the bed's foot rail with the other; mouth open, her eyes seemed to focus inward, concentrating on not letting Joe's grandmother win the prize.

"Vicky, quick! Hang onto Margaret!" Joe rushed to put his arms around Grandma's tense shoulders. "If one lets go, the other's gonna topple."

"Who are you?" Grandma screamed. "Get your hands off me!" She dropped the sweater to twist around and pummel Joe in the chest with both her shrunken fists.

With the sudden release, Margaret gave a sharp squawk and fell against Vicky and partway over the bed rail.

Swallowing bile, Joe yanked his arms back. He dropped low to squat at his grandmother's feet. "Grandma, it's—um, it's Bobby." He heard Vicky catch her breath. "It's Bobby, it's Bobby," he pleaded. "Remember me. I'm your hus—"

"Get away from me! I don't know you!" She shoved past him.

Astonished at her agility, Joe leapt up and lunged to the door. He stood, rooted to the spot, as she retrieved her walker in the hallway, stumped the few steps to her own door, and disappeared. The door slammed.

He moved his gaze to Vicky. She gave him a brief, intense look then turned to the old lady trembling in her arms.

"Here we go, Margaret. You put this on." Her voice and actions gentle, she tucked the thin arm into the dangling sleeve, adjusting twisted fabric. "I presume, I *hope*, this is yours. But who knows. It might be Grandma's."

Joe watched her, his mind a blank.

"Do you recognize it, Joe?"

He searched for the right answer. "No. No, I don't think it's Grandma's. She must think so, though." His eyes roamed the room as he spoke. "I'll get a few like it for her. Then she can lose them and still have …"

"Joe." Vicky helped Margaret climb into bed. She lifted the woman's fluttering, mottled hands to her sunken chest and pulled the cardigan closed over them. "Go sit down. Get yourself a coffee."

He frowned, trying to make sense of what she'd said.

"Joe." Vicky paused to hold his gaze for a second, then smoothed a wisp of hair back from Margaret's worried face and leaned in to press the emergency call button beside the bed's headboard.

Vicky came to him then and cupped his face in her hands. "Go downstairs."

"I need to—" His voice sounded dull to his own ears.

"No. I'll go see to Grandma, if she'll allow it, and make sure she's in her own room. I'll tell the nurse, either way. You go get a coffee."

\*\*\*

An hour later, Joe stared out the car window, trying to concentrate on the passing countryside. It felt odd to be seeing it from the passenger seat. Since leaving Muskegon and its river behind, there was little to look at but trees and more trees. He spotted McDonald's arches over the treetops and realized they'd only gotten as far as Whitehall. He wished he'd driven.

"So, you want to talk yet?" Vicky laid her hand on his knee and glanced at him through the cloud of her wind-whipped hair. She hadn't tied it back, despite knowing it would end up in knots—on a horse she would have, but never in an open car.

"Not really." How many times had he driven this route over the past couple of years? He couldn't remember once being the passenger, and never in a convertible. It should feel good. "What I'd like, Vick, is to go into Montague for a drink. We just passed the exit so take Walsh—no, Fruitvale's quicker."

"A drink? Like a Coke at Twisters? Ohhh, how about a float at Dog N' Suds?"

"No, I meant …" Joe caught Vicky peek at the dashboard clock. "On second thought, let's just get home. I've got work to do." He started to reach for the radio, itching to crank the volume. He dropped his hand. Drowning her out too soon might seem rude.

"Joe, I'm sorry it went so badly today."

He wanted to remind her he wasn't in the mood to talk. That sounded more like Kyle, though, not him. He shrugged, silent, staring at the scenery again. More forests.

Vicky tried again. "Pretty dumb I guess for us to think our news and the ring were going to register with Grandma. We're strangers to her."

Joe chewed the inside of his cheek and willed her to stop talking.

"She's getting worse, honey."

He shrugged again, studying White River as they crossed. "A bad day," he conceded.

"Have you ever seen her like that before?"

"What? Aggressive?" He couldn't look at Vicky. "Yeah."

"You have?"

"Yeah." He wasn't going to say how often. Or that it had become more frequent. He remembered the shock of the first time: he'd dropped in to visit and had found her in the television lounge, sitting beside an old man who was nearly enveloped by the sofa they shared and kicking the toe of her stockinged foot into the sole of his slipper over and over again, telling him no one there liked him. This was the woman who'd nearly cried with disappointment when she caught him throwing stones at her chickens; he'd been five or six and in tears himself after getting spanked by his dad earlier in the day. He'd never hurt an animal since.

When Vicky didn't reply, he knew she was waiting for him to continue. "But it's the first time she didn't know me at all." His throat grew tight and he swallowed hard. "Even as Grandpa."

Vicky squeezed his knee. He covered her hand with his and searched for another line of conversation.

Remembering the cardboard box the nurse had thrust in his arms as they were leaving the facility, he glanced at Vicky. "What do you think's in the box? It wasn't all that heavy." He'd been too distracted to bother opening it in the parking lot. Now he wished they had.

"No telling." Vicky put her hand back on the steering wheel. "The nurse didn't seem to know much about it."

"If Grandma wanted Bobby and Keith to have it, it must be stuff that belonged to them once. Or maybe it's just hers … Heck, if she had it with her, I must have helped her move it in there." Joe sat up straight, turning to the tempest of dark hair; he only caught glimpses of Vicky's face. "Jesus, what if she goes looking for it, and we've got it? She'll freak out!"

"I don't think she's going to remember it, Joe. The nurse apologized, she told me Grandma meant to give it to you a while ago and forgot. That time Kyle came with us."

"Jesus! That was something like a year ago." Joe shifted in his seat, annoyed at the nurse and at Kyle.

"Didn't Grandma think Kyle was a delivery boy or something?" Vicky asked.

"Yeah. She told him to put the pizza in the kitchen, insisted on giving him a tip, and politely led him to the door." Joe felt a stab of sympathy for Kyle. "Just being forgotten is one thing, I guess. Being dubbed the pizza boy is another."

"I don't know ... it was a little funny." With one hand, Vicky held her hair back for a second and shot him a grin.

"Kyle didn't find it funny." Frankly, Joe didn't either, particularly not today.

"No. He did not." Vicky chuckled and took the wheel with both hands again.

Joe studied what he could see of her face. *Was that an amused or fond expression?* He tipped his head back to stare into a Michigan sky as hot a blue as a kid's rubber ball. *As hot as the encounter—heck, fight—with Kyle this morning.*

"Kyle's got more of a temper than I knew. I guess you get to know people better when you live with them." He paused for a second. "He shoved me today."

"He shoved you?"

Joe glimpsed her frown. "Yeah, when I went to Ma's to pick him up, he was all pissed off over not being able to confront her about where the hell Dad is. Then their neighbor, Gillian, was heading out from next door—he showed up on his tractor and we all talked."

"Sorry to butt in, but I've meant to ask: do you think the muddy mess on Gillian's curve had anything to do with Kyle's accident?"

"Yeah, probably—at least partly ... the dirt clots from Gillian's tractors, but also Kyle riding when he was so pissed off. Anyway, this morning, Gillian, got all tongue-tied when he realized something he *almost* told us was something we should already know, but *don't*."

"Wait. Which was what? Sorry."

"That's the thing. We don't know." Joe blew out a deep breath. "Gillian said it was about Dad. He said a cop came to see him before Ma got back from their ski trip. Gillian mentioned a little boy, too, then he clammed up. Neither of us could get him to say more. He told us it's for Ma to tell us. Well, like we said last night, I think she and Dad are over and one of them will tell us when they're ready. But when Gillian high-tailed it back to his tractor, Kyle got all bent out of shape. I told him to chill and he shoved me. He thinks Dad's got a kid somewhere or even that he could be *dead*. And that if I don't get equally bent out of shape, or punch him out when he shoves me and needles me for *not* obsessing about it, that means I've got no balls." Joe hesitated, then finished, "He agrees he's a prick, but says at least a prick's got balls."

Vicky plucked a long strand of hair off her lower lip and chuckled. "He's got a way with words."

Joe raised an eyebrow, silent. He looked away when she glanced over at him.

"What?" she asked. Joe could hear the smile in her voice.

"Nothing."

"You gotta admit it's a funny line." She squeezed his leg again, said, "Here ya go," and turned the oldies station up loud.

# Chapter Sixteen
## July 5th

"Hey, Mel. Hi, Juliet. I want to talk to the brown and white mare. Any chance of that?" Kyle squinted into the glare of the sun.

Mel glanced at his shoes then nodded. "Sure, of course. You caught us between appointments." She smiled. "That is if she wants to talk to you. You go ahead."

"What's your goal for this session, Kyle?" Juliet asked.

"Get some idea why I'm such a prick," he said. He preempted the question he knew was coming. "So, 'self-awareness' again. That's the word I'd boil it down to." He grinned, feeling more than a little self-conscious now.

"Go for it." Mel raised her arm toward the pasture behind the arena, where the team's three horses grazed.

"It might take all day," he joked, heading into the arena. "Break out your sleeping bags for tonight." He stopped and turned around. "Seriously, how long do I have?

"A good hour," Mel answered.

"Ya know …" he started to come back through the gate. "Maybe I should skip this. What can happen in an hour?"

"It's up to you, Kyle," Mel said. "We're here and have the time if you want it."

Juliet asked, "Was the hour you had last week with—was it Maria Horse?—useful?"

Kyle let a half grin speak for him. He turned again and loped to the center of the arena, scanning the surrounding pasture.

There was Maria Horse. She stood, watching him, not making a move to come forward, while the appaloosa mare left her side, ambling toward the open gate between the arena and the pasture.

"Yep. You're up today, Ma. Come on. We've got some things to talk about," Kyle called, his feet planted wide apart. Ma Horse stopped. "Hurry up. We don't have all day."

The mare lifted her head, her eyes fixed on him, nostrils widened.

"What are ya sniffing? Just get in here and let's get on with this." Irritated, Kyle started marching toward her. *Just like Ma. Pain in the neck.*

She turned and retreated into the pasture. With the fence and more space between them, she stopped, but not to graze. Just to watch him.

"For Christ's *sake.*" He glanced over at Maria Horse. She was serene and attentive, and also just watching him. "Maybe I should talk to you again. To hell with—" Then he tripped on a memory from his last session and nearly laughed. His shoulders drooped, and shaking his head, he stuck his hand in his hair for a second. *Pfft, I get it. Angry—again—and this horse feels it.*

"Right. Okay," he addressed both mares.

He tipped his head back and took several deep breaths, concentrating on the blue of the early morning sky. *Okay, everyone, I'm ...unloading my pissy mood onto that cloud there. It can dump a load of rain on us if it's too heavy or it can ... drift off. Drifting ... good. Wouldn't that be a neat trick. Okay, Ma, does that help make you—well, damn. Hello. You were quiet. How can such a large animal move with such grace?*

He greeted her with another soft hello, feeling awkward somehow, unwilling to touch the beautiful creature now only an arm's length away. Proud head held high, her gaze was fixed on something in the distance.

*Why was I okay before with the palomino, but not you? Because I'm thinking of you as Ma Horse, maybe? Last time out here, I marked you as eavesdropping.*

"But with horses, it's just curiosity or concern, right? Interest?" He mumbled, pushing down the thought that could be the case with people, too. *With Ma, it would be judgment.* "Anyway, I guess you've met me halfway here, haven't you?" He spoke to her as he took a small step closer, and registered the shiver that rippled over the curves of the horse's white and chocolate flank. Her tail swished and her gaze moved to meet his. He lifted his hand to within an inch of her muzzle. *You gonna chomp me?* He asked silently. *Dogs like it when you offer a sniff.* He held her eye and stepped another foot closer. *Close enough. Right? No. I hear ya, if we're going to do this at all, we gotta get closer.* He moved his hand to the silky, strong neck.

*Warm, Ma. You're warm from the sun already.* The mare held still. Kyle felt the tension in her. *Is that in me?* He took another deep breath, took his time letting it go. She smelled a little like porridge. He rested the back of his bandaged hand on the boney hardness of her forehead, his fingers relaxed in their natural curl, then tipped them open to trail down to the prickly velvet of her nose. He felt something inside him unravel, soften.

*At the fireworks, you touched my face, Ma. I went to jelly. I don't want that, to be jelly. I'm twenty-eight, for God's sake. Where were any cuddles or touch, when I was a kid, Ma? I'd have loved to be jelly back then.*

Ma Horse lifted her head, her eyes roaming his face. She stepped in and dropped her head, inches from his face.

Kyle caught his breath on a memory. *Right, head hugs, I forgot.* He stepped closer, laid his forehead against hers. *We gave each other head hugs. But Ma, not often enough.* He raised his arms around the mare's head and laced his fingers behind the taut upright ears. Beneath his hands, her mane felt thick, warm, and coarse.

He stood thinking of nothing for a few long seconds, then pulled back and looked at her. The horse kept her head bowed.

"Okay. So, I know you're a horse. You're not Ma," he whispered. "But … let me tell you what I can't tell her."

He laid his bandaged palm against her neck, wanting the connection, his eyes on the horizon. It took a long time for any words to form in his mind. An image took shape first: he sat hunched behind his math homework on the kitchen table watching his mother attack making dinner: yanking open the oven or fridge, slamming drawers and cabinets closed, whirling to yell at him for not setting the table.

*Do you know how scary you were when I was little? And how … far away?* His view changed in his mind's eye: he stood as a skinny, six-year-old in a dim bedroom, staring at a silent bed, flat but for a slight rise along one side beneath a nubby quilt. The only sign a person lay there was the thin, bare arm snaked across a pillow where the head should be.

*You'd be in bed, wasted on your little pills, with a pillow over your head in the middle of a summer day. I snuck into your room so many times. I almost dumped them out once, but I chickened out. Did you know that? Another time, you caught me. I was gonna eat every one of them, just to be a brat. Just so you couldn't. But you heard me: you woke up and slapped them out of my hand, groggy and wasted-looking with black smears under your eyes. No one else saw you like that. Just me. Maybe Dad.*

He glanced at Ma Horse. She still held his eye.

"But, oh," he spoke aloud again. "Of course, Hairy saw you. Wow, you loved that cat. You cuddled and baby-talked to him all the time." He broke off, searching the sky for another cloud, then whispered, "God, Ma. I swear you loved Hairy more than me." A kind of sob-laugh burst from him.

Resting his forehead against the horse's neck, two fat tears fell, darkening her hide.

"Okay, then, here's the big question: Ma? *Do* you love me?"

A warm sense of knowing grew in his stomach, spread to his chest, and tightened his throat. He saw her eyes last night after the fireworks, filled with affection, felt the curve of her hand against his cheek. He took a shaky breath. *Maybe. God, I wish I'd felt it then. Or was sure about it now.*

*How about another question, then?* He cast a nervous glance back toward Mel and Juliet, both sitting on the arena's rail fence, watching. It felt urgent now to keep going. He walked around the horse, out of the women's view, and leaning his good shoulder against hers, felt her brace to meet his weight.

*Why all the secrets, Ma? They drive me crazy. It's like you never trust me to know anything. You want to keep me in the dark, no matter how old I am. Sure, people hide stuff from kids, or think they are, but how about when I was a teenager? I saw what a shit Dad was, but you just kept taking your Valium and making excuses for him. All your pretending made me want to puke and still does.*

He felt Ma Horse shifting, but carried on, talking out loud again. "Now Joe does the same thing. But with you, the big fake is harder to take—given all the orders you dole out like playing cards and with you always keeping tabs on us."

Kyle shook his head once and shoved away from the horse, feeling restless and tense.

"You always expected the worst of me. Always had to tell me what to do." His voice hardened. "And you're *still* doing it, secrets and withholding. Not letting us in. Why the hell do you keep up that wall? What are you—"

Ma Horse stepped sideways, her head high and the whites of her eyes showing all around.

"Hey, hey," Kyle broke off, stepping to the mare he reached to stroke her mane. "What's up? What are you—"

Kyle hands dropped to his sides and he froze. "Afraid of?" A sad smile started, then faded. "Thank you, Ma Horse." Turning to the palomino still watching from a distance, he tipped his head to her. "You, too, babe." He raised a hand to salute her, then softly brought it down to stroke the appaloosa from her blaze to her muzzle. Sending both horses a silent farewell, he turned toward Mel and Juliet.

He started talking before he'd quite reached them. "Well, I feel like a dick. I mean … a jerk."

"Why's that?" Mel asked.

"A great big lightbulb just went off out there." He managed a half grin. "Did you see it?"

"An 'aha' moment, was it?" Juliet asked.

"Yeah, I saw how I scared the horse."

"What did that mean to you when it happened?" Juliet sounded curious.

"Well, I'd been ranting about being scared of my …" he hesitated. This was family business. Vicky had said he didn't need to share with humans. "… scared of someone … when I was a kid. Seeing that big animal looking frightened … it hit me. The adult I was afraid of," he hesitated again, struggling to put this into words. "… was probably just as scared. Now, because I'm pissed off half the time, maybe they're afraid of me." He swallowed. "And I never knew that."

"Okay." Juliet nodded. "Did anything else come up?"

"Yeah. There is something else. I remembered something, that, um…" He took a couple steps backwards, toward the cabin. "I'd kind of like to look up on the internet, while I remember it." He put on a "may I be excused" expression.

"No problem," Mel said. "You go ahead. We're here if you want another session; talk to Vicky or call my cell to sort out a time."

Kyle saluted Mel with the business card she handed him. He dug his phone from his pocket and started entering her number as he turned to stride away, then stopped and faced them again. "Thanks. Both of you."

***

Padding barefoot across the living floor, Kyle rolled his neck and shoulders, stiff from hours on the bed poring over his iPad. He leaned into the kitchen doorway, "Watcha makin', Vick?"

Vicky jumped and a pair of tongs clattered to the floor.

"Whoa! Sorry!" Kyle stepped into the kitchen. "I smelled bacon."

"You scared me." She snatched up the tongs and rinsed them at the sink. "I was a million miles away. I didn't know you were upstairs."

"I was doing some research—the primary model and CMYK color systems. It was a dream Maria once told me; I never knew how creative it was." *Or what I dick I was when she told me about it,* he thought.

"Oh. Well, I'm making BLTs." She squirted cleaner on a paper towel and wiped bacon grease from the floor where the tongs had landed.

"Sounds good." He came to look over her shoulder as she stood up, and registered the sweet scent of shampoo he'd smelled last night in the group hug. *So it had been her hair. Kinda fruity. Nice. Not as nice as Maria's coconutty hair.* He'd loved the smell of Maria's hair. "Enough for three?"

"Enough for five." She ducked around him, grabbed something from inside the fridge, and nudged the door closed with her bare foot. "I'm feeding the Eagala team, too; the human members, at least."

"I meant, enough that I could have three?"

She chuckled. "Wow. Sure. There's enough. Your appetite's back, I guess."

"It was never gone. I'm off the meds and feeling good." He deepened his voice, "Strong like bull." Kyle waited for Vicky's reaction. When she slid bread into the toaster then started slicing tomatoes with no comment, he carried on, "I just tried searching for Dad, too. Asked Siri how to find him and we just went in circles. She was useless; just brought up his contact details from my phone. So I tried Truth Finder and they led me on and led me on till I was ready to toss the iPad over the railing. I'm lousy at this. Anyway, Ma should be telling us what's happened to him." He twisted and stretched, wishing he could take a long swim in the lake to loosen up. "Speaking of Ma, I had another good session with the horses today."

Vicky nodded. "Good. Can you finish draining the bacon for me, please?" She handed the newly washed tongs over her shoulder.

Kyle grabbed them and went to the stove. "Thought maybe I should investigate some of my finer qualities," he started, piling crisp bacon strips onto a platter lined with paper towels. "Joe pointed them out this morning after Ma's neighbor dropped a coupla bombs on us in her driveway."

"Yeah, he mentioned all that."

"He did," Kyle stated. He wasn't surprised, but he did wonder how that conversation went. He pushed the full platter over to Vicky, glancing at her profile. "Not sure now if Joe's character assessment of me came before or after I shoved him." He squinted and skewed his mouth sideways, pretending to ponder. "Probably both."

"Can you man the toaster if you're going to stand in front of it? Be useful." She turned away to start washing lettuce at the sink.

"Something going on, Vick?" He addressed her rigid back.

"I'm just thinking maybe you should be talking to Joe. Not me."

"Why not you? What's wrong with talking to you?" Her back was unreadable, and her voice was no help either. He peered into the toaster instead.

"You know I can't be involved in your therapy. And maybe you and Joe need to talk more than we do anyway," she said.

Kyle laughed. "I think Joe would rather punch me than talk to me just about now."

Vicky turned, hands dangling and dripping water onto the floor. He grinned. *Aha. That gotcha.*

She stared at him. "Seriously?"

Kyle let his grin die.

She leaned against the counter, opened and closed her mouth, then turned her back on him again, shaking her head. "For the record," she said. "Joe doesn't punch people."

Kyle waited for more. The toast popped.

"Get that, please."

He did, his mouth watering at the smell. He put in two more pieces of bread, but kept quiet, watching her be careful with her new ring when she dried her hands. As he waited to hear what she had to say, he wondered why her opinion mattered to him as much as it did. *When did that happen?*

Vicky started spreading mayonnaise onto toast. "All I'll say, Kyle, is your grandmother is the worst I've ever seen her. Or that Joe's seen her. So, especially now, I just think it's better if you tell *him* your personal things … rather than me."

"Hey. I'm sorry about Grandma. But not surprised. What's up with not talking to you, though?" He stepped over and nudged her, grinning down. "Did that stone on your finger breed rocks in your head, little sister?"

Vicky turned around, eyes narrowed. A blob of mayonnaise dripped from the butter knife in her hand onto her big toe. At the sound of heavy footsteps crossing the porch, then the living room, Kyle looked over his shoulder, waiting for Joe to appear. He noticed Vicky move away from him.

*Ah. Now, I get it,* Kyle thought. "Paper towels are over this way," he said under his breath, handing her one. "By *me*, Vick."

***

"Nice." Joe looked from Vicky to Kyle, his face carefully neutral. On his way to the refrigerator, he tossed Kyle a key on a little key chain advertising Pennzoil.

"Nice what?" Kyle answered, catching the key with a small wince.

*Nice, cozy domestic scene,* Joe thought. *And you know it.* He let the question hang there, unanswered. Grabbing a cold beer, he popped it open and leaned against the closed door of the fridge.

"Thought by now you might want a loaner so I don't have to keep driving you around." Joe took a quick swig of beer. "I just changed the oil, checked the tires and brakes. It's the dark blue CRX; not too sexy, but it's automatic, so should be easy enough to handle." He took a long swallow; over the rim of the can he watched his brother's expression harden.

"You know …" Kyle twirled the key on his index finger. His hands seemed fine to Joe. "… I think that's a great idea."

Joe flicked a glance at Vicky's back as she stood assembling sandwiches. Then, watching Kyle pick up a BLT, salute Vicky with it, and lean in to say something against her ear, he stepped up closer to hear.

"Still wonder why I'd rather talk to you today, Vick?" Kyle murmured. With an unmistakable hint of a smirk, he kissed the top of Vicky's head.

Joe gritted his teeth and dropped his eyes. A muscle in his jaw jumped. *Prick.*

"Thanks for everything," Kyle said. "I think I'll clear out now."

Joe started to distribute paper plates around the kitchen table, feeling Vicky's tension, her eyes on him. He listened to Kyle moving around upstairs, followed within minutes by the thump of a small duffle bag landing on the living room floor, footsteps on the loft stairs, then loud meows melting into loud purring—Joe imagined Doughnut enthusing over a chin scratching.

Over the creak of the porch door, Kyle shouted, "See ya around." The door slammed shut on a suffocating silence.

Avoiding Vicky's stare, Joe took another swig of beer, crossed the room, and flicked on the kitchen radio.

Vicky switched it off. "What the heck, Joe?"

"What? It's how we always talk to each other." He heard the CRX come to life in the barn.

"It sure as hell is not." Vicky stood beside him now, frowning. "What's with this passive-aggressive stuff?"

Joe raised his chin. *Taking Kyle's side again … that hurts.*

He moved to lean against the counter for some space. Aiming for casual, he opened a sandwich, broke a piece of bacon, and popped it in his mouth.

"Think I hurt his feelings? Maybe he needs your comforting?" He tried to sound teasing, but only heard pathetic and gave up trying, telling himself he was damned close to not caring.

*No, that's a lie. The truth is you care way too much.*

"Okay, pull your head in, Joe."

He looked away from Vicky's flashing eyes but couldn't escape the chill in her voice.

"I know you have a lot on your mind," she said. "But don't go imagining stupid things and piling on more angst."

*So I'm the one at fault?* He drained his beer and crushed the can. "We're better off. We don't need his anger around."

"*His* anger?" Vicky stalked back to her workstation. "Look in the mirror, Joe."

His focus narrowed to her hands, their choppy motions as she transferred sandwiches from the nicked-up cutting board to a bright blue serving platter. Several sandwiches came to pieces in her fingers. Vicky shoved the mess into the sink and leaned her hands on the edge of the counter.

The twitch in his jaw started double-time. Hearing her take a deep breath, he directed his gaze out the far window, certain he wasn't going to like what came next.

"Kyle's trying to get a handle on his issues, Joe." He knew that quiet voice, more angry than gentle. "What are *you* trying to do?"

*There's the zinger.* Joe's face burned. "Hold it together, Vicky. That's all. To just flippin' hold it together!"

He turned and was out of the cabin, jogging across the yard, before it crossed his mind to say where he was going. *Hell with that. It's not like I'm racing off to a bar.* He snatched the key to the old Camaro from the board inside the barn door.

Jolting and bouncing under the driveway's low, arching trees, he reached to turn the radio to full volume and a pine branch smacked him square in the face. His hand flew to cover his cheek and eye. *Shit!* Maybe later he'd be grateful the soft needles had hit his eyelid, not his eye, but at the moment, seeing dots of blood on his fingertips and smarting inside and out, he felt the world was damned close to shit.

"First, Kyle, then Grandma, now even the damn trees are whaling on me today." Squinting his sore eye tight, he punched the gas and jerked the car onto Jebavy, into the blast of an ear-piercing horn. A motorcycle swerved around him, the driver glaring back over his shoulder and holding his middle finger high in the air, jabbing it repeatedly skyward.

"Jesus Christ." Joe stood on the brake, stalling the car. He dropped his head back onto the headrest. "Hold it together. Just hold it together." The sound of the biker receded toward town and summer quiet took over again. *Not good. Peace is not quiet. Peace is … a problem.* He managed to restart the engine and blast the peace.

"War! Hunh! What is it good for?" *Perfect.* Edwin Starr's angry voice poured from the radio, filling the car and his head. He sang along, not missing a word.

Two and a half songs later, he stood at the Ludington library reference counter, waiting in line to talk to his mother. He remembered years ago, she'd quoted Ray Bradbury saying old books smelled like ancient Egypt; ever since, that's what he smelled when he came to the library.

Breathing in the scent, Joe focused on listening to her advise a gangly teenager laden with books. She encouraged the boy to let her know which ones helped improve his tennis game and with a mumbled, "Sure, thanks" he wandered off nodding.

"Hello, Joe." Ma smiled. "I thought you and Vicky would be at Grandma's still, sharing the big news."

"We got back about an hour ago." His voice sounded robotic even to his own ear.

She studied his face but said nothing. He saw her register his scratched eye. She handed him a tissue.

"She isn't good, Ma." He dabbed at the scratch without interest, feeling awkward standing there. He studied the decorated mini-Christmas tree in the glassed-in office behind her, trying to remember how many years it had been there, hoping no one would ever take it down.

"No," Ma agreed. "She's seemed worse the last four, maybe five times I saw her."

"Sorry?" He stared at her. "You go to see her?"

"Of course, I see her. Regularly."

"I never knew that." *And it's weird I didn't,* he added to himself.

"I didn't know you didn't know." Her eyes moved over his face as she straightened some brochures on the counter. "Does it make a difference?"

It was Joe's turn to shrug. It did, but he didn't really know why. He changed the subject. "I wonder if you could suggest some more books on dementia and Alzheimer's."

"I think I can." She stepped out from behind the counter, rolled her graceful shoulders then clamped a hand on his arm. "Oops, hold on."

Startled, he froze. She used him for balance as she stuck one foot at a time far beneath the counter. Joe ducked his head to see her wiggling her bare feet into sandals; they looked to be nothing more than a few colorful beads and a couple strips of leather.

"There!" She nodded once and let go of him.

Pink polish on her toes? Was this his mother or some imposter?

"Respectable librarian again," she declared, setting off at a brisk pace.

Yep, this was his mother. Joe stayed close behind as she passed several rows of shelves, talking over her shoulder as they walked.

"Bare feet are my only nod to summer while I'm at work." She sounded almost chirpy.

He stopped short twice when she paused to pick up and reshelve a book that had fallen or been left on the floor.

"Sometimes I eat lunch in the children's play area outside. Just so I can dig my toes in the sand and imagine I'm at the beach," she said.

*Nope, this woman is an imposter*, he thought. *My mother never daydreams. Or sounds genuinely happy.*

She slowed, then stopped and faced him. He could see a number of titles on the shelf behind her and disappointment bloomed. Every title he read sounded familiar.

She tilted her head. "I gave you a stack a few months ago, didn't I?"

He nodded, unsmiling.

"And do you remember which ones?"

He started pointing. "This one. And that one. This, one … yeah: *The 36-Hour Day*. That was a good one. And this one by Dr. Ruth was good, too, practical—the same perky voice everyone knows." Guessing her next question, he trailed off.

"What are you hoping to find now, Joe?"

Her kindness almost undid him.

"Just, you know … more ideas." He looked over her shoulder, his mouth twisted, chewing the inside of his cheek. She touched his arm and he stopped chewing. He met her eyes. "I want to know how to *reach* her, Ma," he said. "How to help her recognize me and … I don't know … how to make her *happy* again."

Her gaze was warm, but also sad.

"You read all those other books, right? Did a lot of research on the Internet?" When he nodded, she went on. "So, you know anything you or I—or anyone—can do, is minimal, and the disease will progress regardless, right?"

He refused to nod. He willed her to start gathering books, to find some new articles or research. He imagined growling, "Do your job, for God's sake!" Instead he turned to hunt for a title that didn't look familiar. Maybe he should reread a few of these …

"It might be getting a little late for any of this, Joe."

She stood there in her little skimpy sandals. Books surrounded him—at eye-level, at his feet, in front of, and behind him. Shelves stretched on and on, thousands of books. On every page, knowledge and advice, people's ideas. All worthless. All shit.

A bitter note crept into his voice. "Everyone's trying to just write her off." He shoved his hands into the pockets of his shorts, chewing his cheek again.

"That's the *last* thing I want to do, Joe. The last." She studied his face for several seconds, then started walking again, heading to a different row entirely. "Remember hearing the Serenity Prayer?"

"Yeah, of course." He stopped just short of adding, "Let's skip this, hey Ma?" He regretted ever coming in the first place.

"Probably from Grandma, right?" Ma asked, slowing her steps.

Joe's impatience grew as she stopped, pulled a dark blue, hardcover book from a shelf at knee height, and flipped it open.

"That's right, from her Al-Anon life," he said, suddenly recalling the first few words. "Doesn't it start something like: God grant me the serenity to accept the things I cannot change?"

His voice probably sounded normal to her, but he was starting to feel trapped. He wanted to get out on the road, to speed and to blast music. He wanted a drink.

"You're right," Ma said. "It actually originated way before Al-Anon, but yes, that's where Grandma got it. She relied on that prayer and her fellow Al-Anon members a lot—especially when you were a baby."

"Say again?" *Since I was a baby? This is news.*

"Sure, she was part of Al-Anon for many years. She got as much out of that group and those meetings as your grandfather did from Alcoholics Anonymous; they were both very open about that. The support they got there and from their sponsors was phenomenal."

*That much I do know. Maybe if I don't ask any questions, she'll stop talking.*

Ma went on, "They both started when you were very small, right after your first birthday." She seemed to falter, then stopped. She handed him the book she held and suggested in a soft voice, "Have a look at this. I think you'll recognize a lot of Grandma in there."

"*How Al-Anon Works.* This looks familiar." Joe opened it at random, not so much out of interest, but because another day and time flooded his mind as he flipped through the pages. "I can hear her saying all this." He turned the book toward Ma, underlining several slogans with his index finger as he read them aloud, "One day at a time. How Important Is It? This too shall pass. Attitude of Gratitude. She liked 'Attitude of Gratitude' best, I think." He swallowed. Without looking up, he asked, "But, Ma, what's all this got to do with Alzheimer's?"

"Nothing." She gently took the book from him, her eyes roaming the index page as she continued, "They've got to do with helping you accept we *are* going to lose Grandma, at some point—possibly soon."

Joe shook his head, his shoulders sagging. They stood a short distance from the opening to their row; beyond that: the rest of the world … oblivious. Stupid. A trio of skinny teenage girls in short-shorts giggled past. A toddler lurched by going the other direction, first in then out of Joe's view with an elderly couple right behind, then they were gone, too. A happy chortle reached his ears, and he pictured the baby being scooped up and kissed. It was all wrong.

"Awareness, acceptance, action," Ma read aloud. "That's what Grandma would say to you, now, if she could."

*She would*, Joe realized. *She used to say that all the time, like a mantra to herself.*

"Joe, try going down the street and see if Book Mark carries the daily readers Grandma had … *Courage to Change* or *One Day at a Time*. I mean … umm, if that appeals to you. It's up to you, of course—if you're ready." She looked up, then paused a second, but held his gaze. "They've been helping me. Well, not just the daily readers, but the whole Al-Anon program, the meetings, my sponsor, and such. And not just in dealing with Grandma. I've been going …" she hesitated, "… since November."

*What do I care?* Joe registered her words, but no reply formed. He stood silent, knowing it looked as if he were listening. He allowed her to put the book back into his hand, then followed her to the self-checkout. He agreed that, yes, he could look after her house for a few days starting tomorrow. He didn't ask why. He didn't comment on the short notice. He didn't quiz her about Dad like Kyle would have wanted. He didn't care. He just wanted to get out of there.

He wanted a drink.

# Chapter Seventeen
## July 12th

A quick, hard, crack of lightning lit the cornfields and forests bordering Jebavy Road. Kyle jumped, gripped the steering wheel tighter, and laughed at himself. He angled a quick look through the car's open sun-roof to admire a jagged vein of light forking across banks of dark cloud.

"One, one thousand, two, one thousand ..." He counted under his breath as he drove, anticipating the thunder to follow. *There—unrolling over Lake Michigan. Okay, that took fifteen seconds, so divide by five ... the storm's about three miles away.*

And, he decided, judging by the roiling clouds, moving fast enough to justify pushing the CRX well above the speed limit. With the sunroof jammed open, he'd be deeper in Joe's bad book if he didn't get to the barn quick and ended up caught in the rain. He sure as hell didn't want to be stranded at home with it stuck in the garage till the rain stopped, either.

He heard Maria teasing, *"Try walking or a bicycle. You might learn to like it."* Though it had been almost two weeks since he'd seen her, he hadn't stopped hearing her voice. He'd found himself replaying past conversations with her, trying to get them right. He was starting to get why she didn't want to have kids with him. What he didn't get was why she had stayed with him as long as she had. Turning onto the dirt road leading to the cabin, the coolness of the air beneath the overhanging trees brought up goosebumps on his bare arms. He drove at a crawl, glad for his headlights cutting the heavy gloom ahead. All around him birds battened down their hatches, swooping and calling warnings to each other. He ducked away from branches that reached for him through windows and sunroof and imagined cajoling Joe and Vicky into hosting a murder mystery weekend sometime. *It'd have to be short notice,* he thought, *when the forecast called for heavy fog or a storm like this.*

He started imagining the murder. *A middle-aged woman kills her husband while on a ski trip somewhere out west ... no, wait! The husband kills the wife after decades of putting up with her and then goes into hiding in—say—Colorado's underworld ... where he finds a lover who's a dead ringer—HA!—for the dead wife. He convinces the lover to go Ludington and pose as the dead wife in order to drive his two sons crazy with her frustrating behavior. The sons sense she's not the same woman, though. She's too calm and sometimes almost nice so ... aha! There's one of the sons—the younger, ugly one—standing just ahead in the headlights' beam, eyeballing this car, probably expecting I've busted it. Will you look at that scowl, oh! now it's a cheesy, fake smile. But the audience will know how the ugly one really feels about his brother: consumed with jealousy for an imagined attraction between the older—more studly— one and the ugly one's foxy fiancée. Ho ho! The ugly one now retreats into the cavernous and unwelcoming barn, where …*

Brilliant slashes cracked the sky and Kyle chuckled again as he pulled to a stop on the grass driveway. He cursed himself for forgetting his camera, unfolded from the cramped driver's seat, and stood staring into the drama developing overhead. Scrutinizing, memorizing, choosing the colors and shades he'd use to paint it. He'd find some metallic—

With a boom! thunder clapped, and he jumped. Laughing at himself, he leaned into the car to grab his windbreaker and headed to the barn door.

"Thuffering thuccotash," he muttered. "I've got some therious thucking up and … thun roof thoothing to do."

Joe used to beg for his Sylvester the Cat imitations when they were kids. And they'd both loved scaring themselves with thunderstorms—unless they happened to be camping in them.

Kyle knew the storm had him feeling high, but that—despite evicting him from the cabin—he had Joe to thank for the past week's good mood. Having a vehicle again meant freedom. On top of that, he'd just gotten the bandages off and he had his *body* back. Who cared if most of him looked fish-belly-white, highlighted with scars in an impressive array of pinks.

What he'd learned through Ma Horse last week had kept him pretty level when Joe kicked him out. He hoped those lessons and his new mood would keep him cool through whatever Joe might still want to throw at him, maybe literally. He had it coming, he'd been enough of a jerk to deserve whatever Joe wanted to dish.

Crossing his fingers, Kyle angled his body through the narrow gap Joe had left between the barn's massive doors. He scanned the building's interior and breathed in its signature smell of horse manure, feed, and motor oil. Other than some birds swooping in and out, the far end seemed quiet and dark. While the mini drowsed in her stall, all the other stalls stood empty.

*Odd for a day like this.*

The near end housed its typical collection of vintage and muscle cars. Kyle figured the Olds had gone to its lucky new owner, but he recognized the orange Chevelle, the yellow convertible, and the Camaro—his ambulance. Scuffed work boots and a pair of stained gray overalls stood planted in front of a blue Corvette's yawning hood. A bare bulb encased in a metal cage dangled over the engine, its stark circle of light more intense given the silent dusk surrounding them.

"Whazzup?" came from the Corvette. Joe stepped back from the car, wiping his hands on a rag, and wearing a look of impatient expectation. He pulled out one earbud, holding it at the ready as if to put it right back in, and left the other one in place.

Kyle straightened, but stayed at the door. *Stick with the plan,* he reminded himself. *You earned this attitude.*

"The CRX's sunroof is sick," he said. "Started getting snotty with me off and on, a day or two ago. Now it's on meltdown mode. Stuck on open—a quasi-convertible."

Joe approached, holding out his hand.

As Kyle dropped the car key into his palm, lightning slashed across the sky. "We're in for it."

"Yeah, I'll work on it inside."

Hearing how flat Joe's voice sounded, Kyle wished he'd come earlier to apologize for the shoving and taunting incident. His plan to leave Joe to cool off for a week before trying to clear the air didn't seem to have worked.

The old Joe would have teased, "What'd you do to her, mate?" and commanded, "Outta my way." Now all Kyle got was a mumbled, "Nice tan."

"Isn't it?" He stretched his arms and stuck out one leg to display the best of his lotion slathered scars. "Too sexy for my shirt."

Without a second glance, Joe walked open one of the heavy barn doors, shoving it ahead of him. Kyle moved to do the other, leaning into the weight, liking the feel of doing something physical again.

The thunder came, shuddering in his chest. Shrugging into his windbreaker, he watched Joe park the Honda beside the low-slung Corvette, and wondered for the hundredth time how anyone could work day after day in such a dreary, chilly space.

"Probably a fuse or a switch." Joe climbed from the Honda and grabbed a trouble-light from a series of hooks that marched above his nearly empty work bench then climbed back in, mumbling, "Could be quick, could be a pain."

Kyle tried to feign interest as Joe, head poking from the sunroof, ran his fingers along its inner edge, tried jiggling it, and announced, "Nothing stuck in there and the alignment's okay. I'll try greasing it up."

Swallowing a yawn, Kyle nodded. He watched for a few minutes, feeling useless, as he always did around cars, then found himself addressing a pair of long legs protruding from the open passenger door. The rest of Joe lay contorted on the front seat.

Wielding a small screwdriver, with his head angled beneath the dash near the steering wheel, Joe appeared fascinated by its underside.

*The Michelangelo of mechanics,* Kyle thought. Hoping to get him talking, he asked, "Where are Timmy and Jack? I haven't seen them around a lot this summer."

"Tommy and Jocko. They've been around. They're part-time."

Kyle took another angle, "I forgot to check the doors for any 'Keep out: Eagala in session' signs. We're allowed in here, today?"

"No clients due till around lunch." Joe sounded muffled and not very chummy, more like someone making small talk with a customer. "Vicky and co are exercising the horses way out back on Gillian's land."

"Hope they're back soon, this storm's only a couple miles away." As if to confirm, lightning cracked again. Kyle went still. He noticed Joe pull his head up and do the same, both of them counting the seconds. At 'ten' the thunder rumbled; a mile closer since he'd left home.

He wanted to remind Joe how they'd loved thunderstorms as kids—even now he felt like doing a jig—but he also felt awkward and unwelcome. Joe wiggled under the dash again, mumbling, "They're smart; they'll get home okay."

Kyle dragged a dented metal stool over from a corner into the circle of light and perched at the end of Joe's legs. Sitting without talking for a couple minutes, he wondered why Joe was faking nonchalance; Joe *always* worried about Vicky. *Like one day she'd be swallowed up by the earth and just disappear.*

"So, you gave me a lemon," Kyle teased. "I deserve it. Hope the brakes aren't rigged."

"There's an idea," Joe said. He pulled himself to a seated position with something metal in his hands. "Fuse box—hopefully cleaning the contacts will do the trick."

With a nod, Kyle scooted out of the way as Joe climbed from the car and got busy at the workbench, his back turned.

Seeing his chance, Kyle cleared his throat and started, "Sorry for being such a dick that morning at Ma's, Joe, and for winding you up with Vicky when you told me to clear out." That didn't kill him after all; it was sure easier than saying it to Joe's front. And felt better out than in.

He only got a shrug in reply.

"I had another Eagala session that day," Kyle went on and seemed to get a chin-tip out of Joe. *Jeez ... this is hard,* he thought, and tried to plow ahead, "I guess it occurred to me, a lot of what Ma does—and used to do—might have come from her being scared. You know, buried under having to handle everything

Dad was too drunk to do, worrying about him, his crap attitude, us two ..." No comment still. "So I'm trying to lighten up on her. I went over and replanted some pansies I whacked to hell on her doorstep the other day."

*No high-fives in store for this news.* He wanted to tell Joe about remembering the dream Maria had, but gave up. He blew out a long breath and asked, "So where's Ma been these last few days, anyhow? Her cell goes to voicemail and she's never at her place or the library, no matter when I drop by."

"Out of town somewhere ... back today, though," Joe said. "And no, I don't know where. I didn't ask."

*No surprises there. Ha, here's a topic he'll rise to:* "Hey, how's Grandma doing? Better?"

Joe traded his sandpaper for the screwdriver and climbed back into the Honda. "She had pneumonia last week." His voice betrayed no emotion.

"Wow. That's something like the third time now, isn't it?" No wonder Joe ... didn't seem like *Joe* lately.

Kyle fell quiet, listening to a soft shushing rain begin falling on the barn's metal roof. The shushing changed to sharp tapping. High-pitched hollering—or was it laughing—and pounding hoofbeats erupted from somewhere behind the barn. In seconds, the rain had accelerated to rapid-fire drumming.

Feeling giddy as a ten-year-old, Kyle leapt up and ran to the main doors, then froze as a lightning strike lit the world. With a belly laugh he turned and saw Joe stand, intent on the arena door, and forming words lost under a bone-jarring thunder clap.

Kyle shouted, "No need to count the sec—"

He stopped short as Vicky, Mel, and Juliet rode in from the arena, all shining eyes and glistening skin, astride their rain-darkened horses. Their physicality charged the air and drove him forward. The women and horses tossed their heads to throw off water caught on eyelashes and manes.

A blue-white flash lit the doorway behind them, burning the image into Kyle's mind. Calling an offer of help, he started across the barn to them, but froze mid-stride, just to watch, as the trio swung down from their saddles, almost as one.

Free of stirrups, each woman jumped the last inches to the ground and rushed to close her horse into a stall, then raced past him and Joe to the main doors.

He heard Mel shouting over the rain's staccato fury, "Can't stop! My truck window's open!" Behind her, Juliet just ran, a rain-slick arm raised as if in greeting and farewell. Both women disappeared into the sheeting gray obscuring the world outside the barn.

Kyle stepped back as Vicky flew past, unbuckling her helmet as she ran.

"I'll cancel clients," she yelled.

Joe shouted for her attention, "And—"

She paused, poised to run through the doors, and responded to what Joe hadn't yet said. "... I'll shut any windows in the cabin. Can you—"

Joe finished for her, "... rub down the horses."

Vicky waved, ducked her head low, and disappeared into the deluge.

Kyle went to the door, gripped a thick edge of the rough wood, and leaned to within an inch of the living wall of water.

"Whew ..." Despite the jacket he wore, goosebumps rose on his arms. A shiver ran up the back of his neck and under his hair. He breathed in the cold and the ozone smell, waiting out a sudden flash of desire to haul any one of those women back and up into the hayloft overhead. An image of Maria sprang to mind—lips parted, eyes locked to his, arching beneath him. Knowing she would be the only one he'd really want for a very long time, he ached.

Another lightning flash lit the barn's interior.

"Kyle!"

He turned to see Joe hauling a colorful saddle blanket off Bingo's broad and steaming back. When the thunder quit, Joe yelled over the din of the rain. "Run help Vicky! The loft window sticks!"

Kyle yanked the hood of his jacket up and sprinted into the hammering rain, catching his breath at the icy, raw power of it battering his head and shoulders.

He tore across the yard, whooping like a banshee. Taking the cabin stairs in a single leap, he burst onto the porch, saw Vicky through the window to the living room, and skidded to a stop.

She stood at Joe's desk talking on the phone, T-shirt plastered to every swell and curve, her hair dry on top but the ponytail hanging in wet spirals and dripping rain onto her shoulders.

The door banged shut behind him and he snapped his mouth closed as Vicky looked up. Plucking the wet cloth away from her skin and without seeming to miss a beat in her conversation, she turned her back to him.

*Whew* ... Kyle shook his head, dropped his sodden jacket on the porch floor, and toed off his squelching gym shoes. With his eyes fixed on his soggy socks, he made his way on exaggerated tiptoes, through to the bathroom.

Closing the door behind him with the softest click, he sagged against it for a long minute, then addressed Betty Boop staring out from the shower curtain: "Shit, Betty. *Shit.*"

She offered no counsel or comfort and he took a seat on the edge of the tub, his elbows on his knees and his mind in turmoil.

"Betty, I do not want to go back out there." He eyed her flirty, vinyl figure. "You're no help either, you know."

At least he figured he had a legit reason to spend time in the can; he was as dripping wet as Vicky. He stood, turning side on to the mirror to check his look. *Pretty damn good*, he decided, *but hers? Eye-popping.*

Still stiff, he dragged his wet shirt over his head, tossed it into the shower stall, and rubbed his hair and damp torso with a towel from the crowded rack.

He studied the man in the mirror. *I hear you*, he thought. *But look, that incident was a very long time ago—eight years at least. And a clear case of confused identity; Joe and I have always sounded a lot alike. Plus it was just a kiss—and just that one time, long buried, never to be resurrected or repeated. I doubt she even remembers.*

From the mudroom on the other side of the bathroom door, he heard the unmistakable banging of the cat flap, then seconds later, liquid being lapped up with enthusiasm.

"Doughnut!" Kyle cracked the door open a few inches and crouched there, waiting for her to look up from her water bowl; he reached through to lift the scrawny, one-eyed cat into his hideout. "Great timing, again, little one!" he praised her.

Looking about half of her five pounds, fur matted flat with rain or standing in tufts where she'd attempted to groom, she resembled a miniature Muppet. He cradled her against his throat with one hand and grabbed the towel he'd just crammed back amongst the others. Holding her in one palm and taking his time, he wiped down her face, head, and flanks with gentle strokes.

As his hand moved over her, she nudged her forehead against his jaw with surprising strength and started up a steady purr. *What gives?* Kyle wondered. *I didn't know cats liked this sort of thing.*

Concentrating on the areas that intensified her purring, he asked her, "Is this how it'd feel to be a parent?"

Her ear twitched beneath his breath. Cupping her against his throat again, he jutted his chin over top of her to snug her in and tossed the towel back on the rack.

He caught sight of himself in the mirror as he drew two fingers along the bumpy curve of her spine. A new calm had settled over his face, one that didn't change when he heard movement in the kitchen and sounds of running water.

Taking care not to disturb Doughnut, he grabbed the towel they'd shared and opened the door just long enough to fling it through the mudroom into the kitchen.

"Very funny." Vicky spoke in a normal voice, a smile simmering at the edges. "Get outta there. You don't have to hide away. I'm decent."

Kyle pushed the door open a crack and peered through, aiming to get a laugh, and wandered into the mudroom. Like a one-eyed princess fresh from a spa, Doughnut surveyed the world from under his chin.

She earned a full-watt smile from Vicky, he noticed, but it dimmed to low for him.

"Check the clothes dryer right there for some socks and a shirt," she said. "And stop your smirking."

He cut his protest short at the sight of her wagging finger, glad to glimpse a wry smile as she turned back to the coffee maker.

"No smart remarks, either," she ordered, making no comment on the map of scars he displayed.

"Yes, ma'am." Taking care with Doughnut, who gave a little, *Mip!* of interest, he pulled an armload of laundry from the dryer, and set it on top the machine with her as queen of the heap. With a second *Mip*, she sank into it, kneading, her eyes half closed.

"Be nicer if it were still warm, eh?" Kyle removed one sock, then another from beneath her nickel-sized paws, and pulled them on. "Excuse me." He lifted her to extract a wrinkled T-shirt from the pile, set her down again, and dove into the shirt.

"Coffee?" Vicky asked.

"Yes, please. Ma'am." Hovering in the doorway, he looked from under his lashes like a chastised boy and inclined his head toward the bathroom door as he collected Doughnut back under his chin. "I'll go have it with Betty Boob. I mean *Boop!*"

"Idiot." She finally laughed, filling a faded SpongeBob SquarePants mug and stirring in a heaped spoonful of sugar, the way *Joe* liked it; Kyle didn't use sugar. She turned to look him in the eye. "It never occurred to me anyone would come charging through that downpour."

"Sorry, Vick. Joe sent me to help with the loft window that—" Kyle's eyes flew open, as he started to rush from the mudroom. "Shit!"

"I closed that one before I went out."

"Oh." Kyle pulled a face. *No prize for guessing what distracted me from that.* "Whew."

Doughnut walked onto his shoulder, stepping with care, and wrapping herself around the back of his neck. She settled in, her chin resting on his left shoulder and her tail touching his right ear—caressing, then not caressing, then caressing—and started to purr.

Kyle took his mug from Vicky and watched her touch the pink leather triangle of the cat's nose then turn back to the coffee pot.

Surprising himself, Kyle blurted out, "That kiss between us, way back when, Vicky"—her dark head came up and her hand paused, just for an instant—"I never expected you to come charging into my room in the dark."

"*Your* room? It had been Joe's room for four years. I had no idea you'd decided to come home that night." She finished pouring her coffee.

"So, you thought I was Joe."

"Of course! It was pitch dark in there." She turned to him. "Until I felt the whiskers that Joe didn't have yet, I thought you were spending Thanksgiving break at college with your girlfriend."

"A case of mistaken identity, I always figured that." He started to walk into the living room, taking care not to jostle Doughnut or slop his coffee. "Everyone still says how much Joe and I sound alike—on the phone especially."

"You didn't kiss alike." Her chuckle followed him.

Grimacing, he called out, "Did you ever tell Joe?" before seeing that she'd joined him, cradling a mug of coffee in both hands.

"Of course—right away." She wandered past him and onto the porch. "I never thought to roll down the weather shades in here." She cast a glance at the couch and ran a fingertip along the window ledge then stood staring into the now steady rain. "I knew this was coming, it was just several hours earlier than forecast."

Though he'd have liked to hear Joe's reaction to the kiss, Kyle welcomed the easy subject change. The incident hadn't plagued him; he mostly remembered being so surprised at the time he had just lain like a statue in Joe's bed for the three seconds it took before she'd yelped and was gone. Afterwards he'd been baffled but written it off as "Vicky's most embarrassing moment."

"I wonder if I should go help Joe," she said now. "It must be taking longer with the horses than I thought it would."

Kyle thought—in her baggy shirt, bare feet, and tights—she looked like the little sister he'd never had, and an anxious one.

"He's finishing the Honda, I bet," he said. "So he can send me packing as soon as possible."

Vicky leveled a look at him over the edge of her mug as she came back in and settled into a corner of the couch.

Kyle didn't bother trying to decipher the look or to ask about the big box standing beside the couch; he'd just unearthed an old boot box, stuffed with photos, from the cluttered bookshelf beside the fireplace. Setting his coffee on the floor and easing down into the chair that everyone still called "Grandpa's chair," he started pawing through the photos with one hand, scratching Doughnut's bony head with the other.

"Hell's bells, these are great." He whistled low between his teeth. "Professional quality. A pony Mustang, a Ford Fairlane, the old Chevelle … Joe took these?"

Vicky peered across at the selection he fanned out like a hand of playing cards. "Yep. He calls those beauty shots. Before he delivers any car to the buyer, he gets a good shot to post on the website I made for him. My favorite's the '36 Ford pickup—did you see it? Right, that's it. Isn't that yellow paint job gorgeous? But the wooden truck bed makes it. I'd have liked to have kept that one."

"Speak of the devil," Kyle called in a louder voice.

Footsteps on the stairs materialized into a dripping wet man looking through the window from the porch.

"Oh, honey!" Vicky moaned with a chuckle. She unfolded from the couch and disappeared into the kitchen.

"Here you go; back in action."

Kyle caught the key Joe tossed across the room. *Déjà vu.* "Thanks, dude. That's cool."

As Joe started stripping off and dropping wet clothes on the porch floor, Kyle returned to the photos on his lap, but a sudden image came to mind: sixteen-year-old Vicky telling Joe she'd just kissed his brother in the dark.

*Weird to find out that Joe knew about it all these years—knew about it right when it happened but hadn't burst in to tease him about it … or ever said a word.*

*Why didn't I ever go to him about it?* he wondered. *Griping about Ma keeping secrets is kind of a case of the pot calling the kettle black.* The thought made him sit up and shift in his chair. Doughnut pressed her front claws into his shoulder.

"Ow, sorry. I'll stay still."

Joe mumbled, "Traitor cat," and Kyle looked up to watch him climbing to the loft in his boxer shorts, rubbing his hair with the towel Vicky had brought him.

*You're jealous of me and Doughnut now? Jesus.* Kyle stared out past the porch and into the rain until Joe returned and broke the silence in the room.

"Storm's easing, but this rain's settled in."

Kyle blinked at Joe before registering what he'd said. "Damn." He made a gurgle of frustration and Doughnut opened her eye to consider him. "I wanted to paint. But I can't with the house all closed up."

"You're not getting rid of Maria's murals, are you, Kyle?" Vicky asked. She sat cross-legged on the floor, fishing through the large box Kyle had noticed earlier. As Joe hunkered down beside her, she nudged the box toward him and stood to curl back into her corner of the couch.

*You've never seen them. Why do you sound bummed?* It took a beat before he realized Joe must have been talking about them.

"No. I'll keep 'em. They're finished now. But did you see the sky before this storm started? I want to paint that. And you three coming in on your horses."

"Hey, yeah!" Vicky sat up and leaned forward. "Then you could make copies of your murals and display it all at the arts center in town—LACA would be all over a show like that."

"Hey, no!" He kept his gaze on Joe, watching him pull old-fashioned movie canisters from the box, then went back to shuffling through the photos on his lap, admiring his brother's eye for this kind of photography.

"No really, Kyle. Run a slide show of them or something; project them on walls. Maybe even do an outdoor one in town …"

"LACA wouldn't be interested in me." He yawned, focusing on Joe's photos.

"Why not? Joe told me they're both truly awesome. On par with Carolyn Damstra. You saw her exhibit, right? LACA ran it—"

Joe cut in, "He's not interested, Vick."

Kyle glanced up to catch her reaction.

Looking first at Joe, then him, she kept her hands on her coffee mug and ignored the film canisters Joe offered her. "Ah. The good old 'don't dream' philosophy, is it?"

"Me-ooow." Kyle tipped his head to speak softly into Doughnut's ear. She laid a paw against his cheek, purring. "Share your milk with Mommy, Doughnut?"

"I wasn't being catty—though it's a shame that's considered a bad thing, eh, Doughnut?" Vicky drained the last of her coffee, then met his glance. "I was just stating a fact as I see it, Kyle."

Joe left the room without a word. Seconds later Kyle heard him dialing the kitchen phone. Left alone to fight the battle, he turned to her.

"Hang on, Vick. That's a crock. You think Joe and I don't go after what we want? In the Eagala session last week, I remembered a dream Maria had—I tried telling you about it. I did some research and—"

Joe appeared in the kitchen doorway, with the ridiculous old phone to his ear. Looking from him to Vicky, he seemed to want an audience ... or to curtail their conversation.

"Hi, Ma," he started. "... yeah, we survived, no problem ... you? ... Good. Welcome home ... I'm glad you got in before the storm ... So, I've been going through a box we got from Grandma a week ago. It's old-fashioned movies, the canister kind, you know ... Yeah. Didn't you say once you've got Grandpa's old projector somewh—You do? Cool ... You're right. It is the perfect day for home movies ... Thanks. Sure, see you in a couple minutes."

Joe waggled his eyebrows and disappeared back into the kitchen.

Kyle nodded and whispered across to Vicky, "Did I spy the start of a smile on his dial?"

"Home movies call for popcorn!" She jumped off the couch. "Sorry, Kyle! We'll argue this out later, okay?"

# Chapter Eighteen
## July 12th

Joe finally managed to focus the opening shot of the first movie and laughter and clapping filled the living room as Kyle toddled toward them, a bowlegged, diaper-clad cowboy on a beach.

Vicky's makeshift movie screen, a double thickness of sheets hung over the window between the porch and living room, blocked out most of the rainy afternoon light, but he could still make out the shape of Kyle the man, directly across from him, filling Grandpa's chair.

"Ha, I look like a little fat Frankenstein." Sitting a couple feet from the screen, Kyle leaned in closer and mimicked his baby self's stiff-armed pose. Doughnut stretched a leg in protest then settled back across his shoulders.

Joe gave Vicky's knee a quick squeeze, loving the sound of her beside him, laughing and munching on popcorn from the huge yellow bowl in her lap. She tipped close to announce in a stage whisper, "I think that diaper's loaded!"

From the shadows at the far end of the couch they shared, Ma assured them, "No, it's only water and sand! Their dad always sat in the shallows with Kyle; Keith figured diapers were to keep babies dry, so …"

On screen, Kyle ran into the arms of a young woman with a laughing face. She crouched in front of him, then scooped him up, toweling him dry and kissing him as he squirmed in her embrace.

"Oh, look at you two, Sylvia." Vicky stretched an arm toward Ma, her voice full of emotion.

Joe tried to read her expression—*picturing the day you'll cuddle one of ours?*—then found her leaning low over the edge of the couch, as if trying to match Kyle's action in the movie: Ma had hauled him toward the camera where he flailed backwards in her arms, fearless, then dangled there, apparently transfixed, watching the sky from upside down.

Across the room Kyle adopted a similar pose, nearly on his head in front Grandpa's chair.

"Clearly the day I discovered perspective." He sounded muffled. Doughnut clung to his shoulder, looking more intrigued than disturbed.

"I wish you could hear this," Ma said. "Kyle had the wildest giggle as a baby."

"Where *is* the sound, Ma?" Joe asked. "Am I missing a button here somewhere?"

"Grandpa was hit or miss with recording sound." She rushed her words, like she'd rather stay back on that beach than answer him. "He must not have gotten it that day—aww! Will you look at you, Kyle? Soon as I set you down, you headed straight for that little stranger. I remember this day."

"Waddling a beeline for her in my saggy diapers … drawn, no doubt, to that polka dot bikini."

"I love how useless bikini tops are on tiny kids." Vicky chuckled. "Look at it all hiked up around her neck."

"As I recall, it was her sand castle or bucket you wanted, Kyle," Ma said. "Yep, look at that!" Her laugh trilled, and Joe couldn't help but stare for a second. In the dim light of the cabin, it seemed the slender woman playing on the beach with her firstborn had come to sit with them, remembered joys dancing over her face.

"Oh, what a sweetie!" Vicky cooed. On the screen, the chubby girl rushed to abandon her lumpy sand castle.

"She wasn't into you, though, Kyle!" Ma remembered. "From a squat to a run, look at her fat little legs go … oh, oops!"

"Too fast! Splat! Waaah!" Kyle narrated the tumble and the tears from decades ago. "That'll teach her."

The next few seconds showed a chaotic collage: sky, sand, and water flashed between odd glimpses of limbs and faces.

Vicky and Ma both groaned.

"Oh my. Feeling seasick!" Ma said.

"Reminds me of getting dumped by a horse." Vicky gulped. "Was that a camera hand-off?"

The view settled, this time on a pair of skinny men's legs. Joe leaned closer to get a better look. "That's gotta be Grandpa! Look at those knobby knees." A nice sensation bubbled in his stomach.

"Ha! You're right—and there's the rest of him. Grandma must have the camera now."

Vicky sighed, drawing her legs up under her. "Aw, look at him cuddle that little munchkin all better." She glanced Joe's way, her eyes shining.

He kissed her temple, wondering again whether thoughts of their future children did that to her. *Or seeing Grandpa cajole that little girl?*

"That's just like him. He'd try to comfort any crying child, stranger or not." Ma's voice was warm. "And *also* just like him to scramble into the background—there he goes."

*Please come back*, Joe pleaded silently while Grandpa walked, smiling, straight toward the camera, his hand out in invitation.

As if on cue, the film ended.

"Well, poo!" Vicky flopped back against the couch.

*Right, bummer*, Joe thought. *That was too short.* He busied himself with the projector, too full of memories and images to join in the comments erupting around him.

Kyle snorted. "So, 'the end,' I guess. How smooth."

"Oh, that was fun. Hey, Kyle, can you find one of Joe?"

Ma reminisced, "Grandma was always trying to push Grandpa into the frame, but if I remember right, that's the only time you'll see him in any of their movies. Wow … you know, I'd forgotten these even existed."

"Here's another of me—always a good choice," Kyle said. "Ohh, wait—here's an unlabeled one, bottom of the box."

"Intriguing. Grab that one."

"Not labeled, Kyle?"

"Joe, stick it in … pardon my French." Kyle dropped back into Grandpa's chair and rearranged Doughnut across his shoulders. "Just turn it off quick if it's Grandma and Grandpa getting naughty."

Joe chewed the inside of his cheek as he loaded the film. *Still winding Ma up, Kyle—and this is after declaring you'd give her a break?*

"Kyle!" Ma chided.

"Hell, Ma. Would *you* want to see that?" Kyle stuck his fingers through the projector's beam of light. Barking dog shadows leapt against the white sheet then transformed into squawking geese. "Well, maybe we could just listen if Joe ever gets the sound—"

"Yeah, I'm trying—"

"Oh, honey, look!" Vicky pressed her leg against his. He glanced up and, seeing the movie had already started, stopped fiddling with the sound button. "That's little you in the high chair. Look at those pudgy cheeks."

"Who's that jumping around behind me trying to photobomb?" he asked the room at large. "Ah, one guess." He caught and ate the piece of popcorn Kyle lobbed across the room.

"Oh, your little party hat looks so cute." Vicky poked Joe in the ribs. "Awww, this must be your first birthday."

"Joe. Maybe let's skip this one." Ma's voice sounded odd.

"Why, Ma?" he asked, enthralled with his little self. "Jeez, I must have hated that hat! There it goes on the floor. Hey wait, I hear something—I think this one does have sound. Hang on, let me turn it up."

Over a sudden clamor of recorded voices and laughter, Joe heard Ma speak up from her corner of the couch, sounding distressed now. "Joe, please. Let's choose another movie."

"It's fun, Ma." Kyle laughed. "We want to see it."

"Well, I don't think it's a good …"

Joe caught his breath. "Hey! There's Grandma!" His heart lifted. "Messing up Kyle's hair, like she always did to me, too."

"Even when you were a teenager," Vicky reminded him.

"Joe, please."

*What the heck? Ma's* begging *now?* He ignored her, hoping she'd relax. *This is just too cool.* He agreed with Kyle's comment "talented woman," and wondered aloud at how Grandma managed to bring in his cake, complete with a wax kitten holding a single candle, while five-year-old Kyle hung off her leg like a monkey.

Vicky's touch caught his attention. "Wait … listen," she breathed, leaning to the projector, her head tilted. "What's Grandma asking Kyle? Turn up the volume, Joe."

He did, his grin growing bigger as he listened to Grandma talking over Kyle's grunting monkey sounds.

"*… just think Kyle, now that Joe is one, pretty soon he'll be big enough for you to play together. Won't that be fun?*"

"*No, Grandma!*" *Kyle dropped off her leg and told her from a crouch on the floor, "I just want him to get littler and littler till he goes away."*

Joe and Kyle barked out identical laughs and Joe mimicked Kyle's five-year-old self snapping his fingers. "Even demonstrating my disappearance! Snap!"

"Ha! That's hilarious!" Vicky crowed. She plucked a piece of popcorn from her bowl and flicked it at Kyle. "Weren't you charming even then?"

"Joe!" Ma's curt tone cut through the laughter and his grin fell away.

Frowning, he dragged his gaze to her. She sat poised in the dim light as if ready to leap from the couch.

"Will you listen to me, please? Turn this off."

Her command held a desperate edge that sent a chill down his spine. *What's your deal?* He felt around for the projector's power switch, muttering, "*Why,* Ma?"

Vicky cut in. "Jesus! Is your dad *drinking?* At your first birthday party?"

He looked back at the screen and froze. There his father stood as a young man, gripping a dark green bottle and thrusting it high above the baby chair. One-year-old Joe sat in the chair, belly-chuckling, his head tipped back to watch. A thin column of amber liquid arced past his delighted face and splashed over the wax kitten in the center of his birthday cake.

"Drinking? Hell, he's plastered and going for more." Kyle's disgusted remark almost drowned out Ma, begging again.

"Please, Joe. Turn it *off.*"

Joe barely registered either remark or Ma straining to reach across Vicky; her fingertips groped his hand as she fumbled in the dark for the projector's switch. He kept watching.

"Joe, leave it *runni*—!"

Their father's slurred singing boomed into the room. *"Happy Birthday, dear Josey, happy birthday to you."*

Ma slumped onto the couch, and Joe felt his hands drop onto his thighs. The world narrowed into the event unfolding in front of him.

His baby-self patted little puddles of beer on carefully tufted frosting, then concentrated on his big brother's piping chant, *"Joe-EE, Daddy! Not Jo-SEE, Joe-EE. Not Jo-SEE."* With sparkling eyes, baby Joe slapped chubby wet hands to the top of his head and watched his father thrust the bottle high again to shout, *"Now a toast to my Josey, the most beautiful woman I know, and her most beautiful name! To Jocelyn!"*

A bright green blur—maybe the back of a woman's dress—filled the screen. Then came the distinct sound of a slap, followed by recorded and real gasps.

"*Oh my God*, Sylvia! Did you just *slap* their father in front of those boys?"

"Only ever once … only that day."

Vicky's appalled question and his mother's watery reply washed over Joe. Like a live cable he couldn't drop despite the pain, he couldn't stop staring at his younger self: as his lower lip thrust out, his face crumpled. Streaming tears, he reached fat arms up to be lifted from the chair. Beneath angry adult voices, he cried out, one name after another, till Grandma appeared. She raised him to her chest and called, "Robert! Turn that thing off!"

The sudden glare of the projector's light on the sheet hurt. Joe sat and squinted at it, boneless. The hum of the projector fan heightened the room's sudden silence.

He listened harder, trying to find the sound of the rain on the cabin's roof. It must have eased, now little more than a gentle tapping, the sound of another moving sidewalk.

His eyes followed Kyle pulling the chain on the desk lamp. Only a few actions and fewer breaths remained between now—not knowing—and the pain of hearing the family's oldest secret. He felt as sure of that as the couch beneath him and the warmth of the bare knee pressing against his.

Joe clicked off the projector's light and picked up Vicky's nearest hand, feeling popcorn butter on her fingers. He waited.

Doughnut yawned, stretched, and surveyed the room. His gaze swiveled to her tiny sounds and tracked her in the soft light. With dainty, measured steps, she walked down Kyle's chest and jumped to the floor; confident and languid, she crossed the room on silent paws, leapt onto the couch and settled into Ma's lap.

*Waking the sleeping elephant,* Joe thought. Sure enough, Kyle leaned forward, eyebrows high with expectation, and clapped his hands together once.

"Well! *That* was a fun party, Ma."

Joe glued his eyes to the projector, memorizing the serial number stamped on its metal base. He heard the tears in Ma's voice when she finally spoke.

"So now you know."

"We don't actually, Sylvia." Joe heard only kindness in Vicky's reply. No anger. "Keith was calling Joe 'Josey'? Why? Who was Josey?"

"Jocelyn ... Josey was your father's ... girlfriend ... for years before he and I met. Then again from the time I was pregnant with Joe until ... just after Joe turned four. When she died."

Vicky's grip tightened on his hand. Ma took a shaky breath and let it out long and slow. She continued, her voice so quiet that Joe barely heard the words. "Joe's birthday party, Keith's song, and his toast to her, was when ... how, I found out he and Josey were together again."

"Oh, Sylvia ...," Vicky started, but broke off with a quick glance at Joe as he stiffened. Feeling cold, he turned to look at Ma. Despite the tears running down her face, she held his gaze.

"Did Dad ..." He narrowed his eyes, swallowed, and tried again. "So Dad named me after his lover? And that day you ... so that's why you gave me ..."

Ma cocked her head, her face went slack, and he didn't need to finish. He unwound Vicky's fingers from his, stood, and walked from the cabin into the rain.

# Chapter Nineteen
## July 12th

Kyle pulled the Honda in front of Joe's filthy Camaro, taking care not to leave the edge of the road and become the second victim to the muddy channel at the base of Gillian's drive.

Ten minutes ago when Vicky came back from answering the phone to say Joe had gone off the road, he hadn't been surprised.

"Off the rails more like it," Kyle had scoffed as he stood and glanced at Ma; she'd wilted into the fabric of the couch. "I'll go find something in the barn with a winch on it."

"Never mind about the winch," Vicky said. "It happened outside Gillian's place. Just as Joe was hanging up, the old man showed up in a Jeep with a winch."

*Farmer Gillian to the rescue*, Kyle thought with a mix of fondness and embarrassment. *Just like the old days.*

"But yeah, they might need another hand." She'd spat out the words and muttering about irresponsible alcoholics, begun yanking down the sheets that covered the window.

It appeared they'd managed without him, however. Leaning from the window of a battered and splattered old Jeep, Gillian idled at the end of his long, flower-bordered driveway. Weak sunlight filtered through a thinning mass of clouds.

"Kyle! Good to see you unwrapped." An age-mottled arm crooked along the edge of the driver's window, the old man twisted around to peer at Kyle climbing from the Honda. "Cuppa tea? Coffee? Ruth would love to see you. And I'd like to … well, just come up for a bit? You have time?" Kyle saw the intense blue gaze flick to Joe then back to him. Gillian stressed, "Both of you."

Intrigued, Kyle raised an enthusiastic thumbs-up and turned to hear Joe's reply.

"I'll take a rain check on that drink, but thanks. Please say 'hi' to Mrs. Gillian for me." Joe swung into the Camaro's driver's seat as he spoke. "And thanks so much for your help. I appreciate it."

Kyle groaned and kicked apart a heavy clot of mud. "Baby brother, ya gotta shake this off," he whispered to his own muddy feet.

"Okay, I'll just wander up and let her know we'll see you in a minute, Kyle," Gillian called. Clumps of mud dropped off the Jeep as it started moving up the drive. "Let yourself in the kitchen door."

Kyle waved again and strode to the Camaro. "Hey, dude, how about we find the biggest mud clot around, name it 'Dad,' and kick it clear across Gillian's field? Whaddya say, Josey-Joe?" Grinning, he leaned down to the open window and folded his forearms across the driver's door, then recoiled.

"Hey, whoa! Teasing!" The thunderous look on Joe's face floored him. "Remember, I'm just a dick! Just trying to cheer …" Reaching in to jostle Joe's shoulder, Kyle blanched. "Jesus, you *stink*! No interest in a coffee 'cause you just slammed some drinks, right?" Feeling his stomach clutch at the familiar and hated smell, he scanned the interior of the car. "How'd you get holda booze *so quick*, man?" As he said it, his eyes fell on the open glovebox.

Joe shot out a hand and slammed it closed.

"What're you, *becoming Dad*?" Kyle ground out the words. "If ya can't beat 'em, join 'em?" He registered the sheen of tears in Joe's eyes but was too angry to care. "Illegal and dumb," he growled. "You're *driving*, you idiot. Not to mention how impressed your new fiancée would be."

Joe yanked the car into gear, glaring straight ahead. "Keep the *hell* out of it!"

Kyle stumbled backwards as Joe shoved him from the door. Dancing away from flying gravel and mud spat from the car's spinning tires, he caught Joe's shout over the angry rev of the engine. "Get outta everyone's business!"

Alone in the road, he stared after the car disappearing around the curve. The engine complained as Joe missed a gear.

Kyle dug in his pocket for his new iPhone, his clenched face starting to slacken, and punched in a text to Vicky, "txt me soon as idiot's home." Turning toward Gillian's house, shoulders slumped, his eyes swept the scene around him: trees and fence rails darkened with rain, the sun now burning down from a clean, blue sky. It still looked ominous further east, but where he stood in an enveloping silence, the tarmac had begun to warm and steam.

The far-reaching silence felt familiar. Turning a slow circle, he exhaled and sharpened his focus to the road a few feet away. No skin or blood, no skid marks or shards of debris, but he was sure if he looked long enough he'd find something that belonged to him—or used to.

*Ironic*, he thought, *I bite the dust in front of Gillian's place, pissed off and bawling, then Joe does his version of the same thing, same spot, less than a month later. No one likes a copycat, Joe. Josey.*

"Shit, Dad." Kyle whispered. His thoughts turned bitter. *What the hell were you thinking, or not thinking, as usual … you supremely selfish prick. Who names their kid after the woman they're messing with? No wonder Ma was such hard work—living with you would twist anyone. But, jeez Ma,* seriously? *Give your baby away for years because of his* name? *That's plain ugly.*

He trudged up Gillian's drive, picturing Joe's angry face and wet eyes minutes ago, then seeing an image of the two of them giggling together at a birthday party more than two decades ago.

Just as Vicky's text, "he's hm," came through, he heard a little squeak. Jamming his phone into a pocket, he stopped and lifted his eyes. His spirits followed.

Wearing a baggy floral housedress and a huge smile, Ruth Gillian stood in his path, thick legs planted wide, arms held wider.

You, *old woman, could drive away the darkest of moods,* Kyle thought. Feeling warmth settle into his stomach, he picked up his pace and walked straight into her soft embrace. *Strong, too!* He laughed aloud as she nearly rocked him off his balance.

Ruth held him at arm's length, beaming up at him and shaking her head. Knowing he wore a 'fool grin,' he stood, slightly crouched, while her smiling eyes moved over his face.

Her gaze dropped to his arms. *That,* he thought, *is the meaning of "a cloud crossed her expression."* He wanted to put a hand under her chin and make her look up again.

Instead, she stepped back a little, still gripping his upper arms and let her eyes travel down his scarred legs.

"Kyle."

Hearing the pain in her voice, a lump started in his throat, but Ruth's sudden burst of clucking and fussing washed it away. He left his muddy shoes at the kitchen door and allowed himself to be pushed ahead of her into the fragrant, sun-lit room.

"Make yourself at home, Kyle." She gestured to the captain's chairs circling her polished wooden table and settled into the nearest one, wiggling backwards as if establishing herself there.

Kyle took the seat beside hers, answering her rapid-fire questions: How was he feeling? Would the scars fade? What would he have to drink?

"Lemonade, pop, tea? Coffee? Iced or hot?"

Kyle waited with a smile as Ruth sweetly requested Mr. Gillian to supply them, then enthused with her over the strength and beauty of the storm that had just passed.

He leaned back in his chair and let his eyes rove around a room that time forgot.

*This place, this couple, are a Norman Rockwell stereotype. And God, that feels good. Safe.*

As the old man set a mug of coffee in front of him along with a small china plate stacked with frosted brownies and golden sugar cookies, Ruth demanded, "Kyle! Where are our manners? Have you had lunch?"

On the verge of declining anything more, the unmistakable rumble of his stomach raised a collective chuckle. "Ya got me," he admitted. "Just popcorn so far."

"Popcorn! Well, how about a ham and cheese sandwich? Fresh bread, baked this morning, the first tomatoes from our garden ..." She smiled up at her husband. Gillian picked up the plate of baked goods, put himself in reverse, and backed away from the table, a deadpan expression on his weathered face. Ruth touched his arm.

"No, G, the treats can stay." A quick nod underscored the conviction in her voice. "We'll get started on them!" Kyle saw her hand drop to pat Gillian's leg before she turned her smile back to him.

"What's that saying, Kyle? 'Life is uncertain. Eat dessert first.'" She held up a brownie and saluted him. "I *like* that saying."

Chuckling in agreement, he reached for a cookie and his eye landed on his own name; written in tall, spidery handwriting, it slanted across a small, square envelope tucked into the knitted napkin-holder at the far edge of the table. His smile grew wider. *That'll be a get well card, a little late maybe, but what a nice gesture.*

Sweeter yet was the glimpse of a pale green and brown image painted on the little china plate he and Ruth were working to empty. By the time Gillian eased down into a seat between them, they'd uncovered half of a familiar, beloved bunny family, now faded with time, but still clutching bunches of orange carrots in painted paws.

"Ha! My favorite plate!" Feeling like a kid on Christmas morning, Kyle shook his head at the couple beside him. "I can't believe you remembered."

Ruth leaned over and patted his hand, her mouth full of sandwich and her eyes filled with affection.

"You two are great," Kyle said, shaking his head. "Thank you for all this—for everything."

"Well, Kyle, we've not been feeling as if we've been very good to you at all," Gillian answered. He pulled the envelope from the napkin-holder and, holding it in a gnarled hand, started talking in a hesitant voice. "Ruth and I have been arguing over this for a couple weeks—till her good sense, and some new information, finally brought her 'round." Gillian gave his wife a warm smile. She nodded and smiled back.

"We've both been feeling sick over what happened to you outside our gate," he said. Kyle started to protest, but Gillian raised one arthritic finger. "Ruth was worried maybe you'd grown to be afflicted like your dad, that you musta been drunk to crash on a clear, sunny day like that. Don't misunderstand, now, we always had a lot of time for your dad—both your parents ... They used to be our 'go to' neighbors until his drinking ramped up like it did. You might have some memories of those early years? You do? Good. Well, I felt for your parents and their trials, so I was sorry when they pulled back from us and other friends ... then just seemed outta reach entirely. By the way, I gotta say, it's been wonderful seeing the changes in your mother these past few months." Gillian glanced at his wife for confirmation, she nodded again, and he went on. "For whatever reason, it seems she's a new woman." Gillian cleared his throat and shifted in his chair then went on.

"Anyway, alcoholism is a disease and that's established. Well, no one blames the people suffering from other diseases when they start displaying the symptoms." He patted Ruth's arm, and she shrugged. "That's my view; Ruth doesn't share it."

Kyle smiled, lay his sandwich aside, and leaned forward to concentrate as Gillian continued, "She might have once, but ... well because of that little boy, she can't find it in her heart to feel sorry about your dad."

Kyle swallowed the questions that leapt to his tongue. *In a minute*, he promised himself. *Let's hear the rest of this first.*

"At this point, I figure it's too late for anything but to forgive and start the healing—"

Ruth interrupted Gillian then. "But with your accident out there, Kyle, I started thinking the acorn doesn't fall far from the tree." She took a sip of iced tea, her eyes warm on his, and Gillian jumped back in, crumpling the envelope in his big fist as he spoke.

"Well, we didn't want to believe that. We kept scouring the local paper looking for a police report or a story. When nothing showed up, Ruth here," Gillian took his wife's free hand, "she found the young trooper who spoke to your brother the night you crashed and put the screws to him. Rusty ... nice kid, no match for Ruth; he opened right up, told her you were fine, not under the influence, no indication of excessive speed. So we knew it came down to the muddy mess my tractors made of the road. Conditions caught you unawares, Rusty said. To my way of thinking that makes us responsible. So ... here." Gillian pushed the mangled envelope across the table with a firm shove.

"This can't undo all that," he added and Kyle sat, stiff and still, as the old man's eyes travelled over angry scars. "We're sorrier than we can say about all you been through, Kyle. And it will sure ease our conscience a bit if you accept this."

Kyle opened the envelope and pulled out a simple square of pale blue paper with a single, handwritten sentence on it: "With sincere apologies and much love, Always, Richard and Ruth Gillian." Nodding and hoping the right words would come, a lump grew in this throat as he fumbled to slide the note back in the envelope. A rectangle of paper remained tucked inside; with clammy hands, he withdrew a check, unfolded it, and shoved back from the table.

"But ..." He stared across at two smiling faces and swallowed hard, his heart pounding. "Seriously? This is ... a *lot*."

"We know you teacher sorts don't make huge money. The most important job and all, but there ya go ... seems to be the way of the world," Ruth started and Gillian ... *Richard*, finished.

"You deserve it, Kyle ... and we can afford it. Might not look like it ... but we can."

"Insurance *did* cover the bike and the hospital, Mr. Gillian ... um ... Richard?" Kyle set the check on the table, arm's length away. "I'm okay there, you know, just slow on getting another vehicle. Joe's loaned me—"

"Yeah, yeah, we know about insurance," Gillian waved a hand. "This is separate from all that. It's us trying to demonstrate our apology to you." He pushed the check closer to Kyle as Ruth reached across to pat the scarred forearm nearest her.

"And our affection," she said. "You and Joe are the boys we never had."

Gillian went on, "We've cleaned up the curve and are going to pay attention to it from now on. This is for you."

Kyle fell speechless. Across the table, the couple sat back in their chairs, satisfied looks lighting their faces, and he couldn't think of a single word to say.

"There. *That's* what I've been waiting for—my answer at last." Gillian pushed back from the table and eased up from his chair. He smiled down at Kyle. "Use it to do something you've always dreamed of."

"Sir, Mrs. Gillian, I will." With goosebumps covering every inch of skin, Kyle rose to shake Gillian's hand then bent low to hug Ruth. "*Thank* you, both! I know just the dream. I've just started looking into it, in fact. I'll describe it in detail once I have a better picture myself. You'll be the first to know."

"Well, that's good, Kyle." Gillian squeezed his shoulder. "And keep calling me Gillian if you like; she musta signed that note formal, did she? Ruth's the only one who uses Richard—and that's only when I'm in trouble."

Kyle glanced at his abandoned lunch and went quiet, hating what came next. His smile faded.

"Yes?" From her seat at the table, Ruth leaned forward to peek into his lowered eyes; he felt the gentle encouragement written across her face.

Kyle addressed his question to the old man, who stood at his height, blue eyes fixed on his. "Mr. Gillian. I respect what you said the other day on Ma's driveway, about her being the one to give Joe and me the full story about our dad. But can you at least tell me," he paused to push down cold fear, and blurted out, "is my father still alive?"

# Chapter Twenty
## July 20th

Joe resisted the urge to slap the fat kid hooting up a storm in the front seat of the Camaro. Battling disgust with himself for that fleeting instinct, he grabbed the silver flask the kid was brandishing overhead. As he shoved it back into the glove box under an old map, he tried to cajole the boy into hurrying back to the horses or the bus or wherever young Boy Scouts were *supposed* to be. Playing racecar driver, poking at every knob and button his fast and curious hands could find … the Camaro was definitely *not* the place for eager, young Eagala clients.

*All too flippin' late, of course.* After seeing the troop of boys safely through the barn and down the driveway, presumably to the care of the bus driver and some unseen chaperones, Mel and Juliet had headed back into the barn's hay-scented gloom. But Vicky approached the car, head tilted to one side, her brow creased.

*Great,* Joe thought, *given that look, it's me, not the kid, in for a quiet tongue-lashing.* Sure enough, she didn't look at him, just the kid.

"Hey ya, Gordy," she started in a friendly voice. "You guys are all back here with Mel and Juliet a week from Friday, okay? But the rest of your troop's on the bus now. Quick, quick, buddy, so your friends don't have to wait for you."

The kid hopped out, high-fived Vicky, then waddled at an impressive speed given his bulk down the grass drive to where the bus was idling, most of its windows filled with boys calling for Gordy to "move it, man!"

Joe walked to the barn to pull the doors wide enough to drive through. He chewed his cheek, trying to dream up a legit reason to just disappear inside with his sense of nervous guilt.

Vicky stayed at the car, leaning against the driver's door. Her face neutral, her arms and ankles crossed, she raised an eyebrow as he returned.

"Excuse me, ma'am." Joe gave her a wry grin and tweaked her bare shoulder. "I need to park this thing."

She didn't move. *Jesus, this is worse than a telling-off,* he thought. Mentally squaring his shoulders, he asked, "Okay. What?"

"Come off it, Joe." Her voice stayed even. "You tell me. What's up with you?" It was hard to tear his eyes from hers, but harder to see the message they telegraphed—a mix of disappointment, hurt and—even disgust?

"You're talking about the flask that Gordy kid snooped out? Not mine. I didn't even know it was in there." His eyes flicked back to hers and away, long enough though to see a flash of pain she shuttered down.

Silent, she turned away and started walking to the cabin.

"Vicky, wait!" A jolt of fear made his voice louder than he'd intended. When she kept walking and mounted the steps to the cabin without a word, his fear turned to panic.

"Wait. Talk to me." He jogged after her and stopped her with a hand on her shoulder.

As she stepped over the living room threshold she turned to him, tears streaming down her face.

"Oh, babe, please don't!" Anguish tightened his throat.

"Who are you, Joe Carson?" Her voice broke. "I don't even know you anymore."

The ache in his throat deepened. "Neither do I." He cupped his hands around her shoulders.

"Well, find out." She looked down at the scarred wooden floor and her voice went quieter. "I'm not committing to a man who doesn't know himself … men like that do crazy, hurtful things."

The panic clutched again. "Vicky, I promise. The booze isn't mine. I'm *okay. We're* okay!"

"Joe, stop!" She broke into full-fledged sobbing and with a palm flat on his chest gave him a girl shove—enough to crumble the protest in his mouth and erase every thought. He took his hands away and her head dropped forward like it was too heavy for her neck.

"You've never lied to me before," she cried. "You're lying to me now."

His stomach churning, he chewed on his cheek and stood close to her.

*Do I hold you?* He wondered. *Do you want me to? How do I fix this?* None of the words came out, and he just stared into the sun-warmed tousle of dark hair tipped close to his chest.

Her sobbing slowed and she spoke, so close to a whisper, he had to concentrate to hear.

"In high school we made a pact. I know you remember: if we saw you were following in your dad's footsteps, we agreed we'd break up."

"Wait! Vicky!" The pressure of her balled-up hand against his chest stopped him again.

"You're drinking," she said. "At P.M. Steamers I started wondering … but now … And worse, you're hiding it and lying about it. That makes it problem drinking." She took a gulping breath.

Joe closed his hand around her small fist and took hope from her letting him do it.

"You're *way* in denial," Vicky went on. "About that, about your Grandma, what you learned about your name and your parents' issues ..." She pulled her fist from his and stepped back, finally looking him in the eye. It was his turn to gulp. Her tear-mottled face betrayed nothing but certainty. "The years we've been together, it's been your pattern to pretend, not *deal*, and lately ... it's turned toxic."

She had clearly finished talking, offering him a chance to answer, and he couldn't think of a single thing to say in his defense. He sank down on the arm of the porch couch and didn't watch as she turned away. Staring out at a black squirrel nosing through the grass near the picnic table, his mind remained a blank. He heard her climbing the stairs to the loft, quietly moving around, opening and closing drawers, going into the closet and the bathroom, the hard clack of backpack clips snapping closed. Last: her footsteps on the stairs again.

She stood inches from him, holding her purse, her backpack over one shoulder, and looked outside, her eyes sweeping the view.

*Like she's seeing it for the last time*, Joe thought and bile rose to his throat. He forced it back and took her free hand in both of his.

"Vicky ..." he started, but unsure what came next, he just rubbed his thumb over her engagement ring.

She drew her hand away. "Just give me a hug, Joe." Her voice sounded strong. She'd stopped crying.

"Don't." Joe stood.

"I told you weeks ago about the Eagala conference in Grand Rapids. I'll go early and hang out with my sisters and Penny for a few days." She set her things on the floor and opened her arms.

Joe pulled her against him, leaning down to kiss her neck, her face, determined not to cry. *She already thinks I'm weak. Knows I'm weak?*

She turned her head away. "I think we both need this space, Joe. I know I do. I'm taking a digital detox, too. So don't expect any WhatsApp or text chats."

"I don't need space, Vick! I need you." Jesus, it was true.

"Oh, Joe ... wrong answer." She pulled back, picked up her things, and reached for the porch door's handle. Looking over her shoulder, her eyes sad, she murmured. "You know I won't ... I *can't* do dysfunctional."

He followed her out. *This is surreal. This isn't happening.*

"When will you be back?" he asked.

"I'll call you in a week or so when the conference is over."

"No, *see* me. Come home." It came out like a croak.

"I'll call you."

# Chapter Twenty-One
## July 25th

Kyle watched his coworkers pushing in chairs and stowing iPads under their arms or into purses. Some tried to hide their eagerness to get out into the sunshine, while others didn't seem to give a damn who saw it. Tammy from Admin hooted.

*As planning sessions go, this one went well,* he thought: *short, with a lot covered. Probably because no one can stand being inside a minute longer than we have to—Michigan summers are way too short as it is.*

Under his own sense of urgency to escape the familiar room, he felt an unfamiliar open-heartedness; odder still, he felt ready to show Maria the full extent of it.

He watched as she packed her things into an oversized jute bag he hadn't seen before, splashed with tropical flowers in hot pinks and orange. He liked it. And he liked how tendrils of hair poked out from the turquoise scarf around her head to edge her suntanned face, and how her white sundress would sway into folds as she moved. He wanted to tell her how he'd been inspired by her color-factory dream from months ago, what he'd learned from the horses, and about his dad.

Though seats near her had all been taken when he'd arrived, almost late, he knew she'd seen him.

*Is that why she's taking her time leaving? To give me a chance to leave first? No, let's play it positive: she wanted to let the room empty out to just us, like it is now.*

She seemed shy, cautious, as she came up beside him.

"Hi, Kyle."

Looking him up and down, she grinned and gave a thumbs-up. *Of course,* he realized, *she hasn't seen me since the bandages came off.*

The braided strap of her bag slipped from her bare shoulder. He pulled up the strap, settling it close to the curve of her neck. *Was that a shiver where I touched her skin?*

"Hey, babe." He hadn't intended that, it slipped out, but felt so natural, he didn't correct himself. *Heck, I'm done with being without her.*

Barely aware he'd adopted the grin she'd always liked, he rushed forward to hold open the door for her. As she passed he caught her look of surprise—and the scent of lily of the valley. In silence, they walked down a short, echoing hallway that exuded a summer sense of desertion. Outside, they squinted at each other in the high-noon glare of late July. She took a deep breath, sandwiched her hands together, and pretended to dive into her big bag.

"Into the Tardis—don't get lost." He laughed. "Your sunglasses?"

She nodded and scrunched up her face, sifting through the bag's contents with both hands as if her fingers could see. With an exaggerated sigh, she gave up and her shoulders sagged like a disgruntled kid. Shielding her eyes, she looked up at him, an impish but nervous look playing over her face.

"Come to my place for some lunch on the deck?" he asked. *Do not think through what you're saying,* he ordered himself, *just go with it.* "I've got that sexy white robe of yours—you left it on the back of the bathroom door. Try as I might, I just can't fit into it."

Her startled laugh warmed him through.

*No change there.*

Encouraged, he went on, more serious now. "And I've got something … important … I'd really like to show you." He saw her hesitation, biting her lower lip, but also something in her eyes, like she wanted him to help her say "yes." He rushed on, "I've got that pine nut hummus you love and some of the reddest tomatoes you've ever seen. My mom's neighbor—you know the Gillians?—they gave me way too many."

"Yum. You can bottle those for winter you know. Or make spaghetti sauce or salsa or soup."

*Score!* He took her elbow, ignoring her flinch at his touch. *She's only surprised,* he coached himself. *Hell, I've never done this gentlemen stuff, with anyone, ever. And that's going to change.*

Liking the feeling of the old-fashioned gesture, he turned her toward the parking lot. "No, *you* can make spaghetti sauce or something. That's your gift. I'm gifted at eating." Her smile widened as he steered her down the steps to her bike. "I'd be happy to give you some of those babies." *Jesus! Could I have found a worse way to put that?*

He didn't know he was holding his breath until she finally tipped her head into her sideways nod. Easier than actually saying "yes" and maybe implying he still had any kind of chance with her? He pushed the thought away, exhaling on another grin.

"Good."

Each session he'd had with Maria Horse and Ma Horse, maybe a half dozen now, he'd felt a shift—like he'd shed tangible pounds of baggage. Somehow, so far, probably due in part to a new art journaling habit, he was keeping the weight off.

Minutes later, unlocking the front door to his house as she waited behind him, swinging her bike helmet in her hand, he imagined he could feel the physical warmth of her. His body quickened, responding to memories of times shared in this house. The feeling ramped up—*Wow, zero to sixty*—as he took her hand and led her, silent but unresisting, to his bedroom door. There he let go of her hand and stepped back, waiting for her reaction to the mural.

First, she made a small noise, just a catch in her throat, and her hand flew to cover her mouth. Then with the dancer's grace he had never tired of watching, she moved a little ways into the room.

As she scanned the sunset on the far wall, he studied her profile. Her dark eyes grew larger and her lips parted. With her fingertips now resting at the hollow of her throat, she gazed at the glittering ceiling, then at the sunrise on the wall beside them.

Kyle heard her breathing deepen, matching his, and she turned her back to him. He memorized her pale hair, curling at the edges of her scarf, and the shape of her head as she tipped her chin up a second time to circuit the swath of stars above the bed. She glanced over her shoulder to him, a silent question shining through welling tears.

Kyle jammed his hand into his hair, aching to close the space between them and pull her against his chest. Nodding instead, he willed her to read more into it than a simple, "yes, they're yours" and hoped to hell he'd read her question right. *Do you want them to be for you?*

He took her hand again and led her down the hallway to the kitchen as he tried to shove away his doubts, rummaging for a way to tell her how—even if it sounded hokey—it all felt right: the warmth of her fingers in his, the soft slap of her sandals on the hardwood floor, just being with her.

At the kitchen door, though he could only see the turquoise crown of her head beside his shoulder, he heard her tiny gasp, a barely audible gulp, and once again, the words he wanted only jammed in his throat.

With a sharp, "Oh!" Maria pulled her hand free and went to the wall bordering the sink. Her fingertips traced the wings of the hummingbirds and finches, and the movement of her head followed the flight of the dragonflies.

In a voice just loud enough to carry, Kyle told her, "I had just started this one the night you broke—"

She turned and brushed past him, her footsteps echoing down the hall before he could react.

The clatter of her sandals on the porch steps cut through his confusion.

"Maria!" He quick stepped into the hall bathroom, snatched her robe from the hook, and dashed outside.

The loose ends of her scarf streamed behind her as she pedaled to the corner.

He hesitated and spent his chance to call her back by wondering if he should. As she disappeared from sight, he flung her robe over his shoulder and sank onto the top stair.

Spotting a rabbit hunched in the grass and staring up from his dandelion, Kyle asked him, "So, did that go well or not?"

The rabbit sniffed and went back to eating.

"Yeah, hell if I know, either."

# Chapter Twenty-Two
## July 26th

"Wow, I'm glad you called, Vick. It's great to hear your voice!" Sweaty and disheveled in a grease-stained T-shirt, Joe dropped onto the porch couch, cell phone in one hand and an unopened can of beer in the other. His arrival earned a loud "Mip!" from Doughnut, who'd been absorbed in her nightly grooming. A scruffy yellow mound against the couch's bright Indian blankets, she paused to look him over, blinked her only eye, and resumed the awkward process of licking her chest fur into moist tufts.

"How's Grand Rapids treating you?" Smiling into the darkness of the yard as he pictured Vicky's face at the end of the line, he held the phone between his ear and shoulder to give Doughnut's head a two-fingered rub. She swatted his hand away like an irritated grandmother, then hooked his wrist with her paw, pulled it to her mouth and started grooming his thumb. She released it with a clear look of distaste, and Joe's smile grew to a grin.

Holding his beer at arm's length so it wouldn't spray her, he snapped the tab. Just for a second, he considered squashing a pillow over the can to muffle the sound. No, stooping that low would never happen. His dad had pulled those sorts of tricks—and they'd all pretended to buy them. But as he took a deep swig and readjusted the phone, catching Vicky in mid-sentence, he felt relieved she hadn't heard—or at least hadn't commented.

"… might not be so glad when you hear this," she said. *So,* Joe wondered, *why do you sound so excited?* "But listen, there's a woman here at the conference with a ton of Eagala experience and she's really psyched to check out joining our team. I mentioned her, I think. So I'm staying a few extra days; we're going to some post-conference sessions, to see how we'd work together. I want to gauge how well she'd fit the team and see the extent of her knowledge. If she works out like I'm hoping *and* Juliet accepts my offer to join the team when her internship's over, I could expand the business sooner than I'd thought. Wouldn't that be *so* cool, Joe?" Before he could answer, she rushed on. "We could develop that open space in the barn, like I've talked about. You know how I've wanted to reach out more to military families and to more kids …"

Joe took another big swallow and settled in to listen to Vicky enthusing over her plans. Pleased to find a faded sofa pillow squashed deep into a corner, he jammed it under his head, sandwiching the phone in between, and stretched out long against the cushions. Doughnut stood, clearly protesting the invasion of his bare feet. She arched into what Vicky called "Halloween kitty" pose, and gave a toothy, pink yawn.

Joe raised his head to take another drink, then couldn't resist yawning along with Doughnut. *Wow, am I suggestible or what?* he thought, and hoped Vicky had heard the yawn as "Mm hmm." He looked forward to his turn to talk so he could tell her of his self-imposed nightly limit: two cans, most nights at least, and not a drop in the car. It seemed pretty rough that she didn't trust him with the beers. But this would be his last one tonight, for sure. He wanted an early night, to finally get some sleep ... he was so wiped out.

He endured a thorough and distracting foot sniffing, flinching from Doughnut's tickling whiskers, then, beer in hand, extended his arm as a guardrail, while she tiptoed the cliff edge of the couch. She ascended his pillow and settled in against his head. Savoring her warmth, the rhythm of her purring, and the last swallow of cold beer sliding down his throat, he closed his eyes, smiling at the sound of Vicky's voice in his ear.

***

Joe trudged up the front steps of the cabin, staring at his dust-covered work-shoes, wondering what to scrounge for dinner. He tried not to think how long it'd been since Vicky had last called, though, of course he knew: three nights— *three nights that felt like thirty. Sleep had come easy in the middle of their last phone call—in the middle of her talking for God's sake—but it sure hadn't since.* True to her word, she hadn't even texted.

As he stepped inside the porch, Mel called his name. She waited in the barn's doorway, slapping dust from her jeans, and shading her eyes to watch him cross the yard. Before he'd quite reached her, she started apologizing.

"Joe, I'm really sorry to ask you this, but I'm stuck." She took off her riding helmet, looped the chinstrap over her wrist, and undid her long ponytail. With quick, practiced fingers she braided her hair while studying his face.

Under her scrutiny, he felt like an envelope that may or may not need another stamp. He wondered why she seemed so loathe to ask him a favor. *How much had Vicky told her?*

Mel went on, "I just got a text from my mom, she's dizzy and it's scaring her. This has happened before, and it's most likely just sinusitis, but she sounds upset so I want to go to her. The thing is, I've already let Juliet go to get ready for a hot date she has tonight."

"Can I please, please ask you to feed the horses tonight? I'll tell you just how and who gets what—" she paused, waiting for his assent as if that were an afterthought.

"Of course, no prob; I've done it for Vicky before, but a long time ago."

"Okay." She turned and strode into the tack room, talking over her shoulder. "Well normally, we'd be able to feed them after the evening session because they don't work up a sweat, but that troop of Boy—I mean our last client group, had them running a lot today."

Joe ignored her slip in divulging client identity. He'd seen the Boy Scouts traipse on and off site anyhow with the one called Gordy bringing up the rear as they departed and looking much less out of control than the last time he'd been there. He'd never seen clients in session, but until Vicky could afford to add a private entrance to the barn, he couldn't help but sometimes see them coming or going. He finished Mel's train of thought, "The horses were worked hard by your last group, so they're at risk of colic if they eat before really cooling down."

In her quick glance, he saw, "right answer," and knew he'd just cinched her trust in him. *Vicky must not have badmouthed me*, he realized. *I should have known she wouldn't.*

"So … the bigger three get a mix of seventy percent alfalfa and thirty percent grass, like this …" Mel scooped the feed into two buckets and went to another covered bin. "But, because she's a mini, Bonnet only gets this much …" She showed him what looked like an eighth of Bingo's portion.

He decided it couldn't hurt to show off a little more. "Because a mini can founder easily if they get too much protein. Or don't work off what they do get."

"Head of the class, Joe." Mel beamed at him then called a farewell to each of the horses.

He promised to text if he had any questions, waved her off in her little blue truck, and made a beeline for the refrigerator and his porch.

Lounging on the couch, watching the half-dozen squirrels and chipmunks that played around the cabin, he found they didn't hold his attention like they did when he and Vicky watched together. Instead, alongside the feeling of being trusted, he savored his first beer for the evening.

*Those horses are, without a doubt, as precious as family to Mel. If she can trust me, why can't Vicky?*

The last conversation they'd had, or what he'd *heard* of it, kept surfacing. This time he let it come up, intent on giving it a different ending, one where Vicky said how she couldn't wait to get home, and laughed and told him she loved their life, she'd overreacted and everything was fine—great.

He leaned against the door jamb. "Who am I kidding?" he said out loud just for the company. "That's not how it went." A squirrel paused to glance his way, then continued to nose through the grass. So he addressed it, "When have I *ever* fallen asleep on the phone—in the middle of a conversation? I was just *wiped*. She'll think I was drunk. Hell, *I'd* think that! But I wasn't, and that's what sucks. No wonder she's not returning my calls now—who would?"

"The drinking's not really the problem, you know." Joe took a long swallow. He'd warmed to the one-sided conversation, though the squirrel remained uninterested. "I've been good about that since she left. Just beer now, all other booze *cleared out,* a two-a-night limit—give or take—one alcohol-free day a week, and *none* while I'm driving. Ever."

He took a deep swig and held the still-cold can to his neck. Watching goose bumps rise along his muscled forearm, he realized how sweaty he was, and how hungry. In the yard, his mini confidant had disappeared.

A sudden stab of loneliness drove him from the couch. He went to the kitchen to scrape together leftovers for dinner and started on a second beer. With the stove on low and the radio on high, he climbed into the shower, taking care—more from habit than hope—to first prop his cell on the sink. Pits, pecs, package—and pelt, he decided, rubbing shampoo into his hair. Then, of course, the phone bleated *Funky Town* and Vicky's name came up on screen.

"Yes!" Joe leaned to swipe it on and a blob of shampoo splatted onto the toilet seat. He poked the speaker button, then crossed his fingers for luck.

"Wait, babe! Wait. I've got soap—give me one sec …"

Hair rinsed and shower off, he dripped onto the floor as he dried his hands and grabbed the phone. The sounds of a barking dog and shouting kids filled the little bathroom—the unmistakable noise of her older sister's house, no matter what room you tried escaping to. He hoped the family chaos Vicky adored had cheered her up.

"Thanks, babe. Sorry. You caught me under the shower." Phone against his ear now, he shoved a towel around his lower half.

"Hey, Joe."

At the sound of her voice, flat and without any warmth, his grin and his hope slid away.

"Vick, let me start. Please? I was *not* drunk. I know what it looks like from your end, but I was wiped out. Since you've been gone, I've been working constantly, on top of visiting Grandma."

"And thinking?"

"Well. No ... not a lot." He hopped into the clean boxers he found in the dwindling pile atop the dryer and headed into the kitchen, scrubbing the towel over his hair.

"Listening to lots of loud music instead?"

*Busted.* She knew him too well. He snapped the volume down on the radio and didn't answer.

"Talk to your mom at all, Joe?"

His jaw dropped to blurt, "Seriously, Vick?" but he caught himself. *She'll know the answer anyway, that I have* no answer ... *because really, how is that supposed to work? Something like, "So, Ma, just curious about this thing where you gave me away as a baby because Dad named me after his lover—wanna elaborate?"*

"Strike three," Vicky broke the silence.

*Can't I get anything right with you anymore?* he wondered.

"I counted two." He knew he sounded like a naughty kid, but in truth he wanted to know. "Which one did I miss?"

"Let's see ... would that be your acting all passive-aggressive with everyone?"

"Everyone who? Do you mean that thing with Kyle ..."

She rolled over his protest. "Or when you started slamming the beers and drinking while you're driving? Or when you lied to my face, promising me you were telling the truth? Or ... *Jesus, Joe!* Get a clue! I've been gone over a week and you haven't done anything about getting yourself on track? Don't you want us to work?"

"Hell, Vicky! What's with all this? I proposed to you—of *course*, I want us to work. You're the one leaving me!"

"I was taking time to get my head together and giving you the same. Don't you *get it*, Joe?"

He glared from the kitchen window into the front yard, frustrated that he couldn't think of a thing to say. Again. With the phone against his shoulder and cheek, he swiped his sweat-slick hands against the towel still around this neck and tried to swallow the lump in his throat.

"You *don't* get it," she said, her voice now soft and sad. "I've gotta go ... Bye, Joe."

*I'm* not *saying goodbye*, he thought. *I'm not closing out this call.*

He spotted an early firefly lighting near the picnic table, then another on the arm of the Adirondack chair. He imagined smearing the bugs against the wood, then felt sick at the image.

"Bye," Vicky whispered. After several long seconds of silence, he heard a sigh then nothing.

Panic lurched in his stomach. Letting the phone slip with a clatter to the kitchen table, he sank into a chair, trying to ignore the smell of burning food and a sudden mental image of a moving sidewalk.

The piercing screech of the smoke detector filled the kitchen and he shot to his feet.

"Just perfect." He knocked the device loose from its connection and dropped his fish curry, blackened and crusted to the pan, into the sink. A cloud of steam hissed up into his face as he ran water into the mess.

"What next?"

He reached to punch on the radio then froze, stunned by the blaring refrain from Little River Band's "Lonesome Loser."

"Oh. That's just too much." He snapped it off, grabbed the last beer in the fridge, and stormed out to slump onto the porch stairs.

"I don't deserve this! What have I done?" Less than an hour ago he'd stood here feeling great—trusted—by Mel, at least. Now Vicky's laundry list of his crimes played through his mind on a loop with echoes of song lyrics ghosting through the smoky kitchen.

The last straw for her seemed to be that single, stupid, panic-driven lie he'd told about the flask not being his. No wonder she ran. He sucked: sitting outside an empty cabin in the woods, in a pair of boxers, drinking beer ... Loser. He let out the hurt and anger in a roar.

"And no one to hear me howl like a baby."

Neighs from the barn proved him wrong.

*Oh, yeah.* He yelled across the yard, "I didn't forget. Hang on." As he pushed up from the stair, his empty can dangling from his index finger, he swayed a little. Lunch seemed a long time ago. Other than breakfast food, which he was thoroughly sick of having for dinner, he'd just charred the last edible thing in the house. It also seemed, as he pawed through dresser drawers up in the loft, he'd run out of clean work clothes.

*Living alone blows on so many levels,* he thought, pulling on a dress shirt he'd only ever worn to Rusty and Ginny's wedding. *I am not going to stoop to feeding the horses in my underwear.*

The cabin's brittle silence seemed to follow him to the barn, but not inside.

Inside, his breathing calmed. He made his way around in the heavy gloom, liking the challenge of finding and delivering the individual feed buckets to each stall then returning a second time to check water troughs. Resting a shoulder against Bingo's flank, he listened to four horses munching and slurping.

"Now what, Bingo? Get some dinner and take it to Grandma's?" He stroked the warm muscular neck. "Except she'll be asleep by the time I get there. So … what would town be like tonight? The Mitten Bar maybe?"

He and Vicky were both longstanding Mitten Club members, and had the mugs to show for it, but lately the buzz and crowds of town during summer didn't seem to do it for them. Tonight, though, the Mitten Bar was exactly where he needed to be. Tonight, he needed people and he needed food. He would take it slow getting there.

***

As soon as he entered the noisy throng, Joe wondered what he'd been thinking. The worst kind of lonely had to be lonely in a crowded bar, shoulder to shoulder with strangers jockeying for an empty table, a view of the band, or the eye of a bartender. He searched for a familiar face, thinking how Kyle would hate these crowds.

*The music and the conversations, so many people moving … and whoa—that sure feels like a boob squashing against my arm … still squashing … still there.* He shot a quick look to his left and found, almost at his eye level, a twenty-something redhead smiling at him.

"Hey." She raised her pretty chin and winked a pale green eye. "My friends are leaving and I'm not ready. Share my table? I'll get your first drink."

Joe looked over his right shoulder, then back to her, one eyebrow raised.

Her smile bloomed into a grin; two of her lower teeth leaned in on each other. The boob squish got stronger. "I mean you, tall man in the very cool shirt. What'll you have—maybe a Strawberry Blonde?"

"I like the Dark Horse Crooked Tree …," Joe started, then went red. "But, umm, anything's fine. Thanks." He took a quick step back, commanding his eyes not to flick down for a look.

"Great—our table's there." She pointed to a corner booth near the bathrooms. "Meet you in a minute …?"

Joe just nodded and moved away, surprised and pleased to have found company so fast. After countless stops and starts, mumbling "sorry" a dozen times, he got into the quicker stream of traffic heading toward the men's room.

He'd just reached the last booth when he heard, "So, the bartender told me you're Joe?"

"Yes." *And how did you make it back here almost as quick as I did?* he wondered, *and with not one, but two beers for each of us. You handle bars better than me and have an awful lot of hair ...* Thinking it was kind of red and kind of not, he noticed how the waves and curls poured over her shoulders and heaped onto her—he raised his eyes fast and accepted a beer into each hand.

Still standing, Joe clinked a bottle to hers in a toast; when he set it down after a long swig, it felt much lighter and he remembered he'd planned to eat—maybe a "build your own" from Barley & Rye. But he didn't feel all that hungry anymore.

"Thanks. I needed that," he said.

"You looked like you did." She set down her raspberry beers and took his hand in a strong grip. Her fingers were wet. "Nice to meet you Joe, I'm Xī. Short for xī xì which is Chinese for frolic or a romp. Most just call me Shay. Close enough."

She must have realized he couldn't make a bit of sense out of that.

"My parents' honeymoon was in China. I can only guess they had fun making me." She squeezed his hand a little tighter.

No less baffled, Joe slid his hand free of hers and scooted into the booth, pulling his bottles with him across the table top.

"Anyway, I've always been a sucker for a man looking forlorn and alone."

*And how do I answer that? This is Kyle's forte, not mine.* She followed him in along the bench seat. *And pretty close, too. She smells like beer and ... Thanksgiving, like spices. That hair's amazing. Like autumn.*

"I like helping people," she went on with a smile. "It must go with my job."

*Okay, this is easy.* "What's your job?" He drained his first beer, determined to take the second slower. Shay pushed it into reach.

"I'm an equine specialist." She locked her widened eyes on his and took a drink.

Joe knew that look meant he could ask her to explain—and that she'd really like him to. Mel did the same thing though; he already knew about equine specialists. *Hearing that would disappoint her, letting her talk would be easier. How much have I drunk tonight?*

"I really should know that phrase …" he said and the woman laughed. *Was that funny?*

"In Indiana, I work with horses to help people get their shit together," she started.

Joe wanted to move a couple of inches farther from her. *Would that hurt her feelings?* Brows knit together, he shook his head once and took a drink of the second beer, setting it down with great care. He vowed it would be his last one for sure. *Except I owe a round to … what's her strange name? She doesn't need a lot of encouragement to talk.*

"I came up with some friends for the weekend to see what Ludington's nightlife is like."

*She's bought me drinks and I've barely listened to a word she said. So rude,* he chided.

"It's good. This is a popular bar. My girlfriend—she works with horses, too—she and I …" He stopped to think. *Except wait … ha! this is funny …* "Wait! She's not exactly *my girlfriend* anymore." He shot the woman his own expectant look as he took a drink.

"She's not? Did you break up?" The woman twisted to face him; her eyes reminded him of grapes.

"She's not my girlfriend anymore …" He didn't know how long to hold off on the punchline. But the woman had already started to laugh, a rapid-fire sound that reminded him of something. *Maybe she knew the joke?* He laughed with her, then pulled his chin down close to his throat, and announced, "… because *she's my fiancée.*"

"No way! I don't see any ring on your finger, Joe." She poked his arm. It almost hurt.

Joe frowned. *No ring? Should I have one?*

He looked at his hands cupped around his bottle and felt a hand settle on his thigh, *high up* on his thigh. His gaze dropped to his lap. She had simple fingers, tanned but with no polish or rings; they looked nice against his best jeans. And felt nice.

He looked at her and blinked, trying to focus, thinking again, *that hand feels really nice.*

She laughed.

*A woodpecker!* That's *the sound—like the one busy in the woods by the river lately. Birds are nice.*

"You're one of the good guys, aren't you, Joe?" She wiped her free hand on her jeans and rested it on his right forearm.

Joe lifted his bottle with his right hand and focused on the coppery liquid flowing into his mouth, but could still feel her eyes traveling his skin. Her fingertip trailed from his elbow up to and under the hem of his shirt sleeve. In his lap, her other hand began to press just a little. "I'd be way less lonely up here with a good guy around. I hope you're not a saint."

*"You don't have to be a saint, Joe."*

*Vicky!* He sat up fast, looking over the woman's shoulder into the crowded bar, ignoring her hazy look of surprise.

He'd definitely heard Vicky's voice. *Maybe she came home early after all?*

Lips brushed his jawline; her hand crept higher, following the inseam of his jeans. The woman had moved so close he had to lean back to see her.

"Hey, Saint Joe, you still with me?" He felt her breath on his neck, but if she hadn't spoken in his ear, he wouldn't have heard her over the bar noise around them. "Want to help a lapsed Catholic take up her faith again?"

*"I thought I had to be a saint, Vicky. Who would love me otherwise?"*

He looked down at the unfamiliar hand on his thigh, laid his own hand over it, then lifted hers and placed it on his crotch, feeling a delicious warmth and a gentle grip through his jeans. He looked at the woman. She dropped her chin with a small groan, looking up at him through thick eyelashes.

"Mmm … so, this is a yes?" she asked.

"Yes." Joe nodded. "Yes, I'm a saint. Who would love me otherwise?"

He lifted her hand and dropped it onto her lap. With a scolding little "tsk, tsk" sound, she put it back on him and pressed a fleshy breast against his upper arm.

"I could love you, Saint Joe. Call it whatever you like. I could love you all night long."

He wondered if she meant to be funny—a stupid, porn-movie kind of funny?

"Let me show you," she whispered into his ear. He couldn't smell Thanksgiving on her any longer, just beer.

This was like a porn movie.

He was a saint.

"Saints don't do porn." He didn't know if he'd spoken out loud and didn't look to see her reaction as he slid away from her, hanging onto the sticky edge of the table as he stood. He steadied himself against a couple standing in his way, one hand on each of their backs.

They both turned at his touch then grinned. "Hey, it's Joe. Hi!" the man said and his companion chimed in, "Cool! We haven't seen you and Vicky for weeks!" then glanced at the booth behind them and her brow creased. "Where's Vicky?"

"Dunno, but I gotta find her." Joe dipped his head and, feeling the scrape of fingernails against the seat of his jeans, veered away from the booth and into the crowd.

# Chapter Twenty-Three
## July 29th

Kyle raised his head from the pillow, wondering what woke him, and noticed the pile of snotty tissues on the floor beside his bed glowing a bluish white. The pile started crowing like a rooster; he growled and reached down to knock aside an evening's evidence of the cold he couldn't shake.

With his head back on the pillow, he dragged his phone to his ear. Before his fuzzy tongue could shape a word, a woman's voice demanded, "Kyle, you gotta come get Joe."

"Whoth thith?" Hell, he sounded like something from a kid's cartoon.

"Ginny. From the Mitten Bar. You know: Rusty The State Trooper's Wife?"

*The rusty what? Oh … right.* Groggy with cold medicine, he pictured the trooper who took his accident report—Joe's friend, and registered Ginny's irritation, but couldn't make any sense beyond that.

"Did you hear me?" she asked. "You have to come get Joe. He's on his way to really drunk."

"Hey, Gin. I'm really thick. Got a cold."

"You sound like Rudolph. Get here, Kyle. I couldn't reach anyone at the cabin, and I don't have Vicky's cell number. If Joe drives, I'm calling Rusty. We wouldn't have even served him when he first got here, but that ginger chick must've bought it for him. I just saw him a minute ago and he's looking pretty out of it."

"Shit."

"Right." Ginny hung up.

Kyle scrabbled around for his flip flops and jammed his wallet into his shorts pocket. Except for needing his own house key and a driver's license, the mission stank of déjà vu. He'd once been good at searching the bars in town and had come to hate the noise and smell of those his dad chose. Though he'd quickly learned finding the car *before* the drunk could save a lot of trouble, on his tenth birthday he'd climbed into Ma's car where she waited for him and announced she'd have to hunt for his dad herself. He swore he'd never go drunk-hunting again as long as he lived.

And here, eighteen years later, he sat sneezing in his car, maneuvering into a parking space just a half a block from the Mitten's front door, feeling pissed off, bleary-eyed, and daunted by his prospects of finding Joe either inside or out.

Unlike their dad, Joe could be driving any one of eight vehicles Kyle might recognize, or a new one he didn't. Feeling the way he did, he refused to start some wild goose chase; he'd wad Joe up and toss him in the back seat of the CRX then dump him at Vicky's feet—whether she wanted him or not. He stomped into the Mitten.

A few heads swiveled—the regulars checking for their own kind—but most didn't bother looking up—the tourists. High season in this insanely popular bar had never been his destination of choice; feeling like crap now put it solidly at the bottom of his list. At least, being tall, Kyle could see over the crowd and most of the room. If Joe was standing, he'd stand out; probably half the women in the bar would consider him eye candy, yet he'd be oblivious to them sneaking looks at him.

Swiping at his runny nose, his hair every which way, Kyle squeezed past laughing, flirting, sunburned strangers and waded to the bar. He hailed the spiky-haired woman with John Lennon glasses working behind it.

"Okay, Ginny? Joe'th babythitter reporting for duty."

She tipped her chin and raised her eyebrows in greeting as she finished pulling beers for two blondes. The blondes appeared to write him off with a glance.

*Same to you*, he thought.

"Check the far corner booth, Kyle. Like I said, last I knew he was with some redhead I've never seen before." Ginny set the beers down and addressed the blondes. "Six-fifty each, please."

"Thumb what?" *No way*, Kyle thought. He shoved a hand deep into his shaggy hair.

"*Woman*, Kyle. I know you've heard of those." She turned to the cash register.

"Not in the thame sententh ath Joe."

"Thanks, ladies." She made eye contact and grinned at her next customer. "What can I get you?" Throwing her voice back to Kyle as she poured two Rieslings, she told him, "I don't know how long ago they hooked up, but *she* at least looked pretty into him."

"That can't be Joe, then."

Setting the wine in front of the couple who had wedged in beside him, Ginny just raised her eyebrows again, this time with a head tilt that reminded Kyle of a grade school teacher's silent scold.

*A state trooper's wife would be in the same mold*, he figured.

Raising his hand to ward off further comments, he took a deep breath, muscled his way back to the corner booth, and found what looked like three generations of the same family, all a disturbing shade of barn red, but no Joe and no ginger chick in the group.

*What woman would be hanging with him, anyway? The whole town knows he and Vicky have been a thing since high school. She'd have to be a tourist.*

Kyle checked the john, then, with his head swiveling left and right, shouldered through to the front door and his car.

"Be home, shithead. Be home," he growled as he headed out of town, eyeing every car he passed. He slowed to take the curve at Gillian's corner and, out of habit, glanced up the couple's driveway.

"What the … ?" Slowing more, he peered to the right, straining to see beyond the street light's glow. Big, dark shapes moved through the murky field … *horses, there and there.* He stopped and climbed from the car to look harder, already certain whose they were. He tried to count them, to catch a glimpse as they trotted in and out of the streetlight's range, running deep into the shadows then doubling back toward the road before disappearing again.

He punched on his hazards and ran to the edge of the roadside ditch, squinting as far as the serrated black of the horizon.

"Okay, there's … Ma Horse?" He lurched into the ditch and up the other side to Gillian's fence. The dirt, dry and crusted, jabbed his bare feet through his flip-flops. "And that's … two. Maria Horse! But where the hell's …" he turned a full circle, sure now the mini and the chestnut weren't with the mares. And worse, still no sign of Joe.

He stumbled back to the road, coughing, his rubber flip-flops twisting as he ran; he tore them off his feet, grabbed them up, and rounded the bend. A dozen yards ahead, on his side of the road, a large dark shape crouched, motionless.

Kyle swore and moaned, "Please, *not* a horse. Not a horse." Doubled over with a coughing fit, he ran forward in a stoop and collapsed with relief against the shape, a low-slung car. "Oh thank G—" he almost laughed at his stupidity, then froze, braced against the back of the silent Corvette.

With a glance, he registered the distinctive Grand Sport markings that confirmed the car was Joe's; up here no one but Joe owned a blue convertible Corvette with a white racing stripe. But it was destined for some client, it wasn't really Joe's, and where was Joe anyway? A new wave of fear washed over him.

"No! Joe! Are you in there?"

He whirled to the street and leapt backwards as an SUV sped past, swerving wide and honking for the hell of it. Teenagers yelled taunts from all four windows of the vehicle.

In its wake, something living reared up high over Joe's car, letting loose an ugly, angry noise. Kyle dropped into a crouch, cringing, his arms crooked above his head.

"Holy shit—Bingo!" He scrambled to hunch against the back bumper, covered in goose bumps, and watched with helpless awe as the magnificent animal screamed through an open mouth, hooves slashing the air.

"Oh, please, please don't land on the car. Please do not hurt yourself," Kyle begged.

Bingo dropped onto all four legs, blowing hard through his nose and tossing his head, then turned and galloped into the trees bordering the road.

"Holy shit." Kyle slumped to his knees in the dirt and yelled into the sky, "Thank you!"

He sprang to the driver's window, full of adrenaline, and peered into the open car. With his thoughts racing and overlapping, he struggled to be rational.

*No flattened air bag, but did this car even* have *an air bag?* With a hand gripping the driver's doorframe, he crouched beside the car to look under it. *So low to the ground, there's no way Joe could be … wait, unless it had rolled. No, there'd be more damage if it had rolled. Right?* He felt around the dash—*key in the ignition, but off*—so what the hell?

"Joe, where *are* you?" He yelled, then doubled over coughing. Hanging onto the door again and dragging himself to the hood, he laid his palm on the surface; barely warm. *A good sign or not?* Swearing at the pebbles bruising his bare feet, he ran back to the Honda and tore open the glove box.

"You Boy Scout, Joe." He grabbed a flashlight, and momentum and fear took him halfway back to the Corvette before a sharp stone against his heel slowed him to a fast limp. He focused on the pain, willing his mind to stop—*just stop*—and lay on the grass very close to the car to shine the beam of light under it. *Just in case.*

*Clear.* A stark portrait of lit-up grass and mud clumps, the belly of a racy car and … something awkward way up front … *behind, or was it under, the bumper?* He made his way forward and squatted beside the driver's side headlight, then blanched. Rocking on his heels, he cleared his throat several times and pulled his phone from his pocket.

"Mel, it's Kyle. I need you and Juliet right now." The words gushed from him. "The horses are all out, on the road by Gillian's curve—except I haven't seen your little mini. Joe's car is in the road without him in it." He steeled himself to finish. "And … there's blood on the bumper."

\*\*\*

Joe rose onto one elbow, cringing from the sudden furious sound exploding inside his head. Intense light filled his vision. He twisted away, fisting up hay for protection and raising an arm over his eyes, but it roared louder, came closer, into the place where he lay.

He cowered against the rough wood at his back. The agonizing noise cut out, a slam followed, and angry hands grabbed his jaw, yanking his face to within inches of the thing that cornered him.

"Look! Look, you ass!" The shouting sounded like Kyle. "Is that Bonnet? Did you hit her?"

Joe squinted against the brilliant glare, but rough fingers pulled up his eyelids. His eyes rolled in pain.

"You left *every single stall open!*" Still shouting … still hurting his eyes; he smelled the hay around him and—blood?

"Is that Bonnet?" Kyle yelled again then let him loose with a shove to the floor. "Bingo's somewhere in the woods—"

Joe's eyes started to focus … a car's bumper just above his head … wet with dark smears and what?

"—the other two are running wild in Gillian's field. And Bonnet's missing."

Joe dragged himself up to hang onto the bumper, squinting hard. Short, tawny-colored hairs … gore?

"You *stupid,* selfish *drunk.*" Kyle's feet disappeared toward the sound of another horn outside the barn.

Clumps of animal hair caught in fresh gore.

Joe vomited into the hay of Bonnet's stall.

# Chapter Twenty-Four
## July 30ᵗʰ

The orange light of the rising sun wove through the pines bordering the river's banks, low enough to tip only a few branches. Joe leaned on the kitchen window, resting his cheek against the glass, and raised gritty, sore eyes. A white jellybean of moon shared the sky, fading as he watched.

As much as he wanted sleep, his stomach turned every time his lids fell closed and he saw the ugliness waiting for him in the barn … on the Corvette's bumper. The car he'd driven drunk.

*Stupid, selfish drunk … that's me;* he rolled his forehead on the cool windowpane. *And that's the end of it with Vicky. If I … sweet Jesus … if I killed that little horse, or if any one of those horses are hurt because of me, that's the end of it. And it should be. What a fucked-up mess I am.*

Sinking into a kitchen chair, his head throbbing, he heard vehicles in the drive and dragged himself back up to the window. Mel's pickup appeared pulling the horse trailer and Kyle followed in the Honda. Numb and holding his breath, Joe watched Mel and Juliet unload one mare and then another, leading them into the barn. But no Bingo … and no Bonnet. Joe pushed both fists into his stomach and ran to the bathroom.

Vomiting and sobbing, he bent over the toilet bowl, then stumbled upright and back to the window. Walking beside Kyle, Mel crossed the lawn toward the cabin, her face grim until she caught sight of Joe through the glass and stopped.

Her stare hardened; its fierceness locked his eyes to hers. Kyle dropped a hand on her shoulder, let it slide off, and scrubbing his face with the heels of his hands, trudged into the porch. Joe heard him drop onto the couch with a groan.

For a long second more, Mel stood in the grass, her chin high, her eyes burning his, then turned on her heel and strode back to her truck.

Slumped at the table, Joe rocked and cried as the sun crawled over him and into the room.

\*\*\*

"Hey, slimeball, couldn't you slither to your bed?"

Joe raised his head, squinting against the brightness around him to find the voice that had woken him, then recognized the unmistakable sound of a man peeing.

"Closer to the toilet in case I need to barf," he mumbled.

"No sympathy here." Coughing, Kyle limped into the kitchen, fully dressed but barefoot.

"None expected." Joe stared out at the barn. The nightmare he'd hoped to wake up from remained as stark and real as his pounding headache.

"You stink."

Joe looked down at his muddy and vomit-stained dress shirt. "What the— when did I do that?"

"You trashed it good." Kyle ducked into the mud room and returned with a wrinkled polo shirt he threw across the table. "After you left the Mitten, let's hope. Ginny said you were hammering 'em back with some chick there."

"Jesus ... that's perfect." As Joe twisted out of his ruined shirt, its last remaining button pinged to the floor and skittered under the refrigerator. "The world will know what a dick I was last night."

"You know what, Joe?" Kyle dropped into a chair and pulled up close to the table. "I'd say that's the least of your worries."

Joe's throat started moving. He pulled the clean shirt on and tipped his chin up, his eyes locked on Kyle's face, but found he couldn't speak.

"You gonna puke?" Kyle asked.

Joe shook his head, blinking several times.

"Quit feeling sorry for yourself. Start making it right."

Joe took in a long breath. He turned back to the shimmering green view outside the window. "How the hell do I do that?"

"First: go check the barn; see who's there and who's missing."

He nodded. "I saw you and Mel at sunrise. I only saw the two mares."

"That was a couple hours ago. Juliet was with us, too." Kyle stood. "Let's go look."

Joe nodded again, chewing the inside of his cheek, but didn't get up.

"Jesus, Joe. Man up!"

"Mel hates me." His voice cracked. He squinted up at Kyle. "I think she'd rather it was me on that bumper."

"Do you blame her? Put away the pity, shithead!" Kyle's hands slapped flat against the table. He leaned so close Joe could feel his breath. "This used to be *us*, remember? Us, scared enough you'd piss your pants, with Dad the asshole and Mom making excuses for him. Now it's you, Joe—in both roles! And now it's at least two good women—and possibly two horses—that are suffering." Kyle flicked him hard on the shoulder and straightened to his full height, glaring. "So you feel like shit now. You're used to being the good guy in the world's eyes. Well, last night you were a total dick."

Joe held Kyle's eye and pushed up from his chair, stifling a groan. He crammed his ruined shirt into the kitchen trash can. "You're right, about all of it."

"So out with it; let's hear the whole story, Joe." Kyle turned and headed to the porch. "Besides driving drunk—again—and screwing up with the horses, did you screw your drinking buddy?"

Joe jerked to a stop in his tracks. "No, Kyle! I didn't. God, no."

Kyle bent to slide into his flip-flops but said nothing.

Joe waited at the screen door and worked the inside of his cheek. Outside, the morning was still raucous with birdsong. *The wrong soundtrack for today*, he thought. Shielding his eyes against the brightness, he followed Kyle out and across the yard. The barn door stood open wide.

He glanced at Kyle as they walked in together, knowing they shared the same thought: *it's too quiet in here.*

Then two mares nickered and blew.

Joe went to them. Their big, curious eyes reflected random chinks of the early light lasering through the rough walls.

"Wondering about breakfast? Or your friends?" he whispered. "Or why a big car is taking up Bonnet's whole stall?"

At the sound of the Corvette starting, Joe turned to watch Kyle reverse it into the nearest row of cars, then went into the stall. With disgust, he gathered up his vomit-soaked straw, tossed it in the burning barrel behind the barn, and put down fresh straw.

Kyle checked water levels in all the stalls and started to haul the barn doors closed.

"Wait," Joe said. "Mel probably left them open on purpose." He turned to shove them back and caught a glint of sunlight on metal then glimpsed something blue moving in the trees. It turned into Mel's pickup making its careful way up the wooded drive, pulling a double horse trailer. Kyle walked to meet her.

Joe hung back, standing at the barn door. As Mel parked and swung out of the truck without a word, he studied her face then glanced at Juliet in the passenger seat. Tight-lipped, with red-rimmed eyes, neither woman acknowledged him. Seeing the smudged eye makeup and the silky, fragile-looking shirt Juliet wore, he knew she'd cut short her hot date to join the hunt late last night.

"Did Bingo show up?" Mel asked Kyle. She gripped the edge of the driver's door like a crutch.

Kyle shook his head once and a single whimper escaped her lips. Dashing away the tears that welled in her eyes, she told him, "Bonnet's in the trailer. We found her ripping up grass in a neighbor's yard."

Kyle blew out a breath and nodded. "Good."

Joe's stomach flipped, but he stayed quiet; three found, but one still missing. He started toward the trailer. "I'll unload her. And give them all breakfast?"

"We'll feed them." Mel stepped into his path, her eyes blazing. "And I'm taking Bonnet home."

Joe nodded and stepped away to stand nearby, ramrod straight.

"There's no sign of him, Kyle," Mel said, sounding raspy. She wrapped her arms around her middle, and looked into the soft blue of the sky, rocking a little. Her blue eyes filled again. "I was so sure he'd be back here demanding his breakfast." Her voice cracked and Kyle took her forearm as her face started to crumple.

Joe's stomach lurched. Bingo could be gone. For sure any trust Mel had in him was history.

"Right!" Kyle said. "So let's get busy, Mel! You're wiped out. I've slept a little, so I'll make some calls and get a group together while you catch a few …"

With Kyle taking charge, Mel became a broken-hearted child, standing limp and alone, crying in front of them. Joe had to look away. A dark blur on the sun-dappled drive caught his eye. Giving a loud whoop, he gestured to the others.

"He's there! He's back!" Awash with goose bumps, a swell of emotion surged through him and erupted as a laugh.

Mel spun around.

Snorting and tossing his head, Bingo trotted toward them, in and out of the shadows beneath the pine trees; everything about him rippled with the thrill of a good adventure.

"Oh, my sweet man!" Mel ran, her ponytail flying behind her. Juliet leapt from the truck and rushed to join them. Hearing the cry in her laughter, Joe almost choked.

Kyle punched a fist in the air. "Yes!"

With a sudden ache, Joe wanted Vicky to be there, to hold her hard, to kiss her face, the top of her head. He knew he'd never find the words to tell her about all of this: the excruciating shame, the remorse and fear, then the enormous relief, and for this brief moment, such intense joy.

He also knew, he'd hit his rock bottom. Time now to claw his way up, and he had a long way to go. His head pounded and he wanted to sleep for a month. The nugget of excitement that had just burned with the purest light a moment ago, wavered then morphed to anguish as he watched Mel laughing and crying. She rocked on her tiptoes in the dappled sunshine, her arms wrapped tight around the chestnut's neck, her forehead pressed against it. Bingo nuzzled her shoulder and seemed to prance within her embrace.

"Okay. I hope you can both get some sleep now. I'm hungry as hell." Kyle said. "Can you eat anything, Joe?"

Mel and Bingo held him transfixed.

"Snap out of it."

The sharp nudge to his shoulder broke through; staring at his filthy shoes, Joe followed Kyle to the cabin.

# Chapter Twenty-Five
## July 30th

"Apologize later," Kyle said, not caring that it sounded like an order.

He mounted the wooden stairs and stopped at the top to look down at Joe's whisker-shadowed face. With creases from a shirt sleeve still imprinted on his cheek, his eyes puffy and red, he looked as rough as Kyle could remember ever seeing him before.

The image of one previous time flashed to mind. Kyle had stormed from their parents' house one night, fifteen and full of fury, promising to run so far from home, no Carson would lay eyes on him again, and he'd never have to take another drunken insult from his father. The next morning, after camping at the far edge of the Gillians' property, he'd woken to find Joe curled up asleep in the weeds against his tent, wearing nothing but pajamas.

Countless times since that day Kyle had wondered what he might have done, whether he might've made good on his threats, if his eleven-year-old brother hadn't tracked him and begged him in tears to not leave.

Thirteen years later, it seemed Joe was the one that needed saving from himself. Kyle held the porch door open and followed him through to the kitchen.

"Mel won't want to hear your apologies yet. But I'm guessing she'll soften up. Horse people have big hearts."

Confusion flickered across Joe's face, but with bacon and breakfast on his mind, Kyle didn't feel like elaborating. He turned to start a pot of coffee and a new line of conversation.

"So, when's Vicky due back? Mel said she was off at a conference. Recruiting or something?"

"That's over. She's just hanging out at one of her sister's."

Kyle glanced over his shoulder at Joe, who sat staring out at the barn, then got busy frying bacon. He raised his voice over the sizzle. "And here I thought I was giving you two time to get back on track after your stunt on Gillian's corner. Then I got this cold and spent most of last week glued to the couch binge watching 'Flight of the Conchords.'" He sneezed into the crook of his arm.

"Vicky took off."

Kyle turned to gawk at him. "What do you mean—*took off*? For good?" No wonder Joe sounded and looked like the walking dead. If Vicky took off, of course he'd implode; she and Grandma were the center of his life.

"You said you were giving us time?" Joe said as Kyle took the bacon off the burner. "Well, so was Vicky … apparently. But it's gotten so messed up … I've messed it up so much worse; now it looks like she's decided we're done."

"Why? The drinking?"

"At first. One day after an Eagala session here, instead of getting on the bus to leave, some fat Boy Scout was all over my car—

"A kid named Gordy, by any chance?"

"Yeah, him—and he found a flask in the glove compartment. Of course, Vicky saw him waving it around. I panicked and said it wasn't mine. I knew she'd flip after me going into Gillian's ditch the week before and—I lied. The first time I have ever lied to her."

"Why did you even have one?"

"The flask? It's an old one of Grandpa's. I found it in the barn years ago and left it there. On extra cold days when I'm working late, I sometimes add a little whisky to my coffee. It reminds me of him."

"You and your nostalgia …" Kyle turned back to making breakfast, sliding frozen hash browns into the toaster. *These kind of talks will never be my thing. But this is the guy who once kept me from becoming a teen runaway.* "Wearing Grandpa's deodorant, keeping that ear-splitting landline, using his flask; I bet those boxers you wear are his, too?"

"So?"

"So, I'm *right?* Jesus. Hope you never come across any old tubes of his hemorrhoi—"

"Yeah, well. That day after the home movies, I grabbed Grandpa's flask and, yeah, *after* going into the ditch, feeling sorry for myself, I grabbed it and took a couple swigs—not before. Stupid anyway. Then, *stupider,* I forgot and left it in the glove compartment. I know the law about open liquor in a car, and it wasn't like I kept it there to be handy. I just *forgot* about it."

Kyle scrabbled for the right words, trying to imagine what Maria might say if she'd heard Joe spilling his guts like this. "And you don't think Vicky will believe that? That's why she left?"

"Not just that. Last night she called and brought up that 'don't dream' thing you and I do, and a laundry list of other stuff. I felt her list growing all summer, but at the same time Grandma's been going downhill so fast. Then that movie— it felt so real, didn't it? It *was* so real; Grandma and Grandpa, Mom and Dad, us? *Jesus.* Ma gave me away because I'm named after some woman Dad was cheating with."

Kyle plunked a mug of coffee on the table and turned back to the counter. *Maria could probably sit there and hold Joe's hand, even with everything written across his face like that, but if we're were going to keep talking like this, I sure as hell can't do it face to face.*

"Vick's right," Joe said. "I did start drinking more than I used to. So, now she's worried I'm getting like Dad."

"Are you?"

"If I say no, who's going to believe me? She's going to—heck, *you're* going to call it denial. But I'm saying it anyway. No. I'm not an alcoholic—despite how it looks, despite the horses and last night at the Mitten."

"And driving drunk."

"You don't have to believe me."

Kyle snorted as he went to the table, but didn't answer. He set down a full plate for each of them and realized he'd lost his appetite. Joe didn't even pick up his fork; he blew on his coffee and turned back to the window. Waiting in silence, Kyle almost finished a full mug before Joe spoke.

"I keep thinking, over and over, in a loop: 'Thank God, all the horses are okay.'" Joe looked across the table and started to stir his coffee, though he hadn't put anything in it. The spoon clinked against the stoneware. "But if they're all fine, what did I hit with the car?"

"A deer?"

"Maybe."

"Apparently Michigan has about 50,000 deer-vehicle accidents a year," Kyle said.

"Jesus! Really?" Joe kept stirring and clinking. "But if it was a deer, wouldn't the car look way worse?"

Kyle snatched the spoon away and dropped it on the table. "Depends, I guess." He decided to try the hash browns and talking around a big bite, added, "But yeah, probably. You'd think so." He gulped and lay down his fork. "Joe, where's Doughnut?"

"No, Kyle."

Kyle swallowed again, forcing down the lump forming in his throat and demanded, "I'm asking. Where the *hell* is Doughnut? She didn't sleep on the couch with me last night. Was she here with you this morning?"

Joe shook his head with a moan and everything about him slumped. Color drained from his face.

Kyle charged up to the loft and back down. He fought a strong urge to grab a fistful of Joe's shirt. "So, where is she? When did you see her last? Was she with you at all yesterday?"

"Yoo-hoo!" Ma called. The porch door creaked open.

Joe dropped his head to the table and Kyle groaned, then went to get a third mug, his mind racing as he filled it.

"Joe! There you are—and Kyle. Bonus."

*Bonus?* Kyle handed Ma a coffee as she stood just inside the kitchen doorway, her eyes moving from Joe, to him, then back to Joe. Her smile faded and a deep furrow formed at the top of her nose.

"Are you sick?" she asked Joe, then took a sip of her coffee. With her sunglasses on her head and her white jeans, she looked like a movie star, but she sounded like a TV mom.

Joe raised his head but not his eyes. "Hungover."

"Oh, Joe …" She looked as if she'd just been handed a speeding ticket. "Since when?"

"Since, last night—haven't you heard yet?" Joe said. His face flushed red and he looked into his coffee.

*Please, Doughnut,* Kyle begged, *be at the river or chasing some poor mouse somewhere.* He refilled his own mug, trying to bring his thoughts back to the present, and informed Ma as he sat down again, "And I'm at the tail end of a cold. Enter at your own risk." He coughed into the crook of his arm for effect.

Ma shrugged. "This is probably not good timing, then?" She sounded tentative, but setting down her coffee and her purse, tucked away her sunglasses, and took a seat between him and Joe.

"Did you want to talk to Joe alone?" Kyle pushed back his chair. *I'd much rather hunt for Doughnut than revisit that home movie debacle. I'll start in the deeper corners of the barn then—*

Ma's hand flew out and touched his wrist. "No, Kyle. I'm glad you're both here."

Kyle pulled up to the table and thrust a hand into his hair. *You touched me twice in the same summer? When has that ever happened?* Across the table, Joe sat silent, his head in his hands. *On the verge of melting down.* Kyle wondered. *Picturing those bloody hairs or fur or whatever on the Corvette's bumper? Fur the same color as Doughnut's …*

"Okay." Ma wrapped her hands around her mug. "I told Joe, but I don't know if he's told you, Kyle, after the trip to Utah—

"Utah, is it? That's where you and Dad went skiing?" Kyle glanced at Joe. *I was searching for Dad in Colorado.*

"Yes." Ma faltered, frowning, then carried on. "I started going to Al-Anon. You've heard of it? Right?"

"For drunks?" Kyle tried to concentrate on Ma's words instead of imagining Doughnut hunkered in front of the Corvette trying to hold her ground on the road.

"No, you're thinking of AA. That's for alcoholics. Al-Anon is a twelve-step program, too, and it's adapted from AA, but it's for the people who've been affected by someone else's drinking—the families and friends of alcoholics."

Maybe she noticed Kyle throw a glance Joe's way.

"Like the two of you, as kids." She hesitated, but didn't look at either of them. "And now, as well. Like Grandma … and me, too." She took a deep breath. "It's all about support, helping us change our own negative behaviors and attitudes—focusing on our *own* issues," pausing just a beat, she added, "instead of on the alcoholic or everyone else's business."

Kyle crunched a piece of cold bacon and watched her massage her shoulder at the base of her neck. Years of resentment toward her ways—the anger that had fueled this summer's campaign for her to get real, to cut out all her secrets and falseness—all started backing up in his throat.

"Okay. Anyway," she kept massaging her shoulder as she talked. "Since November I've been going to every meeting I can. The talking and support, the whole structure of it has been amazing. It's helped me deal with … everything around your dad."

Kyle took another bite, hoping to cram down the bitter words filling his mouth and ordering himself, *don't be the dick Joe said you are. This might be what you've been hammering away for. Think what you've learned from the horses. Listen.*

"An old-time member with a lot of recovery under her belt is working with me as a sponsor, kind of like a confidante or mentor. We've been working through the twelve steps together and I've come to Step Nine. The previous step asked that I make a list of anyone I had harmed, and that I become willing to make amends to them all. The amends come in Step Nine." Her massaging hand stilled and she met Kyle's eyes. Joe still wouldn't look at her. With another deep breath, she said, "Thinking deeply about it, with my sponsor's help, gave me such a different perspective on the past and all the huge mistakes I made with you boys and I … want to make amends to you both."

"How do you do that, Ma?" Kyle dug for the memory of the gentle acceptance he'd felt from the horses, to soften his expression and offset the engulfing coldness he felt toward her.

"By owning my part in it." She shifted in her chair but held his eye. "Not blaming your dad, his affair, or his drinking, and doing my best to change my own behavior, starting by apologizing."

The sun shone through the kitchen window onto Ma's face. Kyle studied the myriad small lines around her eyes and mouth. Probably not laugh lines. The image of her crying as she listened to Frank Sinatra came to him and he nodded.

"Joe ... I want to tell you how very sorry I am that I let Grandma keep you all those years. I went to get you a few hours after that awful birthday party. But when she didn't want to give you back, I didn't demand it."

Joe finally raised his eyes to Ma, his mouth twisted as he chewed the inside of his cheek and his forehead creased.

It was clear Ma saw Joe's intensity, too. Questions flickered in her eyes as she studied his face, but she kept talking to both of them in turns as if, having started, she couldn't stop.

"She made such a good case for keeping you—saying I had my hands full with your father drinking again and with Kyle to chase after. She could handle a baby, she said, but not a four-year-old, too. You, Kyle," she bit her lip and smiled at him, her eyes soft, "were always running on a thousand watts right up till you fell into bed, filthy, on the nights I couldn't catch you to bathe you."

Kyle squinted as the sun moved onto his face.

"After learning about your dad and Josey, I was such a wreck." Ma gazed at the table in front of her as if seeing the scenario unfolding in the scarred oak. "I thought he'd kicked the drinking before we got married, so to learn differently and find out about Josey at your party like that, Joe, well ..." she let the sentence die, squeezed her shoulder for a moment, then rushed on. "I believed your grandmother when she said it'd be better for you. And I'm not blaming her. At the time, at least, I thought she was right. I was—a mess. I started using Valium to get through the crisis, then started needing it more, relying on it, and became more of a mess."

As she turned to address him, Kyle leapt up and collected the mugs from the table. She went ahead anyway.

"Kyle, I can't imagine what it was like for you, seeing me that way. If you hadn't come into the world with so much feisty resilience, I don't know how you would've turned out."

He topped up and returned each mug, then put away the empty pot and sank back into his chair. While the anger and bitterness hadn't gone, it had diluted, changed to an odd mixture that included detached fascination and an unfamiliar desire to hear her out.

"Then, Joe," Ma tried and failed to hold his gaze, "you started growing extremely attached to Grandma and to Grandpa. I lost any confidence that I was strong enough to deal with an unfaithful, alcoholic husband, and still be a good enough mother to manage two little boys—one of whom clearly preferred his grandmother over his mom." Her little laugh didn't cover the catch in her voice. Joe looked up again.

"As time passed, it started to feel selfish to take you back. Then your dad went and got you. And that was that."

Ma's gaze moved over Joe's taut mouth and narrowed eyes. "It wasn't until a couple weeks ago when I saw your reaction to the movie that it occurred to me I wasn't the only who'd suffered with my decision; I realized how much I'd hurt you. I never knew that. I never should have let you spend one night away from me." Her voice choked again. She dipped her head for a second, then raised her face to Joe's. "I thought I'd done the right thing. Can you forgive me?"

Kyle looked from one to the other. Joe sat rigid as stone, silhouetted by the sun behind him, then started shaking his head.

The color drained from Ma's face, and she pressed her fingertips to her mouth until Joe spoke. She leaned in to hear him.

"So, it wasn't about my name?" Joe sounded incredulous, and barely audible. "That you didn't want me around because I'd always remind you of Josey?"

"What?" Ma looked baffled then she gasped. "You thought that's why Grandma and Grandpa had you? The name your dad chose?" Her chin came up and her eyes widened, making space for the sudden tears glistening there. She swallowed hard and grabbed Joe's slack hand, squeezing it as if to push her answer into his skin. "Never."

Joe crossed his arms on the table and cradled his head on them, face down.

"So! There ya go." Kyle clapped his hands once.

Ma ignored him and addressed the top of Joe's tousled head. She reached for a tangled lock of hair but stopped and pulled back.

Kyle hadn't given her childhood a lot of thought until that moment. Watching her toy with the strap of her purse, he wondered why he hadn't and how touching got so hard for her.

"Joe, I never knew I'd made the wrong decision until the other day." She slid her bag onto her lap and folded her hands over it. "As cliché as it sounds, I thought what I'd done was for the best. I truly did."

Ma sat up straighter and turned again to Kyle. He pressed his lips into a tight line but stayed in his chair.

"And that holds true for this next thing." Taking her wallet from her purse, she removed a folded square of paper. "It's about that 'don't dream' saying between the two of you." She unfolded the paper as she spoke and extended it to Kyle.

Kyle turned his head and looked back at her from the corner of his eye. She bit her lip and the paper trembled in her hand, hovering above the table, like an unmade decision. He leaned forward and took it from her, more gently than he wanted to.

The paper was soft, the creases so deep, it kept folding onto itself as he tried to read it. He flattened it on the table and read it through twice, its meaning sinking into him like ink spreading through water.

"Our mother took her parenting advice from a quote by Pearl S. Buck." He shot a look at Ma, then read it aloud for Joe. It felt like chewing steel.

*"There are many ways of breaking a heart. Stories were full of hearts broken by love, but what really broke a heart was taking away its dream—whatever that dream might be."*

"So, don't dream?" Joe raised his head from his arms with a look of utter disbelief. "It was you who started us saying that?"

"You determined to raise children with no dreams." Kyle wanted to pin her to the wall with his words.

"Only to save you pain. To keep you safe," Ma whispered, her tears spilling over. "I'm so sorry."

# Chapter Twenty-Six
## July 30th

Joe sank onto a moss-covered rock, pulled off his work boots, and gave them a lame knock against each other. Debris caught in the lugs dislodged and fell to the carpet of pine needles that floored the woods. He opened one hand then the other and let each shoe drop wherever they landed. With his elbows on his thighs, he eased his pounding head into his cupped hands. Trying to gauge how long he and Kyle had been walking the woods calling for Doughnut felt like too much effort.

*Who's to say she even knows her name is Doughnut?* He wondered. *We never consulted her.* A branch snapped nearby, and he swiveled his head to watch Kyle push his way through the undergrowth, leaf dust on his face, a broken twig caught in his hair, and sweat darkening his T-shirt in large patches.

"You look like I feel," Joe muttered.

Kyle frowned, scratching at mosquito bites on his arm.

Joe checked his cell phone for missed calls despite knowing what he'd find. The vet clinic and the animal shelter had sounded sympathetic when he'd checked there for Doughnut, but didn't offer much hope anyone would bring her in. Vicky hadn't called either.

"Where else, Joe?" Kyle sat on a neighboring rock.

"We've searched every one of her favorite hang-outs—that I know of, at least." Joe spoke to the inside of his eyelids, the heels of his hands pressing on them to make sparks of light. "The loft, the barn, every field around it, all along the river here … and we've probably passed by or looked into just about every tree on the property. The ditch by the roa—" He heard how lifeless he sounded and stopped talking. One more word and he'd break down.

With two fingers hooked into each sweaty boot, he picked them up and dragged himself off the rock. Barefoot, the walk back to the cabin would seem even longer, but maybe if he focused on his feet, he'd stop seeing that bloody fur dried on the Corvette's bumper. He wanted to check again, to convince himself this time that the tawny yellow fur they'd scraped off Doughnut's favorite spot on the living room couch didn't match what was on the bumper. But it did look like a match. Close enough that, seeing it, he'd nearly thrown up again.

"We'll do this again tomorrow," Kyle mumbled.

Joe managed a slow blink in reply. Though the woods weren't dense, the shadows around them had grown longer and he felt wobbly and shaky. He couldn't remember if he'd eaten anything after Ma left, leaving her bombshells in her wake. He and Kyle had left her news in the kitchen, too; she'd dumped so much on them. Too much to think about, much less talk about, and not important enough to warrant further delaying the hunt for Doughnut. She had still evaded their biggest question, going silent and rushing out when Kyle demanded: Tell us about Dad. What's happened to him, Ma?"

Despite a headache and lack of sleep, Joe's thinking had cleared, burned as clean as if he'd had a fever. Going over what Ma had told them didn't seem terribly painful now. It hurt more to picture what he'd likely done to that yellow scrap of a cat he'd shared his pillow with since spring and fallen in love with almost from the start—a bubbling-in-his-stomach kind of love that made him scoop her up and babytalk her with no one around to see it.

As he and Kyle trudged out of the woods in silence, birds swooping overhead in a cloud-feathered sky, he wondered what that little cat brought out in him: joy at her antics and innocence, protective feelings at her vulnerability, disbelief at the many unfathomable things she did. She was brave, oblivious to his concern and to most dangers of the world. He felt a wild kind of pure love for her, similar but somehow … smaller … than what he'd seen between Mel and Bingo on the driveway that morning; that had seemed to be a love almost human, one that involved respect and intelligence, yet, despite the animal's size, also dependence and vulnerability.

And he'd almost destroyed that. Might still have destroyed the small animal he loved. He thought about Kyle's assumption earlier: that while he watched Mel celebrate Bingo's return, he'd been working up to apologize to her. In reality his mind had been reeling, thinking of the anguish he'd caused and how it so easily could have been heartbreak.

Because of the choices he'd made and perceptions he'd gathered and woven into a smothering blanket of self-pity. He'd been stumbling around under the weight of it for … way too long. Like Ma, he hadn't thought of himself as good enough. Maybe he hadn't turned to Valium, but he'd been leaning on others for strength. First Grandma, then Vicky, hoping they wouldn't notice, and trying to cultivate their love for him so he wouldn't have to stand alone—basically living as a victim, feeling helpless against the moving sidewalks of life. But, going by last night, victims also commit crimes against others. He wasn't a saint and he wasn't blameless—or a victim. And he knew what he had to do about it.

As they'd searched the barn earlier, Kyle had told him about visiting the Gillians: that he'd at least learned their father was alive. Kyle concluded their dad's lack of contact meant he didn't give a damn about them. So, Kyle had decided to quit searching for him, saying without rancor, "Screw him."

*Maybe that qualified as feisty resilience*, Joe thought. He paused to rub his heel where he'd stepped on a prickly weed. *Or maybe it's a defensive wall. I want resilience, but not a wall.*

With Ma, he knew he now had a second role model nudging him by example to a gentle means of change. He exhaled with a wry smile and looked over at Kyle waiting while he massaged his foot.

"Some food, some sleep," Joe said as they started walking again. "Then, if there's a meeting happening somewhere tonight, I'm going to look into a new way of thinking."

"AA you mean?"

"Maybe … I will if it turns out that's what I need. No doubt I'd be following in Dad's footsteps if I keep going like I have been." He followed Kyle up the steps and into the silent cabin. "But it never got to be where it was just about drinking. I could stop and I did. A lot of nights I had just one beer or none and didn't even *want* any. But I did start using booze as a crutch, instead of dealing with stuff. So, I'm going to man up. I'm going see if Al-Anon," he shot Kyle a grin, "can help me find my balls."

Kyle grinned back, a crooked, tired-looking grin. He knuckled Joe's shoulder, then gripped it.

"What?"

"Joe. We're being so flippin' stupid." Kyle blew his breath out and shook his head. "That can't be Doughnut on the bumper. She's too little. If you hit her at all, you'd have creamed her."

"Oh, Jesus." Joe groaned. "And we'd have found her in the ditch."

"Or all over the road." Kyle shook him by the shoulder. "And we didn't."

\*\*\*

"So, Vick, I'm sitting here on our porch couch with my tall, cold glass of iced tea," Joe said with exaggerated emphasis, "watching our resident raccoon amble around the edge of the woods in the moonlight."

"Mm hmm …," she murmured. "I can see him."

Joe pictured her in the dark at her tiny studio across town. She'd be curled up in her oversized reading chair by the window, as he'd seen her dozens of times over the years, the street lamp through the blinds leaving ribbons of light across her face. They'd once moved the bed beneath the window to make love with striped bodies.

"Any sign of Doughnut, yet? Mel saw Kyle searching the barn for her."

"None. I'm still searching, though. Kyle helps sometimes. One of the horses could've stepped on her that night."

"And I think she's just off on a lark," Vicky said. "She'll show up."

Joe wished he could agree. And wished he knew what to say next. Because he had felt ready for this call, he'd imagined it would be easier than it felt so far. Talking just didn't come easy. He reminded himself of his new favorite slogan, "Easy Does It," and said, "It felt like the right time to call. I've really missed you."

"I miss you, too, Joe." She hesitated, then asked, "How are you?"

It hurt to hear her being so cautious, but felt a lot better than the blast of anger he'd earned when he'd called to confess the incident with the horses. He'd wanted to be the one to tell her, to start his new life with a spine. And though there'd been a chill in her voice, she had managed to thank him for that as she'd hung up. Mel had been the same when he'd gone to apologize to her.

"Funny you should ask," he teased Vicky now. "A couple weeks ago, the day after my dickiest day, I finally dug out a couple of those Al-Anon daily readers."

"And?"

"And I opened them up at random, like Grandma did sometimes, just to see what came up. Both readings were about denial."

"Oh, yeah?" Her soft laugh made him smile.

"Of course, I remembered what you said the day you left—about my pattern of pretending instead of dealing with stuff, and how it had turned toxic. So, I went to an Al-Anon meeting."

"And ..." Vicky sounded as if she was holding her breath.

"And I bawled."

"Joe."

"Like a baby. It wasn't even when I was talking; it was from what other people said about their own experiences. Their stories all rang so many bells, Vick." God, it felt good to be talking to her again, rather than trying to catch glimpses of her whenever she came to help run an Eagala session. But even more, it felt great to be legitimately proud of what he had to say. "So I got a sponsor that night. Since then I've seen or spoken to him every ni—"

"I'm coming home, Joe," Vicky interrupted.

"Home, here? Really? When?"

"Right now." She laughed again. "Well, okay, I'd better get dressed first."

"No, don't bother with that."

"Seriously, Joe." A smile shone in her voice.

"Seriously, Vicky."

"You know we have a lot of talking—and healing—to do yet," she said.

"Yes." He paused and with a hint of wicked in his voice, suggested, "We can do that naked."

He heard her catch her breath, then let it out. "Yes, we can. We can absolutely do that naked."

# Chapter Twenty-Seven
## August 15th

Kyle eased between the auditorium's back doors and, hoping to soften their harsh metallic click, turned to slow them as they closed. He caught sight of his reflection in one of their reinforced windows, the crease between his eyebrows, and his thick dark hair standing up on the top and sides from jamming his hands into it. *Like I'm trying to cram my brains back in,* he thought. *Too late for that, apparently, or I'd never have let Joe talk me into an Al-Anon speakers' meeting. This might be Ma's thing, and Joe's too, it seems. I'll stick with the horses.*

Scanning the room, he saw a surprising number of people scattered in clusters and pairs throughout the rows ahead. His eyes fell on Vicky's familiar head of tousled dark hair, two rows from the back, with Joe in the aisle seat beside her.

As if sensing Kyle had arrived, Joe stood, urged Vicky to scoot over one seat, and turned to send him a silent invitation—or maybe a plea—to come take the open seat.

*On the aisle and bolting distance to the door, I can handle that,* Kyle decided, taking slow steps to avoid drawing attention from the front of the room where a handful of men and women—a surprising number familiar to him—milled around near a wooden podium. Most conferred with each other while new arrivals hugged, and a white-haired, bird-like woman set out water glasses and a small pitcher.

Kyle lowered into his aisle seat, rolling his eyes at the high-five Joe offered. Vicky leaned forward, wiggling her fingertips in welcome as he dragged his palm across Joe's with no enthusiasm.

"Ma'll be glad," Joe said.

Kyle shrugged and glanced around. "Thanks for sitting in the back. I'll try to stick it out till she talks, but when I get a gutful, I'm out of here." He tipped his head to the room and a stream of latecomers filling in most of the gaps near them. "I can't believe there are so many *families and friends of alcoholics* in the area."

"This isn't just Al-Anon," Joe said. "It's hosted by the area AA groups. Al-Anon's participating in it. It's both."

"So every alky and their ala-nutters are going to tell their stories? Pfft!" Kyle started to stand. "I'm leaving now!"

Joe gripped his shoulder, smiling, and pulled him back down. "Just the braver ones talk. It took a while before Ma got up the nerve and volunteered."

"What's the big deal? Hasn't she been going for eight, nine months now? Isn't she almost done?"

Joe's smile grew wider. "I'm learning nine months in the program is nothing. A lot of members have been going for decades. There's a saying they finish every meeting with: 'Keep coming back. It works if you work at it.' Ma's dead set on getting the most she can out of it, so she's jumped in with both feet."

Vicky leaned forward again and nudged Joe's shoulder with hers. "Don't go thinking she's 'graduating' soon or anything like that," she whispered. "People don't really outgrow twelve-step programs. And why would you want to? It's self-care that's not self-centered … and free to boot."

"I'm thinking it's like exercise," Joe agreed. "It's good for you; stop doing it, and you'll just go flabby again."

Kyle shrugged. Vicky drew back against her seat in mild surprise then, with a fingertip, turned Joe's face to hers and kissed him full on the mouth.

"Did Ma ever say why she's so hot on us being here?" Kyle interrupted the mutual beaming to his left.

"To give us her point of view?" Joe suggested. "Moral support, maybe?"

"How about *you* tell *our story*, from the kids' point of view? Tell our missing father's while you're at it, too." Kyle bristled, twisting in his seat and felt the old anger rising up. "I'm sure Ludington would learn some shit they never knew about our upstanding family."

Vicky squeezed Joe's thigh and jutted her chin to the stage.

"There ya go," Joe lowered his voice. "Looks like Ma's being introduced to go first."

*A ponytail and a tie-dyed sundress?* Kyle thought. *She looks about seventeen years old.* "Good. I won't have to sit through a bunch of 'poor me' stories," he said.

"It's not like that, Kyle. Really …" Joe started but Vicky nudged his leg and gave a quiet "shh!"

"Right," Kyle muttered, yet he and Joe leaned forward in their chairs at the same time.

With a direct view of Ma from where they sat, Kyle saw her eyes dart from her sandals, to the wall at her right, flick over the audience, and down to the sheets of paper trembling in her hand. He swallowed hard and found his own palms sweating.

She stepped up to the podium and began, her voice unsteady, "On her way to deliver dinner to a friend with a broken arm, my mother's car was broadsided. Three days later, she died. I was seven."

*Wow. What an opening.* Kyle held his breath. The audience went dead quiet, coughs stifled, squirming stilled. Ma glanced up with a weak smile. "Okay, everyone: *breathe*—and so will I." She waved her notes at them. "That was a few years ago, after all."

Thin laughter stuttered across the room and Kyle sent the audience a silent *"thank you."* From the corner of his eye, he saw Joe lean into Vicky.

Ma continued, "My dad started drinking after that. Slowly at first. Then it became his top priority, till it killed him eighteen years later. As a kid, I became overly responsible. By the time I was a pre-teen, I was making appointments to keep him well, out of court, and out of the car when he'd been drinking. Otherwise, I had my nose in a book to escape life. If my sons had known me then, they might have called me a brainiac. I read or I studied and, if I hung out at all, it was with the nerds."

Kyle twisted in his seat. *Did anyone use that word anymore—other than for computer geeks?*

"Books saved me—hiding in them meant I did well in school." Ma sounded at ease now, the librarian used to talking to strangers. "I got a scholarship to study library science. In my senior year, listening to music in some coffee shop on campus, I met a great-looking guy by the name of Keith Carson." She aimed a mischievous smirk over the edge of her notes. "Some of you might know him?" Most of her audience smiled or laughed. Hearing Gillian's throaty rumble, Kyle spotted his unmistakable profile several rows ahead and realized most of the people in the room would have known Sylvia and Keith Carson for years or even decades.

"Well, not long after that, here I was in Ludington, meeting Keith's mother, Joy—an absolutely lovely woman," Ma said. At the mention of Grandma, Kyle felt Joe sit straighter beside him. "And Keith's father, Robert—who felt oddly familiar somehow—and guess why?" Kyle watched knowing nods bobbing around the room.

Ma shared the punch line. "Right … like mine, Keith's dad was an alcoholic. When I met Robert, he was a happy-go-lucky man who let Keith's mom manage everything of importance in the family's life. You would have thought I'd see warning bells and red lights. 'Run away! Run away!' But no … Keith had this crooked half-smile I couldn't see past. Even his own mom seemed to warn me away from him. And Joy's warnings weren't especially subtle, with things like 'take care with Keith, he became a drinker in high school.' Or 'take your time so you know what you're getting into.' Or even, 'are you sure you want to risk having an alcoholic marriage?'"

Kyle couldn't resist checking whether Grandma's warnings rang bells with Joe and Vicky; it seemed not. They held hands, their eyes glued on Ma.

"Joy kept telling me, 'You're so young, so smart, so pretty, you'll have lots of choices.' But then she fell in love with me, too."

*When did Ma become such an entertainer?* Kyle wondered. She stood grinning, waiting till the little burst of laughter died out. Then her voice became somber.

"After that, Joy's tune changed and became more like: 'You're great for Keith, he's so much more settled than with …' um, the woman he dated before he met me." Kyle nodded at Joe's nudge, thinking it was big of Ma to leave Josey's name out of the story. If she'd died when Joe was four, how many in town might still remember her?

"Joy also said, 'Make sure Keith is great for you, too.' Well, guess what? He *promised* he'd give up drinking."

The audience shared her wry laugh—as if everyone there had the same story.

"Mm-hmm …," Ma nodded. Baffled at how she was making this all sound so matter-of-fact, Kyle scanned the audience again. *Not a hint of pity—or self-pity—in the room.*

"We all know how reliable an alcoholic's promises are. At that point, he may have only been a …" Ma resorted to the air quotes Kyle despised, "… 'problem drinker.' He did dial it way back, enough that I married him. With a champagne fountain at our wedding. I'd always wanted one of those." She threw an answering smile to those chuckling around her and resumed, "Our first four years were great. A year of just us, then a sweet baby boy we named Kyle." Ma's eyes swept the audience and Kyle slouched low in his chair, out of her view.

"We had three years as the perfect happy family and then, when I became pregnant for a second time, changes starting creeping into our relationship—subtle at first, then not so subtle. Keith started leaving me at home to meet up with 'an old drinking buddy' who'd gotten in touch after no contact for years. It was the old girlfriend. My fears about this friend—which I couldn't bring myself to voice—plus the reality of Keith's drinking, a new pregnancy, and a very energetic three-year-old were too much."

As Ma's joking tone fell away, the audience went quiet, respectful. Drawn forward again, elbows on his knees, Kyle rested his jaw on his fists, and squinted at her.

"Many years later, I learned that one of the key risk factors around a new mother developing post-partum depression is lack of support—say from her spouse and family. I was probably depressed even before our second boy was born. And I certainly was afterwards." Kyle heard Joe groan and saw Ma take a deep breath. "But I wouldn't admit it. I just kept struggling, putting on the mask, not even asking Joy for help. It all fell apart when Joe turned one, and—long story short—the affair, the drinking, it all came out and I ... came apart.

"Fast forward through three years of hell. Joy took over parenting my youngest, my oldest suffered through haphazard, inconsistent parenting on my part and, sometimes, downright cold or mean treatment on Keith's part. That is, when Keith was at home and not with his ... girlfriend." Ma paused, then raised her chin and spoke a little louder. "I started to rely on Valium to get me through. Even when his friend died and he brought Joe back home to us—on the day he learned of her death, in fact—Keith kept drinking off and on. But mostly on. He tried AA now and then, but didn't commit to it. His father, Robert, had gotten into AA hours after he and Joy took over Joe's care and, as far as I know, never had another drink from that day on."

A burst of enthusiastic clapping interrupted her.

"With Joe back home and two children relying on me, I finally woke up." She cleared her throat. "I realized I had to get off the Valium and I did. That was no mean feat, let me tell you! By then I was suffering from what I'd now call a severe Al-Anon deficiency." This time Ma talked over the rippling laughter. Ducking her head to check her notes, she started ticking a list on her slender fingers.

"I was: overly responsible, a perfectionist, an expert in denial, controlling, short-tempered, sharp-tongued ...""

Kyle ground his teeth as he listened, each word a hook pulling a long-buried feeling to the surface—fear, sadness, longing, confusion—still sharp, real. With each feeling a stark memory arose: a slamming door, being yanked into line by the wrist or arm, being left to cry, being taunted or ignored. He shifted in his seat, claustrophobic, and cast around for somewhere to escape the sight of Ma. He caught Joe and Vicky exchanging glances.

"I notice a lot of heads nodding," Ma said.

Kyle noticed, too, and welcomed the familiar surge of anger the crowd's reaction provoked in him. More powerful than he'd felt in years, closer to a fury, it engulfed him, knotting his stomach. He gripped the arms of his seat and fought an urge to grab someone—anyone—by the collar and yell, "Confess it all and it's fine? Bygones? Is that it?" He wanted to spew a torrent of outrage and accusations. *Those are words! What about the kids who lived it? Who got the brunt of your sickness before they barely had words?*

Ma had started talking again. Frightened for the first time by the strength of his reaction, Kyle forced himself to listen and breathe, but he couldn't look at her. He watched his fists on his knees, clenching and unclenching.

"… over the years both boys were at home," Ma went on, "and since then, too, I built up so many 'I'm sorrys' it became embarrassing. But rather than saying them, or better yet, upping my game, I pretended saying 'sorry' wasn't necessary. Someone shared a little ditty last week: 'it's not old behavior if you're still doing it.' Isn't that good? Why keep saying, 'Sorry, sorry, sorry,' when I keep on doing, doing, doing? Like an echo."

Kyle looked up. Something in Ma's tone cut through, the same unfamiliar catch in her voice as when she'd tried to make amends to him and Joe at the kitchen table.

"Those of you my age might remember that famous line from *Love Story*: 'Love means never having to say you're sorry' … well, I twisted that idea every which way; for the most part, I think I walked on those I loved." She blew air through her lips and Kyle found himself doing the same.

"Saying sorry is not easy," Ma said. She paused too long, staring at the podium. When she spoke again, he strained to hear her. "Are you kidding? Saying sorry to any of you? Or those I love and have hurt? My sons … will they ever forgive me? My husband … will he? Or even saying 'sorry' to myself. God knows. Literally, *God knows*."

Unbidden, Kyle recalled Ma Horse in the arena, the whites of her panicked eyes as she side-stepped, head high and nostrils flared. Afterward, he'd struggled to explain to Juliet what it had taught him. But as he refocused on Ma fidgeting at the podium, her throat working, he remembered and felt his anger drain away.

Ma pressed two fingertips against her lips and tipped her head back to blink at the far corner of the ceiling. Kyle rolled his shoulders and stretched his neck, half wanting to leave yet wondering if she knew he and Joe had come.

She took a deep breath and a sip of water, then leaned into the microphone. "Whew. I have such a headache all of a sudden."

Her audience offered a gentle laugh.

"Here's the good part. Through Al-Anon, I've learned I must both make amends, *say* those 'sorrys'—including to myself—*and* change my behavior. But also, that I now have the support—from those of you in my meetings, my sponsor, the literature, and a new connection to my Higher Power—to finally do it. On top of that, I have community, the love of strangers in Al Anon around the world; I can see how *they've* done it. Through them, I can know by working my program, I can make changes, and can trust, *with practice*, they'll stick."

She shuffled her papers. "So that brings me to today. Oh, sorry." She smirked and dipped a shoulder. "See, I can say 'sorry'!" Someone shot her a thumbs-up and smiles mirrored hers.

"This is where Keith's story kicks in. So I'll finish with this. There were a number of sober patches in our marriage, some lasting several years. But in my deluded mind, thinking everything was up to me, I never went looking for my own recovery till last November—and, shall we say, I had help in that." She flashed a smile at the front row.

Kyle poked Joe's arm and sat up taller, craning to see Ma's friend.

"I've heard a lot of people profess everything in life happens in the time it's meant to happen," Ma continued. "Including when any one of us decides to make recovery a priority. I'm eternally grateful my time is now. I'm still new enough at it to wish I'd got started a whole lot sooner, but no one can rewrite history— though I've heard some politicians try really hard—and 'now' is all we've got. *Now* I have a solid program. So, for getting me to where I am today: on the road to serenity and the emotional healing that *anyone* can benefit from, I'd like to thank all of you, and I'd like to thank," Ma gestured toward the front row, "my husband, Keith Carson."

"What the—?" Kyle slapped Joe's knee and half rose to stare as their father walked to the podium and Ma stepped aside.

"Jesus Christ," Joe whispered, and Vicky fell back in her seat, her hands clapped to her face.

Seeing Joe's gaping mouth, Kyle snapped his own closed and pushed his fist hard against it, holding back all he wanted to shout. Through his fingers he hissed, "Did you know about this?"

Joe just shook his head, eyes fixed on the stage.

Kyle hissed again, "Look at him down there—still the suave ladies' man, but the bastard's gone totally gray." Then he shut up to listen.

Keith leaned down to the microphone, pulling on the collar of his white button-down.

"In, what to me is Sinead O'Connor's most powerful song, "Famine," she says, 'If there ever is to be healing, there has to be remembering, then grieving so there can be forgiving.' This is going to be about all that. Hi. My name is Keith and I'm an alcoholic." Waiting while most of the audience replied, "Hi Keith," he dropped his eyes to the sheet of paper in his hand, swiped his palms against the sides of his trousers, and went on, "And I've just finished serving ten months in Utah's Summit County Jail."

Kyle jackknifed hard into his chair, thumping his tailbone on the back of it and felt a second jolt as Joe did the same.

The room crackled with whispering and stabs of indrawn breath, then dozens turned to shoot sympathetic glances at him and Joe. Hands in fists, Kyle locked eyes with Joe; he looked as ill as the morning the horses were missing, blank and dead-eyed. Worse, he looked like he'd lost twenty years and reverted to the little boy who'd stood shaking beside Kyle clutching his hand as they watched their father fumble to remove his belt to use on their backsides because they'd played tag on his newly seeded lawn. Hazy, in the background of his memory, Kyle saw Ma turning away, crying.

For the first time since that long-ago afternoon, he grabbed Joe's hand, gripping it hard as Keith started talking again.

"I guess by your reaction, keeping a secret in a small town can be done after all—"

*You'd know*, Kyle thought. *You've had plenty of practice.*

"—thank you, Sylvia, for keeping one *last*, but very big secret for me." Keith glanced at the front row and paused again, chewing the inside of his cheek.

Kyle glimpsed Joe doing the same.

"My wife began the story that has turned my life around—this time for good. So I'll tell you the rest of it, the part I begged her to leave for me to tell anyone, including our sons ... when I got up the guts to do it."

Keith cleared his throat and fidgeted with his papers for a moment before looking out from under dark lashes.

"Pfft!" Kyle almost spat, recognizing the "shy charmer melting hearts act" that years ago he'd dubbed the "outside angel and inside tyrant."

"My probation officer has given me permission to attend and speak at this meeting, but I'm due back in Park City by midday tomorrow. I served time for ..." Keith hesitated, took a deep breath and rushed on, "... child endangerment while intoxicated."

Kyle felt as if he'd been punched. He tasted acid in his mouth and his squint hardened to a glare. This time he didn't register how the audience reacted; he only heard Joe's sharp gasp and felt Vicky's cool hands wrap around his and Joe's locked fingers.

"Sylvia and I had been in the ski lodge there at Park City—you know one of those stone and glass and fireplace kinda showpieces featured in brochures for romantic, couples' getaways. That's probably what we were both hoping for—a happy jolt to get our marriage on track after nearly two months of living apart and years of … what she's just described. It was Thanksgiving weekend and the first vacation we'd taken alone in over a decade."

"Well, it was the end of our first day there, late in the day, lights coming on all over, beautiful people everywhere starting to chill out or gear up for a party. I was drinking and … probably flirting. But not with my wife."

Kyle shook his head. God, he manages to look sheepish, at what—fifty-three, fifty-four?

"As you'd expect, Sylvia wasn't exactly thrilled with me and, um, we started arguing. I probably needled her into it. You know, a case of the guilts over being a dick … Of course, once she was good and mad, I took that as an excuse to storm out and blast on up the mountain again. Free and goofing around on my own like a single man while she suffered alone in the middle of a happy crowd.

"I managed to behave well enough for long enough to get on a lift. There I was, half pissed-off, half having a hilarious time; flailing around on the lower slopes near the lodge, and one hundred percent drunk as a skunk."

"Then I heard a child's belly laugh. You know the kind? A toddler's? Infectious, makes you laugh yourself." His voice cracked. "Pulls you to it."

There wasn't a sound in the room. Kyle pulled his hand free of Joe and Vicky's and dug his fingers into his hair. He stared at the stage dreading the story unfolding.

"I was drawn to that laugh. My skis turned that way. If I was thinking at all, it was that I wanted in on their fun. Have a laugh with that cute figure of a woman and that little nugget of a kid crouched on the front of her snowboard. It was their last run of the day. They were heading to the lodge for hot chocolate. They saw me coming—at the last second. Out of control. She knew what was about to happen and tried to react. To grab the boy to her. She screamed. The child stared into my face."

Blinking through his own sudden tears, Kyle saw his father choke hard, drop his head, then continue in a harsh whisper only audible because of the dead silence.

"I see the look on his face. I'll never forget it. Never. Or the sound …" Tears fell onto the podium and the abandoned speech notes.

Kyle rubbed damp palms against the knees of his jeans till his hands were hot; he itched to get away from the horror of the story. Too real. He felt the boy's terror and pain, the young mother's anguish; he was living it. He was the child.

The boy was his, Maria the young mother. He found himself rocking, his breathing harsh and loud, and surrounded by turning heads and pain-filled glances. An elbow pressed his arm and he turned to Joe and Vicky leaning toward him. He erupted from his seat and pushed out through the rear door of the auditorium.

The hallway was too bright. Walking fast, his vision blurred as tears brimmed. He heard the auditorium door bang behind him and Joe call his name. He broke into a run and slammed out through the fire door to the dimly lit parking lot, dodging and weaving between rows to his car at the far edge. He collapsed into the driver's seat, Joe's voice quieter, more distant now.

Kyle yanked the car door closed and howled. "You bastard! You bastard!" He slapped his hands flat-palmed against the car's ceiling, pressing hard, pushing against it. Head thrown back against the car's headrest, his eyes darted unseeing around the dark interior. His breath came in huffs, the soundtrack to a parade of torturing images in his mind. Him, aged four, running to the living room, squeezing in to flatten himself behind the tall bookshelf, his parents yelling, his mother's voice vicious, his father's loud and slurred. The Utah toddler crouched, waiting for impact, then silent and bloody, crumpled in the snow, the young mother panicked and shrieking. The child he had ached to parent with Maria: peals of laughter following the baby's trajectory as Maria tossed him into a blue summer sky then, giggling and nuzzling his silky smooth neck as she caught him, and twirling, spinning, breathless with joy.

The mossy trill of Maria's laugh mixed with their infant son's and his anger bled out, replaced by a piercing sadness so intense he struggled to breathe. Gripping the steering wheel, he gulped hard once, twice, a third time. Sudden fear squeezed his chest.

A figure caught his eye, hovering in the shadows beyond the passenger door, melting back.

"Hey! Who's there?" His breath was back. Ragged, but enough. Scrubbing his sore eyes dry with his cuff, he leaned closer to the window, but saw nothing. Maybe someone moving across the unlit side road?

*Joe?*

He slumped against the seat, his breath slowing, coming quieter, his mind blank, clean. Everything felt heavy now … his arm … the car keys.

*Concentrate, man,* he thought. *Get yourself home.*

He dragged the car into gear and pulled onto the road, remembering too late to search for who had been there with him, watching over him as he grieved.

# Chapter Twenty-Eight
## August 16th

Joe took in a lungful of cool, fresh air and checked his watch. "Well, Ma and Dad will have to leave for the airport in about twenty minutes if he's going to make his flight." Vicky brushed a fingertip across his unshaven jaw, and he stopped chewing his cheek, then shrugged and confessed, "So, okay ... I guess I thought he'd make time to stop here before he went back."

Both awake early, they'd brought a pot of coffee out to the picnic table after breakfast and now sat facing the river, the rising sun barely warming their backs.

"Maybe he's at Kyle's," Vicky said. "Since we had time with him last night at Ma's. Or maybe he's still with her. They'd have had a lot of ground to cover in a very short time."

"I wonder if she let him stay."

"He's sure as hell *not* at my place!" Joe and Vicky both jumped and turned at the sound of Kyle's voice. "And there's no one at hers. I was just there, pounding on her door. By the way, you guys need a watch dog. You didn't even hear me drive up. Anyone could sneak up on you with all the nature racket at this hour."

"Nice, isn't it?" Shading her eyes, Vicky aimed a grin in Kyle's direction.

"Well, g' morning. You look like crap," Joe said. It struck him how much Kyle looked like their dad ... a younger, more chiseled version of the time-worn, ladies' man in that auditorium last night.

"Thanks. You, too." Kyle dragged the heels of his hands over his face. "At least I have an excuse–slept like crap."

*Okay, what's coming won't surprise me,* Joe thought, *new venom from old wounds.* He refilled his own coffee mug and handed it across the table.

With a look of thanks, Kyle went on, "I was wiped out when I went to bed. Then all night I just kept seeing that poor kid's face—Jesus!—and dreaming of you and me as kids, how Dad was—"

"Well," Joe cut in, "you've got the answers you were chomping for all summer. Where Dad's been and who Ma's mystery kid was ..."

Kyle plunked his mug onto the table and gawked.

Joe stopped. "Wait. You're just getting this now?"

Vicky jumped in, "Kyle, you missed an amazing story. Your mom sent presents to the little guy the whole time he was in the hospital."

Kyle pursed his lips, shaking his head. "That's what she was up to? Unreal."

Vicky gave a gentle shrug that said: *doesn't surprise me.*

"End of story?" Kyle asked.

"Nowhere near," Joe said. "Ma never brought up the presents; Vicky did—afterwards. But Dad talked—in front of everyone and then with just us at Ma's—about the kind of father he was to us as kids …" Kyle narrowed his eyes and raised his eyebrows, but stayed quiet, so Joe continued, "He didn't hold back. He described how badly he hurt Tony—internal injuries, a concussion, broken ribs, and two broken legs." Kyle growled and Joe raised his voice just a little as he went on, "Dad said what he did to that child is going to stay with him forever—"

Vicky interjected, "—and that he expected a lifetime of shame, self-loathing, and regret. Quote, unquote."

Joe finished, "He said he welcomed that jail sentence and was ashamed it wasn't longer."

"Damn right!" Kyle hissed. "He should rot in there!"

A sparrow landed on the edge of the picnic table, cocked its head at each of them, then flew into the woods.

Joe took a deep breath. "Well, he's out now, on probation in Utah."

"What I don't get is why I didn't find this online." Vicky looked from Joe to Kyle. "A drunk skier mowing down a child on the ski slopes would have been big enough news to hit the papers."

"They wouldn't have suppressed his name would they?" Joe asked.

"Heck, no," Vicky said. "Not for something like that."

"How did you search? Did you use Keith or Robert?"

"What do you mean?" Vicky frowned. "Keith."

"That's his middle name, babe. You never knew that? His first name's Robert, after Grandpa. I don't think anyone ever called him that though. Even Grandma."

"No. Way. I did *not* know that." She shook her head. "Or maybe I forgot. I'm sorry! I should have let you do the searching yourself."

"No. *Ma* should have told us," Kyle said. "We had a right to know. Her and her warped sense of loyalty."

"Well. We have the story now. First hand." Joe leaned across the table toward Kyle and enunciated, "Dad said what was *worse* was what he did to you and I as kids."

"And he said all that in front of everyone," Vicky added. "Not that he physically hurt either of you guys, but that he—"

"Was a total shit?" Kyle cut in. "Drunk or wrapped up in himself? Never asking us a thing about our lives? Berating us when he paid us any attention and calling it teasing …"

"Yes!" Vicky nodded. "That he was a shit! That how he behaved forced your mom's life and your lives to center on him … his lies and alcohol, his selfish needs."

Joe took over. "What was worst in his view was that he stole our chance for a decent, normal childhood with the kind of dad we deserved."

"Aw!" Kyle pretended to play a tiny violin. "He shouldn't give himself such credit. We overcame."

"That's exactly what I thought!" Joe said, then glanced at Vicky and added, "Even though, really, we didn't, you know."

He arched and stretched, wishing Kyle could finally give it up and climb out of his pissed pool. *Life's hard enough*, he thought, *Grandma … Doughnut …*"

"So he goes to some AA meetings in jail and comes back here telling his sob story, expecting everyone to feel sorry for him?"

"No!" Joe said. The clear disgust in Kyle's tone got under his skin. He took a deep breath, mentally running through Al-Anon slogans until he hit on "Think."

"Come on, Kyle." He lowered his voice. "Listen. You weren't there to hear the full story. Dad isn't after sympathy, and he isn't full of self-pity. If you'd stuck around last night, you could've seen that. He doesn't feel he deserves pity from anyone. He feels for how he was with Ma and us, and feels for that little guy and his mom …"

Kyle snorted. "Yeah, I can just imagine how he feels for the kid's mom …"

Joe looked away, squinting. *What the hell? Born feisty, Ma said. Well you can have it. I want to heal.* He welcomed the squeeze Vicky gave his hand, relieved when she interjected again.

"He says he's after forgiveness and starting over."

"With who? Me and Joe? We're in our twenties, for Chrissake!" Kyle flung the last of his coffee across the lawn.

"Who knows, Kyle …," Joe shifted his position on the picnic bench and pulled his hand free from Vicky's. *After all your grousing this summer, why didn't you come have it out with him last night? Answer your phone and come to Ma's for pie?*

The crunch of slow tires on gravel broke into his thoughts.

"Okay, that's Mel and Juliet." Vicky rose from the bench beside him, brushing her fingertips along his jacket sleeve. She curved a hand above her eyes and waved, then turned back to address Kyle. "Look. I know they planned to go riding before our first Eagala session today. If you want to try and work this out in the arena, I'll see if they're willing to ride later and give you a session now? Up to you …"

Almost feeling his churning and struggling for self-control, Joe read Kyle's angry glance toward Bingo out in the paddock; the parade of expressions crossing his face seemed to telegraph, "Spend even *more* time on that bastard?"

Kyle finally jerked his chin up at Vicky and Joe let out a long breath.

"Good." Vicky strode across the lawn to Mel and Juliet. From the bottom step of the porch, a chipmunk started his sharp, staccato call—like shooting staples, Kyle had once said—drowning out whatever discussion accompanied the three women's shrugs and nods. In less than a minute, Vicky beckoned to Kyle with a thumbs-up. He dropped his fist on the table with a thump, and went to join them.

*Thank God.* Joe wished the team luck, wondering who'd need it most— probably Bingo.

Vicky disappeared into the cabin to do her own thing. He looked forward to the same—an easy, straightforward hour detailing the Fairlane for its new owner in Pentwater. He knew Tommy or Jocko would have fought over the chance to take on the task but, next to finding just the right car, detailing had always been his favorite part of his business.

As soon as Kyle, Mel and Juliet appeared near the arena fence Joe headed into the barn's dim, fragrant stillness and snagged the ignition key from the board. To farewell the Fairlane felt bittersweet. It helped to remember that after months of searching for a buyer, he'd found a collector who recognized his asking price was fair and hadn't balked at paying it. He reversed the car out onto the concrete pad beside the pebble driveway then ducked back into the barn to fill a bucket with the clay bar, chamois cloths, and waxes he'd need.

"Fucker!"

Joe dropped the cans he held and bolted through the barn toward Kyle's shout. Halfway through the arena door, one work boot already planted in the hoof-printed dust, Joe grabbed hold of the rough wooden frame to slow himself down.

He exhaled with a huff, shaking his head. *You don't need any help —from me at least—that's up to Bingo. I'd say you've met your match, mate.*

Fascinated, he watched Kyle's attempt to catch Bingo. With all the taunting and lunging going on, he thought it looked more like a challenge to a bar fight. Bingo seemed to have accepted by leaving the paddock and coming into the arena to reply with his own taunts. In response to Kyle's aggression, the chestnut did little more than toss his magnificent head and sidestep the lunges.

Kyle charged, the massive horse trotted toward the barn, and Joe tensed to jump out of his way. Ten feet from the door, Bingo doubled back to the corner where the barn's outside wall met the nearest fence and Kyle ran after him at full speed, red in the face, waving his arms and shouting. Bingo twisted one way then the other, dipping his head then throwing it high as Kyle leapt from side to side, arms thrown wide and blocking the path out of the corner.

"Shit! Watch out," Joe breathed, "look at his eyes! He's warning you this time."

Bingo flattened his ears, his nostrils flaring, and Joe threw a frantic look to Mel. She and Juliet watched, but more with avid interest than concern, it seemed.

Bingo reared up, pummeled the air with his hooves, then dropped down, breathing as if through bellows, and ran past Kyle to the farthest fence.

Kyle rose from the crouch he'd assumed and turned—an ugly look on his face, one that seemed to shout not fear but triumph.

At the sight of it, Joe rubbed away the prickles that rose on the back of his neck. *You wanted that. You're punishing Dad.* He sagged back against the door frame and a noise burst from him: "Hunh!"

With a heated glance his way, Kyle stalked, tight-mouthed, through the settling cloud of dust to pursue Bingo. Mel spied Joe, too, and shouted one word: "Go!"

*Crap! What was I thinking?*

He knew better but had utterly forgotten: unless given permission by the client, observing an Eagala session was strictly out of bounds. Hands held low in quiet surrender, he backed through the arena door, but not before he saw Mel reach a hand up to flip her ponytail as she turned back to Kyle and Bingo.

Thinking how horse-like that gesture of annoyance looked, an equine version of giving him the finger, Joe chuckled and announced to the empty barn, "Mel, you are so cool." With his mind racing, he squatted to collect the supplies he'd dropped in the sawdust.

*Loyal to a fault to those in your care, eh, Mel? Unfortunately for me, despite what Kyle says about your big heart, I expect that same loyalty's going to fuel a long-term grudge against me for endangering Bingo and company. How many times can I say, "I'm sorry?"*

He slowed, then paused, sitting on his heels, his hands full. Scraps of thoughts came and went like puzzle pieces he didn't know where to put. *Ma is loyal to Dad— to a fault. Now she's about forgiving and compassion. What about Vicky? When's she gonna be okay again with me grabbing a beer from the fridge or ordering wine with dinner? If Grandma's mind worked well enough for her to understand what her alcoholic son had done, how long would it have taken for her to come to terms with it? Big hearts ... compassion and forgiveness ... In his screwy way, under all his taunting and nastiness, is that what Kyle's really digging for out there with Bingo?*

Joe stood up, hugging the cans and brushes to his chest; something to think about or share with his sponsor, but not now. He turned toward the Fairlane.

# Chapter Twenty-Nine
## August 16th

"Bully! Just like Dad! You might have size on your side, but that's about all." Kyle massaged a stitch in his side. Since the crash, he wasn't used to this kind of workout.

The horse puffed and blew, huge eyes fixed on him.

*Now what? Now what.* He threw his head back, catching his breath, and noticed a hawk fly overhead, heard the honking of some Canada geese. His breathing starting to quiet, he glanced back at Bingo—still haughty, head held high, watching him.

*So you go swig a beer or two, now? Stomp off to Michael's to have a laugh over your tough little son.*

Bingo averted his eyes.

*Embarrassing you, am I? Well, I heard about it years later … how you'd brag about me grabbing your beer bottle from beside the recliner and running to dump it out. You'd look like fury at first, then burst out laughing and go get another. You liked me being feisty. That's when I got your attention. Calling me Kyle the Kid, egging me on when I mouthed off at Ma or you even.*

Bingo, sauntered closer in the casual 'you don't see this' attitude of a child, then stopped, his gaze still angled to the river.

*Now what … I'm supposed to meet you halfway? Is that it? Forget what's past? Pretend it never happened? Don't you "win" then, Dad?*

Intense, Bingo eyes cut to him. Through him.

*Yeah, okay … you win that point; with a jail sentence, a conviction, on your record. What a trophy that is. You'll be welcomed back to Ludington for sure. Ha. No town's going to be as quick to forgive and forget as that AA crowd. I wouldn't want to be in your shoes. Your hooves. Jesus, what you did to that little kid! My God! How'd Joe and I get off all those years without you hurting us?*

Bingo shifted and settled, blowing softly, his head low. *Shit luck, right? I can't see you hurting any kid on purpose; you'd rather have not hurt that one, either. Duh. Of course not … Maybe that's the best I can say: you never hurt us physically. Wrestled and raced us, sure, but only when you were sober.*

Kyle warmed to the memory. *Okay, so that was a blast—you chasing us all over the house or through the yard and into Gillians'. Jeez, Joe would squeal! Those were the best days.*

Bingo stepped closer.

*Never baseball, though, or catch. I remember you told us Grandpa never played ball with you, or showed you how to throw. Too drunk, you told us. At least with you. Ma said he quit—just like that—when Joe arrived. Too late for you, eh, Dad? You'd have been what—pushing thirty then? You caught his love of booze, though, eh? Didn't Grandma always call it "the family disease." Funny too, it's a kid—and not your own—that put the brakes on it for you, too. And you think it's for good this time?*

As Kyle grew calmer, he noticed Bingo inching forward. In minutes, a warm, prickly-soft nose pushed against his raised palm.

*Whaddya know … Damn. That's wild.*

Scratching Bingo's muzzle, then leaning against him, shoulder to shoulder, Kyle rested his head back against the warm, solid strength.

*Why can I manage to have a beer and it's just a beer? It doesn't need to be a six-pack or a bender. I didn't inherit your allergy and I've no idea why not. I guess you'd rather not have inherited it from Grandpa either. Or grown up with that, like we did.*

Kyle laid his forehead and palms against Bingo's flank, taking in his dusty scent, feeling the quiet rise and fall of their breath sync together.

"I'm sorry, Dad."

# Chapter Thirty
## August 16th

By noon the day felt much warmer, but deeper patches of cool shade lay among the dappled sun and trees bordering the river. It already had begun to smell like fall. Joe shrugged out of his faded army fatigue jacket and draped it over Vicky's shoulders. He wondered when her mood had changed and if he'd regret asking what was bothering her.

Though he hadn't seen her then, he'd heard the sounds of controlled chaos as the morning's Eagala session ended and she, Mel, and Juliet herded a noisy crowd of Boy Scouts on their way. Shortly before that, he'd sent the Fairlane on its way with the car's happy new owner and pocketed a very respectable check. One that should bring his new "Act Like the Big Dogs" Transporter Fund close to the goal he'd set, close enough that he was itching to tell Vicky. The prospect of having his own transporter felt exciting. So did picturing the extra time it would give him. And she had been the engine behind it.

Yet, despite the rest of Saturday stretching ahead of them, it didn't feel like the right time to share his news. She didn't seem quite *there* with him. She'd hardly spoken since they'd begun their daily search nearly half an hour ago, watching and calling for Doughnut. Joe picked up a blue jay feather and tucked it into his shirt pocket.

He and Vicky had talked through the previous night's bombshells, sifting through timelines, tying up story threads, and sharing their horror at what that little boy and his mom had endured. He was surprised how basically relaxed he felt about his parents. It had occurred to him as he'd finished up the Fairlane, all that he'd learned about them made no difference to what he'd lived. Sure, he knew their reasons and stories now, but none of that changed his experience. He'd always have the childhood they'd given him, both good and bad. Understanding them better felt good, sure, seeing them more as people than just as his parents was long overdue, he figured. But the best part had struck him while he talked to his sponsor just before lunch: he didn't feel bitter toward either of them. He wanted to move forward, to stop looking back and hanging on so tightly to the past.

Vicky's uncharacteristic quietness started to worry him. They still weren't back to their overall auto-pilot … that steady undercurrent of connection and affection he'd relied on for so many years. He blamed his own sense of remorse and guilt and maybe Vicky's tentativeness. He'd damaged the trust they'd had from the start. What lay between them still needing repair felt suffocating.

He remembered the slogan his Al-Anon sponsor always used to close their Zoom calls: "One day at a time." Today, Joe had suggested revising it to "one minute at a time." The challenge came with figuring out how to apply it.

*This is only her fourth morning living back here again. We're in the early hours of our new start. And ... at this minute, we're only looking for Doughnut.*

"Doughnut!" he shouted, trying to picture her trotting toward him, tail curled over her back like a question mark. He couldn't see it.

Kyle's conviction those tawny hairs on the Corvette couldn't be Doughnut's, and Vicky's stubborn belief their cat was still alive, both failed to light any spark of hope in him. Still they checked websites, called the shelter, hung signs in town, and searched twice a day. *After all*, Vicky had insisted, *Doughnut came to us as a stray. Maybe she's just wandering again.* Joe had agreed, keeping his darker thoughts to himself. It had been more than three weeks since he'd seen the cat; that seemed reason enough to be pessimistic. He had cleaned the gore off the bumper long before Vicky moved back from her place. *Maybe if she'd seen it, she wouldn't be so hopeful.*

*Stinking thinking.* He almost growled out loud. *This is not staying in the moment.*

"Sorry I've gone so blah today, Joe," Vicky said.

"Wanna talk about it?" He lay his arm across her shoulders. "Doughnut!" he called.

"I wish I could ... it's work-related." Vicky touched her forehead to his upper arm for a second then, to Joe's surprise, went on. "A boy I thought had made such great progress seems to have gone backwards. I'm baffled at what's gone wrong." She shook her head. "Anyway, I'll talk with my supervisor about it. Doughnut!"

He started to remind her: trust the process, trust the horses, as she'd said so many times before. She put a quick hand against his hip. Steps ahead on the leaf-strewn path, a brown squirrel sat on its haunches, frozen in fear, its tiny clawed paws drawn against its narrow chest. Joe matched Vicky's silence, holding his breath until the animal leapt away into the undergrowth.

The little creature seemed to lighten Vicky's mood. She slipped into the jacket he'd hung over her shoulders and gave him a little hug.

"I love their charm school posture." They started walking again. "Don't they seem extra busy lately? Can they be getting ready for winter, already? Doughnut!"

"It's coming fast." Joe pulled out the blue jay feather from his pocket. "Did you notice this?"

Vicky's face lit up as she took it. "A flight feather—look at that. They're molting already." She stroked it against her wrist. "Mmm ... I love fall."

"Kyle starts teaching again in a couple weeks. Doughnut!"

"And we haven't done anything about the end-of-summer bonfire." Vicky scanned the sugar maples to her left.

"I was hoping you'd want to still, but I wasn't sure."

"Are you kidding?" She poked his shoulder. "The occasion of our first kiss? Nothing's breaking that tradition, Mr. Carson. Doughnut!"

"We've never missed a year." Something seemed to open in his chest as he said it. He took her arm to stop her walking. "Vicky, do you still want to marry me?"

Her eyes went soft.

"You worried me, Joe. But I never stopped wanting to be with you always— married or not."

A little rougher than he meant to, he pulled her into a hug and buried his face in her hair.

Her face pressed to his shoulder, Vicky said, "What you went through because of your dad's drinking ... Kyle and your mom, too; I do know I could never handle walking into an alcoholic marriage—"

"And you aren't." He led her to a rock big enough for them both to sit on then slid his hand up her neck and into her hair, cradling her head in his fingers. "I've shaken your trust, but I'm going to show you. I'm learning so much about myself in Al-Anon. Things I never told anyone because I hadn't put it together myself."

"Like ...?"

"Like how I put people up on pedestals and decide I'm in charge of keeping them happy." Joe slid his hand from Vicky's hair. "My first memory is that."

"What happened?"

He took a deep breath. The river murmured past, oblivious.

"I was alone with Dad in our family's old car. He was driving fast, crazy, and I was giggling my head off, sliding all over the back seat. I'd never been in a car without being strapped in a kiddy seat before and thought it was a blast being thrown from side to side. Then he stopped somewhere, got out of the car, and left me behind. I thought it was part of the game. Still excited, I waited and waited, hiding in the footwell of the backseat. Until I had to pee. I got out and went inside this smoky, smelly place. I know now it was a bar."

Vicky squeezed his knee and covered her hand with one of his. "My shoes stuck to the floor when I walked, and I couldn't see Dad at all. Only lots of crotches and belt buckles. I panicked then, ducking around and between all the legs. Some people got annoyed. Someone spilled something in my hair. I started crying, but I kept going until I found him."

Squirrels chittered overhead. Beside them birds or chipmunks rustled in the leaves.

"Dad was alone at a table in the corner crying—really hard—drinking and crying. It scared me. I stood beside him, begging him to take me to the bathroom. When he saw me, he thumped his beer down and pulled me onto his lap and hugged me so hard it hurt. I wet my pants on him." Joe gave a little laugh, but Vicky stayed serious, her eyes fixed on his.

"When he realized I'd peed on him, he shoved me off. I hit my back on the edge of the table and landed on the floor, wet and sticky with pee and beer, bawling my eyes out. But the worst thing—by far—was seeing my dad crying up there in that chair. That was awful."

Vicky laced her fingers in his. "Of course it would be. It'd be terrifying."

"End of story: I crouched under the table hugging his legs and patting his knees, over and over. Finally he dragged me back onto his lap and rocked me. He kept whispering my name until he got quieter and quieter. At least I thought he was saying Joey—of course it was probably Josey."

"Oh. It was the day she died. And he took you back from your grandparents."

"Right. His lover's namesake." Joe tipped his head back to gaze into the hard blue sky above the trees.

"You were four, Joe."

"Yep. Four and trying to make it all better for my cheating daddy and his broken heart. But I didn't know any of that. Just that I had to make him stop crying and make him happy again."

"You're not four anymore."

Joe looked at her and smiled. She smiled back.

"No. I'm not," he said. "And I'm not four*teen*, either, trying to make him happy or earn his praise and permission to come hang out here at the cabin. I'm *twenty*-four. So, screw it, no more pedestals. Everyone can handle their own problems, and I'll start dealing with mine."

Vicky rested her forehead against his.

Joe took a deep breath. "It's trickier when it comes to you and me, Vick."

"I hear you."

Joe swallowed hard. "Your turn, then."

"Okay." Vicky sat up. "Full disclosure: I liked being on your pedestal, Joe. A lot. It scared me, though. I think I freaked a little once we got engaged." She paused, staring at her engagement ring. "The day you roared off after the home movie thing, Kyle told me not to start making a case against you and it pissed me off. Because he was right. That's what I was doing. When Gordy found the booze stashed in your car's glove compartment, it gave me a legit reason to take off."

*You wanted to leave me*, Joe thought. *Ow.* "You wanted off your pedestal?"

"Crazy as it sounds, yep. Now I realize, I want *real*. Not perfect anyone. I was spilling the beans to Mom and Penny after the Eagala conference. Griping about you, the drinking, everything that's happened this summer, and it all came out. But the thing is … they said pretty much the same thing Kyle did. They read me the riot act for *my* behavior. They didn't excuse your lying, or driving when you were drunk, but they didn't see you as an alcoholic or an alcoholic in training, rather as someone swamped by some big stuff." She touched his cheek. "And the only one supposedly on your side—the well-educated, self-righteous, mental health professional—ran at the first chance she got."

"Wow." Joe chuckled. He'd won some backers in Vicky's family. And even Kyle had stood up for him? *Wild.*

"So. I was never perfect … just … up on myself and liking your attention. Scared, too." Vicky shifted a little on their rock. "Overall, not much use to you from up on that pedestal. Think you can still love me at ground level?"

"Hmm." Joe smiled. He stood and drew her up with him. "Happy to try it at ground level."

"Now, there's a can-do attitude." Vicky pulled the collar of his shirt away from his neck and drew the tip of her tongue along his skin. "You know I never wanted a saint, Joe."

Joe stilled.

"Umm, about that, Vick." He unlatched her fingers from his shirt and wrapped his hand around hers.

"Joe?" She searched his face, her eyes clouding over.

"There was some woman, Vicky. At the Mitten Bar."

"Whew." She dropped her shoulders in a quick slump then flashed him a grin and pulled her T-shirt from her jeans. "You scared me for a minute."

"No. Vicky. I'm serious. I have something I need to tell you."

"No, Joe. You don't." She faced him again. "I already know. The woman, Shay, figured it out. You talked about your girlfriend—your fiancée—enough, she figured out you were talking about me, her prospective new boss."

"Shit! I never got that. *She* was the one you wanted to hire?"

"One and the same. She called to quit before she started—and told me why. If she hadn't though, I'm sure Sue and Terry Dodds would've spilled."

"The Dodds were there that night?"

"Standing right in front of your table, apparently. They were surprised not to see me with you."

"I thought I heard you. You were calling me a saint."

"Is that why you left?"

"No." His face burned. "I said saints don't do porn or ... sleep with porn stars ... something like that."

"You called her a porn star?"

"I hope not ... I might've? Definitely implied it." He cringed. "What a dick!"

"My sweet man's rejection style ... She didn't tell me *that* part." Vicky chuckled and crouched to spread his jacket on a grassy patch a few feet from the riverbank. "I love how you stayed who you really are despite being drunk. You've no idea how much that means to me."

"Say what?" Joe crouched beside her so he could see her face. "You're impressed with how I acted?"

"With her, yes. I am. I'm sure plenty of people would use being drunk as an excuse to cheat, or that they'd worry more about some stranger's feelings than about their own partner." Kneeling now, she leaned in to nip his cheek between her teeth, then kissed the spot. "Plus, you told me about it yourself."

Joe pushed his hands into the back pocket of her jeans. With earthier sensations taking hold, he lost track of the odd bubbling feeling in his stomach. A grin pricked his mouth as he felt a measure of their old assumed trust slide back into place. Then a thought came to him.

"But you've lost your new team member because of me, Vick."

"Don't worry about that. I want a team that fits well ... and fits this little community. If it takes a while to build—" She shrugged. "It takes a while. And that's another thing, Joe, I promise to channel my rampant ambition a little—keep you part of things, plan together, not just inform you, and then push, push, push."

"Maybe stay in Ludington?"

"Maybe." A sultry tone wove around the word. She pressed against him.

"Maybe in the cabin, even?" He watched her lean back and pull her T-shirt over her head.

"We'll decide together." She held his gaze as she unbuttoned his jeans. "I know there's a bonfire to plan for tonight, but ..." Her fingertips slid under the hem of his shirt to raise it, grazing his stomach, and he caught his breath with a hiss.

"Sizzle," Vicky whispered. As she pulled the fabric over his head, he smelled Old Spice and heard her murmur, "First things first."

# Chapter Thirty-One
## August 16th

"Mrs. Brown, you've got an ugly daughter." Kyle danced his way across the lawn toward Joe and Vicky. The real lyrics of the Herman's Hermits' song blasting from the sound system on the porch overpowered his lousy tenor.

*What a turn-around*, he thought. *Thanks to Bingo, some sleep, a hard workout, and now, a night like this ahead of us: a meal I don't have to cook, friends, and a big bonfire.*

Joe took the moment a notch better. A wooden spoon for a microphone, he finished their boyhood verse in an English accent worse than his own. "Girls like her, they give me quite a scare."

Vicky grabbed for Joe, laughing, trying to clap her hand over his mouth. "How *old* are you guys?"

Kyle dumped an oversized tub of Best Choice potato salad onto the crowded picnic table, surveying the platters and bags already there.

"Vegetarian sausages. Black bean burgers?" He high-fived Joe and glanced around the yard. "I don't see any veggies in this crowd."

Squat glass jars, with a handful of sand and little candles poked down inside, hung from several trees, wired to low-hanging branches, and clustered on every flat space in view, including several mismatched, rickety tables. A folded Indian blanket covered most of the picnic bench at his knee. Nothing matched … from polka-dotted and flowered cushions on wooden benches and kitchen chairs to the striped tablecloth just visible under the feast-worthy pile of food. Kyle caught sight of Tommy and Jocko dragging old wooden pallets to the unused paddock behind the barn, readying for the bonfire later.

Mel climbed from her little truck, calling hello to Rusty and Ginny as they pulled up behind her; in response, Rusty loosed a split second blast from the siren and gumball light. Every conversation and movement paused, then resumed.

At the arena fence, Juliet stood holding hands with some guy Kyle had never met, pointing out Bingo and the palomino grazing in the distance. The Gillians sat near the river, both sunken deep into the Adirondack chairs and deep in conversation with Sue and Terry Dodds.

"Pretty cool, Vick; you two manage to pull this off every year without fail."

"Except for my Grand Rapids peeps not making it this year, we did okay."

Kyle returned Ruth Gillian's eager wave and started toward the two couples.

"Wait, Kyle. I've got a surprise for you … there will be a veggie here—at least one."

Vicky's words snagged him. A sudden thrill coursed through him. "You invited her?"

"She asked if it was okay and I said of course. I ran into her while I was shopping for tonight. Kyle, I hope it's—"

"And in fact, there she is," Joe cut in.

Kyle spun around—the hell with playing cool. Behind him, Vicky teased Joe. "I've got a surprise for you, too, Joe Carson."

"Can I have it now?"

"No, not now. Too many people around …"

"This sounds worth waiting for."

Kyle tuned out. At the edge of the drive, Maria looked around with a happy smile, stepped from her bike, and wheeled it to the corner of the barn. He didn't know what to do but watch. The dress she wore, layer on layer of some kind of floaty material, made him think of rainbow sherbet.

*Oh, God. Good enough to eat.*

As she stood unclipping her helmet, the sun shone through the fabric, outlining her legs. Kyle swallowed hard. At the same instant, she caught sight of him.

She moved toward him across the grass, swinging the helmet by its strap and grinning with the tip of her tongue caught between her teeth. He could smell her shampoo or something as she stopped, hugging distance away.

"Hi." She bit her lower lip, looking both delighted and shy at the same time. He ached to wrap his arms around her. But he no longer had any right to hold her.

He buried his right hand deep in his hair, wishing he'd cut it, wishing he'd worn a better shirt.

"Hey, Maria. Good to see you." Understatement of the year.

Vicky stepped up. "Hello, you! I'm so glad you could come."

Kyle watched their hair swinging together as they hugged, dark curls and light, feather-like ones entangling, then separating. Maria shrugged off her little backpack and he shot a hand out to support it as she dug through.

"Somewhere in here … under my squished-up jacket and other sundries … I've got a couple of specialty doughnuts *just* for Joe … some peaches … Okay, there're the strawbs …"

With the lightweight pack resting in his palm, Kyle felt her searching hands move inside the orange canvas, the pressure of her fingers against his, but nothing more. She didn't squeeze his hand through the fabric or rub a fingertip along his palm. She didn't flirt like she would have done not so long ago—or was it decades? A hovering sadness threatened to corrode his excitement at having her there. If he let it.

"Voila!" Maria held three peaches high. "And not even bruised. These are sooo juicy they're going to drip all over us. Shall I go—"

"Enjoy yourself? Yes." Vicky took the fruit, smiling. "I'll chop these up and hide those doughnuts." She poked a finger into Joe's pouting mouth and addressed him over her shoulder as she headed to the cabin. "Want to start the grill? Your mom said she'd be heading over around now, I think."

Left alone, Kyle faced Maria with nothing intelligent to say. As she stuffed her bike helmet into her pack, he took in the hint of a tan on her face, the same dozen or so freckles he remembered across her cheekbones. She had her hair in a way he didn't remember: sort of half in a ponytail and half not. But he blamed his sudden stupidity on the smooth turn of her neck, the place where it curved into her shoulder, an expanse of silky skin broken only by the skinny straps of her dress … She used to love when he'd—

She smiled up at him, her eyes bright and expectant. So large and dark, like the eyes he bared his soul to so often that summer. Remembering Maria Horse brought a rush of topics to mind: Maria's summer … her reaction when he showed her the murals and the news he had about them … what Gillian's check to him was going to mean … her work … and just … her.

"Can we go for a walk?" Seeing the answer on her face, he took the pack from her and tucked it under the picnic table. The Archies' "Sugar, Sugar" faded behind them as they ducked under low-hanging branches and picked their way to the leaf-strewn path hugging the river bank.

Wanting to completely escape people and oldies music, Kyle led Maria to where the river widened to run shallow and gentle. The air pulsed with a layered cacophony of katydids, crickets, and cicadas. It even smelled green.

"There." He pointed to a series of mostly flattish stones meandering from the near bank to a downed cedar ash on the far side and glanced at Maria's pale green canvas shoes. "You shouldn't even get a shoe wet."

"I'm sure I won't." Balancing easily on one leg at a time, she slid the shoes off and waded into the stream.

Kyle watched her, a rainbow moving over water.

*No wonder I still love you.*

The thought arrived unadorned. It made no difference where they'd been or where they were headed; none of that changed the simple fact he loved her and hadn't stopped.

He left his shoes on and followed her, stepping across on the rocks. She brushed drops of water from her feet as he settled in beside her on the tree's trunk.

"Pretty feet." For a second, it was last January—the Sunday she'd convinced him to go skating in Scottville—and they were on the floor in front of Joe's fireplace, warming up afterwards. She was sitting between his knees, her back to him, as he sandwiched both her cold, bare feet in his hands. He leaned forward to huff warm breath on them, squashing her body between his chest and her own knees. She squeaked.

He blinked and came back to the sunlit woods. "I always loved your feet."

Catching the clear "you did?" look on her face, he felt a quick twist of regret. *Did you have any idea how I felt about you?*

Chirps and rattles and lispy trills punctuated the woods. Sounds he loved and knew she did, too. But tonight, they weren't enough. Kyle fired out questions about her summer, only registering about half of what she told him—"part-time lifeguard," "lots of reading on the beach, biking, and yoga," "volunteering as an English language reading tutor," "a weekend in Chicago to see the museums," and where she'd "found a place called the Doughnut Vault that Joe would go nuts over"—while he lined up the next thing to ask. He nodded when he should, his eyes moving over her face, smiling to see her hands conducting her voice.

She told him about stumbling onto these amazing mosaic-filled potholes that a Chicago street artist had created—and they'd reminded her of him—then described the Shedd Aquarium and falling in love with the lacy sea dragon she'd seen there. "It's like an ancient piece of lace that's all battered by the wind or the sea, and yellowed with age." He could see it. "How can that fragile thing even live? You'd love it. It's exquisite."

Distracted by a movement above them, they both turned to watch a downy woodpecker enter its snag. Kyle drank in the sun sparking off the river. The air smelled fresh, filling him inside. *This*, he thought, *is heaven.*

Maria stopped mid-sentence and he realized he'd voiced his thought aloud. He bared his teeth in an embarrassed, Snoopy-style grin and made her laugh.

"Well, what about you?" she urged. With another twist of regret, Kyle noticed she didn't include the playful nudge that used to be her style with him. "I know your bandages came off before I saw you last, but are you all healed?"

"Yeah, pretty much. It doesn't hurt or anything, just kind of tight in some spots where there are scars." He looked at his palms, wanting to offer them to her, to feel her fingertips explore the shiny, deep pink marks. Fear stopped him; fear that she wouldn't touch them if he did offer.

He cupped his hands over his knees. "I guess the biggest news is that the Gillians insisted I accept an apology check from them for the accident. They're convinced the muddy clumps outside their gate are the reason I lost it. Said they'd feel better if I took it and, in their words, 'make a dream come true.'" The look of eager excitement on her face stopped him. "What?"

"Your art! Right? You're finally going further with it?"

"Well, sort of … I've been in touch with the School of the Art Institute of Chicago—"

"Goosebumps!" She showed him her arm and nudged his shoulder.

A delicious sensation, like hot chocolate flowing into his stomach, surged through his body. He nudged her in return and grinned.

"—to talk about entrance requirements. And I'm in the process of getting together the portfolio they ask for." His face grew warm. When had he ever blushed … in his entire life?

"I'm scheduled to exhibit at LACA in Spring and—"

Maria stood up and sat down. "No way!"

"Way!" He belly laughed. What she made him feel was too big to contain. He'd never seen anyone's eyes shine so bright—and for him. To stop himself from pulling her onto his lap, he talked in a rush. "So, I'll submit some slides of new stuff I've got planned—I think I'll check out those lacy sea dragons of yours—plus the stuff I'm doing for LACA and, um … those murals I, um, I did for you …" *Damn, there goes that moment.* He studied his scruffy gym shoes and trailed off. "With a huge dose of luck I'll be in Chicago next fall."

"Kyle." She had twisted toward him, her excitement distilled to pure sincerity. "The murals were …" her hands fell open on her knees as if helpless, her voice dropped to a whisper, "… supremely awesome."

The hot chocolate feeling flowed through him again, then a thought cooled it: *so why'd you rush to get away that afternoon?* He couldn't bring himself to ask though he knew his face showed his confusion. She had to see it. And she didn't offer to explain.

He'd never felt claustrophobic out in the woods until now, sitting there with not one clue what to say. He was about to stand when Maria broke the silence.

"I saw you last night."

"Ah," he croaked. The gentleness in her voice seemed stuck in his throat. "You were there for the tell-all? I didn't see you." *That feels like a month ago, not yesterday. At least this topic's easier than us—or the lack of us,* he thought. He fiddled with a dead branch poking out near his hip, snapping off a random twig.

"No. You kind of hotfooted it out the door toward the end of your dad's speech."

"Yeah." Without meaning to, he went a step further. "It was rough." He rolled the twig between his palms.

"I came to you in the parking lot."

"You wha—" then he remembered: *the figure in the shadows. So it wasn't Joe after all.* "Oh."

"No one should be alone with that kind of grief. But I couldn't decide whether you'd want me there ..."

*So you came to do the right thing, to comfort someone in distress. Not me,* someone. *And it helped. You helped by just* being there—*even when I didn't know it was you.* He swallowed hard to get past a deeper tightness in his throat. "Yeah, well, I think I had a migraine afterward."

"I didn't know you got migraines."

The bark of his laugh sounded false. "That might have been my first."

"It must feel good to have some answers though, right?"

He paused, remembering all the griping and ranting she'd heard from him about his dad and the family secrets. And now, here they sat together in the woods, talking like this. All thanks to Bingo.

"My mother sure kept his secrets for him. She always has." He tested his twig's brittleness, bending it back and forth. The last red-gold rays of the sun soaked them both and painted the woods around them. "What I don't get is how she could be so loyal to an alcoholic who cheated on her and was such a jerk."

"You could ask her?"

Though she'd put it as a soft suggestion, it seemed to be more than that. Wistful?

He tilted a grin at her. "I guess. Communicate? That'd be something new for me, right?" A smile leapt to Maria's face. With a quick nod, he gave her shoulder a nudge. "She seems more open to talking lately—blames that on Al-Anon."

Maria slid in a quiet, "It's working for me."

"What's working? You mean …" Seeing her lower lip caught between her teeth confirmed it. "Seriously—you, too? Huh."

She raised a shoulder in an answering shrug and smiled, but didn't offer more.

Kyle started picking bark from his twig. *How could I know so little about your past after being together over a year*, he wondered.

Another penny dropped.

*That's what Ma meant. About you hanging out together and that's why you came to pick her up that morning; it was* your *secret she kept that time … Jeez …*

"That little toddler's amazing," Maria said. "You know that he's forgiven your dad for what happened?"

"Did he? The kid he crashed into?" Kyle quirked an eyebrow at her. "No, I must have left before he got to that part."

"Yeah … I think children have a kind of magic in them. They know the secrets to life—like letting go what doesn't make them happy."

"No kidding." Kyle nodded. "So he forgave Dad. Wow." He twisted his twig into a spiral. "It took me a pretty intense Eagala session to get there. But it already feels like I might've, too. Feels good."

"You've been doing Eagala? That's so cool!"

The lump rose again in his throat, thanks to the delighted grin shining in her eyes.

"I read or heard something …" Her expression dialed back into a thoughtful look and her hands stilled as she concentrated.

He cleared his throat. "In Al-Anon?"

"Yeah, I think so. A quote from Nelson Mandela—something like …" She tapped the air with an index finger, reciting: "Resentment is like drinking poison and then hoping it will kill your enemies."

That struck a chord. Nodding, he tossed the twig away and looked over her head into the trees for a long time, then dropped his eyes to find her studying his face.

"Why'd you come to me in the parking lot last night?" he asked.

"I felt for you." He waited and she went on. "I still feel for you. I always will."

"Sorry for me, you mean?"

"No, Kyle. I love you."

*Oh, babe. If only.* He pulled in a long breath. "Why do I feel that statement has a really big 'but'?" *Yeah … see that wry smile on your face now.*

"Because sometimes you are unbelievably perceptive." She caught her lower lip between her teeth then released it. "It's 'and,' though, not 'but.' As in: and I think there's someone better for you than me out there, and someone better for me than you."

*Shit, no.* "The new, improved break-up speech?" He swallowed and pushed his palms hard against his thighs. "You did this twice now. Only one do-over's allowed."

"I botched it so badly. Let me say this, okay?" She took a deep breath. "I couldn't leave it like it was. Because the first time … "

"On the phone?"

"No. That was awful, that was panic talking. No, the second time, out on the lawn …" She tried to gesture in the direction of the cabin, but got it wrong.

"When you came to make amends?"

"Yeah, and botched it."

"So you feel a third go is required?"

"It's called *closure,* ya big pumpkin head! Let me talk!"

"Here's the thing, Maria. Do you get the sense that maybe I don't want to wrap things up and wipe away all hope?"

Her face started to crumple, but she didn't look away. Hope flared in him. He slouched a little so their eyes were level.

"I know, Kyle." Her voice cracked. "And I'm not all black and white about this, either."

"So what color are you?"

"I'm … pink."

"Pink?" A bubbling sensation in his stomach threatened to come up as laughter. When he was little, rolling on the grass with one of Gillian's puppies, he'd dubbed that feeling "love bubbles." He'd never felt it for a woman, even Maria, until now. "So you're not even one of your primary colors … or your good old CMYK color system?"

"You—"

"—remember that cool dream you had? Yeah, I do."

"But you only made fun—why do you remember it?"

"I was a dick. Underneath, I was impressed … I remembered the whole thing in an Eagala session—how you'd joined me in the shower that morning, your eyes all sparkling, talking a mile a minute. You told me you'd just had an amazing dream. That you were in some enormous factory and everything was white—white everywhere you looked—except suspended midair in the very center of this huge room there were three geometric shapes: one blue, one green, and one yellow. You were so excited! I remember you said: 'The *primary colors*—it was a *color factory*! Isn't that so cool …' and then I—"

She stood up, her expression begging him to stop. So he did. But they both knew how he'd replied, his back to her as he'd rinsed shampoo from his hair: he'd raised his voice over the noise of the water and said, "And you're a *teacher*? What are the three primary colors?"

He'd hardly been able to hear her answer, joyless then, thanks to him. "Oh. Yeah. Red not green. Okay, so I'm stupid."

And his final knife thrust. "Well, maybe your *dreams* are stupid."

"I was *such* a prick to you, Maria. I talked to you the way Dad talked to us when he was drunk; I just soaked up those scripts and spewed them onto you like I was getting revenge on him or something, dishing up poison for everyone around me and burning an enormous hole in the center of *my* life." He squinted up at her, willing her to get his meaning.

She sat beside him again. "You're harder on you than I was, Kyle. I'm over it now. I mean, I understand. It's okay."

"No, it's not. I don't know how long ago I hit my rock bottom, but it seems I never bounced off … I just lived down there, snarling and sniping, trying to drag everyone else under, too. That night at the picnic table, when you told me I'd never said 'sorry' to you for anything—Jesus—that knocked me between the eyes. You woke me up that night." Kyle looked up from his shoes and watched Maria pull a long strand of her hair against her mouth, creasing her soft lower lip as he went on, "When you left, I nearly imploded in front of poor Doughnut. She knocked my head on straight with her little look. Then I went and asked Vicky for my first Eagala session."

Maria's hands drifted to her lap.

"And that dream of yours? I remembered that in my second session and ran straight from the arena to Google 'color systems.' Reading about additive and subtractive colors and CMYK percentages and Pantone and all, well, your color factory with everything all mixed up in one place … it got me all fired up over color and light—how they work together." He paused, distracted by the sparkle starting in her eyes; he felt those bubbles in his stomach again.

"Researching your color factory started me thinking about the Art Institute. So when the Gillians gave me that check, I knew right away what I'd do with it.

"So, woman, *if*—and this is a big capital 'if'—I ever become a fine artist, I can thank you for the spark and the whole chain of events that finally got me going." Kyle swallowed hard and felt his cheeks grow hot.

Beside him, Maria just sat, her hands quiet on her lap and her face relaxed. He followed her moving gaze, watching the river, then a nesting squirrel, then a circling hawk. They watched a chipmunk skitter along the far path. It stopped directly across from them, quivering and sniffing, its tail standing up poker straight, then dashed back the way it had come. Her eyes moved to meet his.

"This isn't how I'd thought this would go," she said. Her voice and eyes were soft.

"You had a little speech ready?"

"Yeah, I guess … sort of."

"And now?"

"I feel quiet. Sad."

"Sad. So you … haven't changed your mind?"

She gave the tiniest shake of her head.

He pulled in a lungful of air. "We're too different."

"I *love* your 'different,' Kyle. That's not it. I think we're too alike. Both too dented to fit together over the long haul." Her eyes started filling.

Each word lodged inside him. "I get it."

"You do?"

He nodded. "We both need to get healthy and … find … another healthy someone."

A kind of a laugh-cry burst from her, like a bubble of tension popping. "You're amazing."

He tilted his head, acknowledging her praise and his defeat. The fizzing in his stomach had quieted, but not died out. He expected that feeling would remain for the long haul. His eyes roamed her face and he felt a grin start on one side of his mouth; he gave her a slow wink and stuck out his tongue.

Her eyes went to his lips.

"Ach. Look!" She gulped and her voice dropped a notch. "While you were thinking I was remembering your mouth."

"Oh, woman," he shook his head slowly. "Don't go there. These last minutes the sun has been setting in your hair and it's killing me." She stared at him. "Right now … it's glowing and your shoulders are golden—like an aura or something."

"Kyle. Can I kiss you?" Her question materialized, quiet as smoke.

"Goodbye?" He knew the answer.

A tear ran down her cheek.

He swallowed hard, but kept his voice steady. "Only if I can kiss that tear away first."

She nodded and more tears spilled out. Kyle whispered a clipped, "Mine." A perfect mimic of the seagulls they'd loved in *Finding Nemo*. Another laugh-cry burst from her. *That's it,* he promised silently, *only laughter from now forward. Never again will I hurt you.*

Twisting his body toward her, careful against the roughness of the tree, he closed the inches between them and felt the crackling charge between them grow. One hand resting on the warm curve of her lower back, he cupped the other along the side of her face and stroked her temple with his thumb. His fingertips caressed the downy side of her neck just beneath her hair—her favorite spot to be touched and he heard her breath catch.

Resting his forehead against hers, he told her, "You're kissing the old Kyle goodbye, Maria." He pulled back and laid his lips against a teardrop on her jawline, turned her face and did the same on the other side. He could feel her holding her breath. "You won't be seeing that Kyle again. But he loves you and always did." With the tip of his tongue, he traced the path of another tear down her cheek, tasting its saltiness, then captured the last one from the corner of her mouth and closed his eyes. "Goodbye."

Kyle slid his hands from her and sat up straight. Her tears flowed unchecked and the sound of her breath vined around him as she leaned close, one hand lying as a soft curl on his thigh. She rested her forehead against his and their breath mingled.

Kyle's heart squeezed; this was the gesture she'd used in their early months together, sitting on his lap to deliver a statement she was intent on making.

She drew back and studied his mouth. He barely heard, "And here is your last kiss from the old Maria." Her mouth touched his upper lip, his lower lip, then he felt her hovering there, so nearly touching, an exquisite sensation, as she breathed, "I love you, Kyle," and brought her lips to rest on his. His breath, his blood, rushed to welcome her, the world centered to a pinpoint focus on that touch and that moment … until she eased away and spoke against his mouth.

"Goodbye."

# Chapter Thirty-Two
## August 16th

Joe let the porch door slam behind him and paused on the top step to shout for Rusty. By the primitive flicker of tiki torches and Vicky's jar candles, he saw animated conversations abruptly stop all across the yard and shadowed faces swivel to him. He spotted Rusty rushing to meet him and ran down the stairs, calling out, "That was Ma on the phone—some teenage idiots are egging her house right now, yelling about Dad being a drunk and a menace to babies."

"I bet I know every punk who's there," Rusty said. "Ride with me. I'm in the blue goose."

As he and Rusty ran to the driveway, Joe saw people turning to them and rising from their chairs, their expressions anxious or agitated. Vicky stood with the Dodds beside the picnic table, openmouthed with anger. She missed the mark twice as she tried to jam the lid back on a crock pot. Joe veered over to pull her into step beside him.

"I'll ride separately and take Vicky," he called to Rusty.

"Wait!" Ginny caught up with them outside the barn and grabbed Rusty's hand. "I'm coming with you."

Gillian waved his hand to catch Joe's attention. "Loan us a car, Joe, we walked over. No one's treating your Ma like that!"

"Pick from the biggest I've got in here," he told Gillian, then lowered his voice to Vicky, "Babe, can you get the lights on."

Friends collected outside the barn doors. Joe registered stamping and snorting from the far end of the building, the horses picking up the crowd's tension.

Visibly bristling, Mel stood at the front of the group, her eyes glued to him. "I want to help, Joe."

Joe looked back for an instant. "Thanks, Mel ... a lot."

Rusty added a gravelly yell before he disappeared with Ginny, "Watch your speed everyone but ... a little's okay; I'll vouch."

"Gotcha. Anyone who wants to can hop in the back of my truck!" Mel turned and ran, her red ponytail flying behind her. The dark of the treed driveway swallowed her. The Dodds ran after her and Juliet followed with her new friend.

As he and Vicky swung into his Camaro, Joe heard Kyle start doling out instructions, "Pile in wherever there's room. We'll follow the rest."

Joe leaned out his window. "Tommy? Jocko? I need you guys to stay behind and keep this place from burning down. Keep the bonfire under control till we're back—and all those little candles everywhere, okay?"

At the main board, Kyle tossed out keys like Halloween candy, then jumped aside as the Gillians roared out, the old man and Ruth both leaning into the dashboard as if they powered the car.

The outside ringer for the cabin's phone jangled on the barn wall an arm's length away.

"Ow!" Vicky clamped her hands over her ears. "Who would that be—"

"Can one of you get that inside, please? Jocko?" Joe shouted as engines fired up around them in the wooden building. "And take a message; we'll be quick."

Reversing out of the barn and around in one expert sweep, Joe caught sight of Jocko sprinting toward the cabin. Foot on the gas, he bounced down the rutted drive after the patrol car's tail lights. Exiting the chilly tunnel of white pines, he jolted to a stop and strained to make sense of Rusty's cigarette-graveled voice calling back to him.

"Seeing my light will send 'em running for clean pants quicker than your crowd. Let's go!"

Joe accelerated onto Jebavy Road and glanced in the mirror, squinting against the glare of Mel's and Gillians' headlights as they waited for Rusty to lead. Through the trees more light glittered from vehicles streaming along the driveway.

"Joe. Tell me."

He'd forgotten Vicky there beside him. "I don't know much, Vick. Ma steps out her side door, about to lock up to come here, when a raw egg smashes against the edge of it. Splashes her in the face. She nearly took it full on."

"How scary! I bet she jumped a mile. What brats!"

"That's one word for them. Drunk, too, she thinks. I'm sure they are ... hollering stupid things; there's three or four of them ... with that many—and drunk—who knows what they might try, besides egging the house." He pressed the accelerator to keep up with Rusty and found it already to the floor. Vicky hung onto the dash with both hands, but didn't complain.

"Christ! You're right." She nodded at the tail lights ahead of them. "Rusty using the car off-duty like this—is it legal?"

"Don't know ... I'm not reporting him."

"Good move leaving Tommy and Jocko behind," she said.

"Yeah. They'd only be into kicking butt." A brawl on Ma's lawn wouldn't help anyone.

"Oh yeah, that, too ... but I was thinking more about the bonfire in the paddock; they had it really raging just now. Hopefully by the time we rescue Ma and get back it'll be more of a marshmallow fire."

Joe concentrated on slowing at Gillian's curve, pleased to see the drivers behind him following suit. That curve had had enough action this summer.

Before Rusty obscured his view, his headlights picked up a shape on the unlit road ahead—an open-sided Jeep, easy to jump in and out of. Where it huddled, the roadside maples and conifers stood thick and close, enough to hide it from Ma's house. But they'd parked it in the wrong direction for a quick getaway.

With a piercing double blast from his gumball light and siren, Rusty slammed to a halt beside the Jeep and jumped from the patrol car. Joe pulled within inches of the kids' bumper, flashing his high beams. Ma had every one of her outdoor and front window lights blazing.

"Good thinking," Joe muttered, laying on the Camaro's horn.

Lit by the glow pouring across the grassy yard, figures froze in place, raised arms pausing mid-throw or clamped to their sides. With a volley of nervous shouts and half crouching as if to avoid a grenade blast, the teenagers stumbled away from the house in confusion, lumbering toward the trees that hid their vehicle.

More of the posse swarmed up behind Joe and Rusty, all higgledy-piggledy; Mel's truck and the Gillians' panel wagon bumped nose-first a few feet into the yard and their headlights spot-lit the boys. Kyle swerved wide to clear the blue goose and box in the Jeep on the other side.

Joe pulled Vicky up Ma's front path at a jog, then dropped her hand and bounded up the steps to the concrete stoop. A transparent, gelatinous mass pockmarked and slid down her door's large window. Egg yolk and shell fragments streaked the wooden frame. Through the gooey glass, he saw Ma, her hand poised to open wide for them, her upper half backlit by the glare of the hall light. But she hadn't called hello or said anything at all.

Joe's anger twisted into alarm. "Ma? You okay?"

Still silent, she opened the door for him, and he caught sight of her red-rimmed eyes and wet face.

"Oh, Ma!" His voice cracked as he stepped to the threshold. "Did they hurt you? They're just stupid kids. It's over."

She creased her forehead and tipped her head to the side. Joe no longer saw fear or relief, only sorrow in her eyes. And her gesture, as she opened her arms to him, seemed more about offering comfort than seeking it.

"Joe."

Hearing the anguish in her voice, he knew. It wasn't the vandals—it was Grandma. He wouldn't be sharing news with her tomorrow, or ever again.

\*\*\*

He moved within an anesthetizing shell of music. It had enclosed him the moment Ma spoke his name on her doorstep; it was peace. He'd shadowed Ma at the nursing home as she went in to stand beside Grandma: sunken into her softly lit bed, she looked just as she had for such a long time. Ma and Vicky had stroked her hair, adjusted the soft blanket she lay under, pulling it up to her chin. Outside Joe's shell, on *their* side, faces and scenes exuded tension and grief—inside, familiar melodies and lyrics swirled: opalescent, tranquil.

Peace.

Joe had gazed at Grandma, but hadn't reached to touch her, hadn't spoken. He'd simply thought music to her and she'd heard him. He'd felt that with a quiet certainty.

*Had Kyle been there? Yes.*

An image arose: Kyle and Maria, silent on the window seat, holding hands. He had no memory of the Dodds, Gillians, or any of the rest. They'd melted away while the music in his shell lulled him. His eyes felt heavy, his whole body sluggish.

He sat behind the wheel of his car now, calm. None of his passengers talked; probably asleep.

They passed Ma's place, every light still on, egg dripping from the eaves and window ledges, the vandals visible moving around inside. He felt curious, but too tired to stop.

Only a little farther to the cabin … just about where the sky glowed a dirty, burnished gold … sunrise already? Very pretty, the glow grew brighter against rising cushions of charcoal-colored cloud, and a soundtrack of sparking and cracking—loud enough he heard it mixing with the music in his head. Breathtaking showers of embers rained onto the car. Fireworks? That wonderful smell of campfires … wood smoke … white pines popping and snapping. He drew in the scent, savoring it, then turned off the main road, enthralled.

Here the tunnel of the driveway blazed, trees pirouetting in a slow motion ballet with limbs stretching to the sky above and far enough gone he could easily see through to the skeleton of the barn at the far end. The century old timber faded and brightened, pulsing like the music that hummed and vibrated in his ears. There, through the glowing frame of what had been the barn's front wall, the roof busily burned itself up, resting on the floor in places, and in others, tenting over cars or gates and horses' stalls. To the right, as he drove closer, beneath the swaying trees, a horse—Bingo—ran fully aflame through the arena to the river, screaming, his proud head held high and his neck extended. A figure—a woman—also alight, chased Bingo, silent as she ran, her ponytail a meteor streaming behind her.

Then he heard Vicky's voice and the cry in it broke through his shell. His fascination morphed to revulsion and he screamed her name long and loud, but she only answered, "Joe! Joe!" and he couldn't find her amid a hailstorm of embers and ribbons of fire. He twisted to be free of his seat belt, to get from behind the wheel, flailing at the door that wouldn't open.

"Joe! Wake up! Baby, wake up, wake up!"

Choking for air and blinking against the interior light of the car, he clung to Vicky. She knelt beside him on the Camaro's tiny backseat, hugging his arms tightly to his sides, rocking him. Ma leaned over from the driver's seat, her tired face contorted with concern. Hovering outside the car at his opened door, Kyle's and Maria's faces wore the same masks of worry.

Joe let his eyes slide closed and felt Vicky collapse against him, her hair falling across his face. He tried to focus on her distant murmur, "Yes, Sylvia, please come stay tonight. We'll see you at the cabin when you get there. Kyle, can you drive us, now? And, Maria, thank you. I'll drop off your things tomorrow."

Doors slammed and the car's overhead light no longer shone through his eyelids. As the car moved forward into a chorus of cicadas, the cool breeze, smelling of autumn, lifted his hair, and Vicky's arms stayed tight around him.

***

Her fingers lifted his hair and stroked his face.

"Joe? We're home, sweetie." He heard her hesitate and when she spoke again, seconds, or maybe hours later, her voice sounded odd. "And there's someone here who wants to talk with you."

He kept his eyes closed. He'd melted into the darkness of the Camaro's backseat; a night here … no, a year here … would be good. The pleasant honey of a deep, female voice seeped into his ears from some distance away. Despite the thrum of cicadas in the woods, her words were clear, but they made no sense to him.

"Sorry, to surprise ya'll, Miss Vicky, but when ya didn't call for us this evening, he just insisted on coming over regardless. He was that eager to set things right, once we found him out. Seems he would've staged a sit-in, waited for ya here all night if he had to. That fellow—Jocko?—and his friend set us up comfy on your porch with some of your party snacks. I only sent 'em both home a minute ago. Hope you don't mind."

"It's okay, Claudia. Don't worry." Vicky's voice got stronger, as if she was coming closer to him. "Just hang on a sec." Then she was pulling him from the car, her strong fingers dragging him by the wrist like a badly-behaved dog.

He stood, surrounded by the hammering of cicadas, trying not to sway, feeling the coolness of the night on his skin. Vicky pressed her hand to the small of his back, shoving him forward a little. "Joe, look, honey."

Trying to oblige, he lifted his lids as far as he could, halfway. Across the yard, in the flickering light of a single Tiki torch, stood that fat, little Gordy kid, lasering him with those huge eyes.

Joe blinked and looked again. Still there. Gordy … the little octopus that had invaded his car and unearthed his flask—how many years ago? Maybe not an octopus tonight—more like a miniature tank chugging over the grass, hugging a backpack to its flabby front and heading straight for him. A woman who had to be its mother stood in the shadows by the porch steps, arms crossed high over a ship's prow bosom.

As the tank stopped—inches before colliding with him—he resisted flinching and looked down. It spoke. And it sounded shy.

"I owe you all a big fat 'sorry.'" The voice trembled a little. "Especially you, Mr. Joe." With great care, the tank set its precious cargo on the ground, squatted down, and, folding back the flap, dug into the backpack with careful hands. The pack seemed to resist. Then it meowed.

"Mip."

Joe's eyes sprung open. The kid stood, thrusting his arms up to Joe's face. Eye level and dangling from her armpits, Doughnut's single eye stared him in the face.

"Sorry, for stealing her, Mister." His trembling voice turned tearful. "I really liked her."

Doughnut stretched out a skinny leg and lay her paw on Joe's nose. He heard a burst of noise and wondered if it was him or the kid blubbing. With both hands, he lifted Doughnut to his face, then stood still as she stepped out of his grasp onto his shoulder, and settled herself around his neck awaiting her ride into the cabin.

# Chapter Thirty-Three
## August 17th

"You want some 'Not-Doughnut' stew, Ma?"

Kyle knelt against the living room couch, keeping his voice low. He'd heard Vicky settle into the loft bed just a few feet above their heads, with the sound of a kiss, but no words spoken, so Joe must be asleep again. Doughnut would be a furry halo at his head and, with overcast skies, it would be utterly dark up there, other than the insipid glow of that ancient Daffy Duck nightlight, always on the ready to welcome anyone shuffling to the bathroom in the night. By the look of him, the plastic faded and scratched, Daffy could have started his career lighting Grandma and Grandpa's way when they were as young as Joe and him. *Did Dad play with that thing as a toy?* he wondered. *Did he pick it out ... beg them to buy it for him?*

An era had finished tonight with an old woman dying alone in a quiet nursing home filled with people she may not have recognized from one day to the next ... any more than she'd recognized him, her eldest grandson.

Ma's whisper brought him back. "Sorry, Kyle? 'Not-Doughnut' stew? Am I dreaming this?" In the darkness, he felt more than saw her pull herself out of the near corner of the couch.

Kyle waited until he'd guided the warm bowl into her searching hand before releasing it.

"You're awake. Ruth brought venison stew to the bonfire tonight. Blame Vicky for the name." He chuckled. "It's a doe, not Doughnut."

He lowered himself onto the floor beside the couch, leaning his back against it, his shoulder inches from Ma's. With his bowl balanced on a bent knee, he glanced around the cabin as he blew on the stew to cool it.

Earlier, someone had built a fire, the season's first. Now, it smoldered in the hearth, little more than embers and his favorite smell in the world. The only light in the room came from its glow and a forty-watt lamp that, for some reason, always sat on the floor of the porch.

Kyle held his breath for a second then smiled. Under the silence, he could hear Doughnut's busy purring in the loft, ecstatic to be home and sharing Joe's pillow.

Kyle told Ma, "Gillian found the doe floundering at the back of their farm with a broken ankle the morning after Joe's little incident with the Corvette."

"Which I know nothing about."

Mouth full of stew, Kyle let that comment go. He swallowed. "Well, unfortunately the timing coincided with a particular Eagala client of Vicky's deciding to make off with Doughnut."

"Poor little guy. Vicky said he'd fallen crazy in love with that cat."

"Yeah, well … the whole time Gordy had her locked up like Rapunzel in a tower, Joe and Vicky and I went nuts hunting for her. And for a while, Joe and I were sure he'd killed her as the finale to his drunken night at the Mitten."

"Do I want to know about that?"

"Ahh … probably not. Water under the bridge." He laughed.

The poke in his shoulder felt like the end of a spoon. "What's funny?"

"Me suggesting we brush something under the carpet," Kyle said.

"Ah." The way Ma dragged out the word told him she got his point. She enunciated each word of her reply. "Yes, a bit too much non-disclosure over the years."

"And recently."

"You mean about your dad?" Kyle took another bite of stew. Ma went on, "True to an extent, but in a whole different category. Keeping your dad's whereabouts a secret came from a healthier motivation."

"Which was?"

"Less about hiding issues that embarrassed me or covering up for him—which I've done plenty of over the years, I don't deny that, and I admit *at first* that was exactly my motivation for not saying he was in jail, *and why*. But I got past that with help from Al—"

He interrupted with a familiar twinge of irritation. "And you still wouldn't tell us."

"I know it's subtle, and you might call it rationalization, but I wanted to respect his right to explain for himself. I came to understand the depth of his remorse and shame and wanted to honor his request that *he* be the one to break the news of what he'd done. That's the truth, Kyle."

"But where did that leave Joe and me?"

"Not knowing where your father was."

"Or if he was even alive."

"What? Seriously?" A puff of breath crossed his cheek as she leaned closer. He turned his head toward her, but in the shadows could only see her eyes reflecting a glint of light from the porch. "Now, that's a case of F.E.A.R as False Evidence Appearing Real." Her astonishment seemed to have changed to amusement.

He mulled over her acronym, annoyed. *You couldn't have put yourself in my shoes? Or Joe's? Offered even a nugget of info?*

"You never said a thing except 'don't worry.' You could have at least told us he was in jail."

She sat quiet for a moment and he waited, struggling not to think, knowing if he did, he'd close up and reject anything she might say.

"I could have, Kyle … I'm still not sure I should have. It would have meant breaking my word. But that meant you and Joe suffered. And that's something I didn't think through well enough. I'm learning how rotten I've been—how little empathy I've shown—most of my life. Maybe my whole life."

In the silence that followed, Kyle imagined scribbling cutting replies across a huge canvas before painting them out with Maria's gentleness or the calm of the horses. Then Ma tipped the balance.

"Can I ask you a really huge favor, Kyle?"

If her voice hadn't sounded so thick with sadness he knew he might have scoffed; instead he shrugged. "What's that?"

"Can you be me for a minute? Not to hear an excuse, but … maybe to understand? So you hurt less?"

She sounded *real*—the way he'd always wanted her to—mask off and guard down … for the first time? He waited.

"When my dad started drinking, I was seven. I learned to focus on him, entirely on him, to keep us safe. I watched for his cues and tried to anticipate and meet every need, or I'd suffer the chaos that resulted if I didn't. That's how I lived life with *your dad*, too. I know you saw that. And I know you hated how much I tried to control your life, too. Yours and Joe's. Uncertainty and lack of control terrified me. A temper terrified me."

Kyle remembered the skittishness his anger had caused in Ma Horse and felt a sharp stab of remorse. Ma went on before he could get his head around it.

"For me, Utah was the last straw. After seeing Tony in an ambulance and your dad in jail—I couldn't see anything else. I guess at first I was suffocating in my own shame and fury and grief. But the habit of protecting my alcoholics, distorted as it was, was still a lifelong habit. One I'd never recognized till Al-Anon … and it didn't leave any room for me to wonder what you and Joe might be thinking. After I got more sane … I don't know. Truly." She swallowed hard and let out a heavy sigh. She sounded on the verge of tears. "But I never—ever— dreamed you'd think I would *hide it* from you if your dad had died."

*Yet, I did think that. Joe didn't, but I did.* He squirmed at the next realization: *I never actually* asked you *if Dad was alive or dead, just like Joe never checked his assumption that you sent him to live with Grandma because you didn't want him around.*

"I had no idea how little you felt you could trust me. I'm so sorry, Buddy."

*Buddy!* He'd forgotten that old nickname. She hadn't used it much and had quit when he started middle school, but when she did, he'd always liked it … the idea he could be her buddy.

"Well. Maybe it's warped for me to think you'd chase me down to say, 'hey, didja know your dad's alive!'"

Ma knuckled his shoulder and he felt ten years old again. He heard a quiet chuckle in the dark; he liked that sound a lot more than the shaky tears.

"Ma, the night I crashed the Suzuki, we saw you on your porch. I'm sorry we drove past."

"Old history, Kyle." She paused. "But thanks for saying that."

"Were you sitting there missing Dad?" *Now where did that come from?* he wondered.

"No—*you*, actually. I was hurting for you and Maria, hoping I'd look out and see you two driving up with her on the back of your bike … or just back from getting ice cream with her."

"Hmm. Thanks." Maybe it was the softness of the room they sat in, eating stew together, but something made this line of conversation important. He stepped further along it. "There was another time, you *were* missing Dad …"

"NPR played a Frank Sinatra song; I went to your dad's desk to listen when it came on."

Kyle leaned back, trying again to see her face. He heard the delicate sounds of her eating.

"Right. I had something for you to give to Maria. You didn't hear me come in."

"But I heard you leave." She set her bowl on the carpet beside him and lifted a heavy lock of his hair, then let it drop. He shivered. "That was the afternoon I decided to finally go see your dad in jail. I hadn't visited until then. I needed to know where we were going."

"And you found out?"

"No. I decided. There's a difference."

"What did you decide?"

"Can I tell you in a minute? I'd like to say some stuff before I get to that."

"Sure." Kyle set his empty bowl in hers and turned to lean his shoulder against the couch. His eyes had adjusted to the dark and he could see her sitting with her knees drawn sideways, hugging a pillow to her middle.

The sudden hum of the refrigerator underscored the silence in the cabin. Even Doughnut must have dropped off to sleep.

Ma spoke in a whisper, but so close to his ear that he heard every word and sometimes felt her breath on his jaw.

"In the weeks after your father put that little boy into the hospital, there were times I thought I'd die from self-hatred. It was as if I'd done it. I felt so identified with him. I even felt his shame and self-loathing. Both of us survived that time only thanks to all the people that collectively held us up from sinking into oblivion: Al-Anon for me and AA for him."

"He got that in jail?"

"He was lucky. Way too few jails offer alcohol abuse programs, but Summit County does. He also ordered a bunch of literature from AA's on-line store. The jail has something called 'Publisher Only Rule' so to be allowed the books before his release he had to agree to donate them to the prison. At least he had them when he most needed them. I guess—well, I hope—he's gotten a new collection since."

"So did Dad put you onto Al-Anon?"

"Are you kidding? I wouldn't talk to him for months after he went to jail. I hate to say this, but there were even times *I would rather* that he had died on that mountain. Tracy visited him almost from the start—"

"Who's Tracy?"

"Tony's mom, the little boy he—"

"Wow, no shit! Sorry … go on."

"Apparently Tony kept trying to send your dad artwork for his jail cell until they realized he hadn't been given any of it. Turns out stickers and glitter and such are classified as contraband so they were being diverted to Keith's locker."

"That's wild."

"Innocence hasn't much of a chance in jail. Anyway, to answer your question: no, it was Grandma who suggested I go to Al-Anon—a very long time ago, years, in fact. Then I went to see her in the nursing home after coming back alone from the ski trip. I stood in front of her—with my husband in another state, in jail—feeling so defeated and baffled as to what to tell her. She just smiled and stroked my cheek. I don't even know if she knew me or was just admiring my complexion."

Kyle reached up to nudge her knee in lieu of the grin she couldn't see.

She finished, "I started Al-Anon the next day and got a sponsor the following week."

"I picture Al-Anon like a mini gang of therapists all in one room zeroing in on each other."

"Ha! No, not at all. There aren't any professionals in the groups, at least not there for the purpose of leading it. That's the beauty of it. The members take turns chairing and everyone shares their experience, strength, and hope."

"I don't get how that'd work. The animals run the zoo?"

Ma's laugh startled him. They both stayed still for a moment, listening for sounds from the loft, before she answered in a low voice. "The program itself provides the structure. So, no, there's no one in charge to make sure we stick to it. We do, though. Because it's helped countless people around the world for decades and we want that same healing." Kyle felt a quick touch on his shoulder. "Sorry. I say no one's in charge, but that's wrong. Like AA, Al-Anon is first and foremost a spiritual program. The fundamental key is recognizing there's a Power greater than each of us—whatever you want to call Him, Her, or It. I've found what everyone told me at the start is true: the more quickly someone taps into that Power, the more quickly and more deeply they begin healing."

"What? Like some cosmic slot machine pouring out blessings?"

"No. For me, it's more like a best friend. With, I don't know…" She paused. "With more wisdom and compassion than I'll ever have—and with my best interests at heart. Everyone defines it for themselves. I call my Higher Power 'the Universe' and I've come to believe we're all connected. I don't care if people say God, sometimes I do. I guess to me it's interchangeable—just words."

"So it's another 'take it on faith' thing? 'If it's God's will … blah, blah' …? 'In God's own time' … 'if He or the Universe, whoever, *deems it shall happen*,' and all the rest?"

Ma stayed silent.

"I know I sound cynical, but in our own way, didn't we all pray to this same God while Dad was drinking? For how many years? I *begged*, Ma."

"And what did we ask for? For Dad to stop drinking?"

"Well, yeah. Of course."

"We wanted Dad to stop drinking, but he didn't want to, did he? He wasn't asking for help for himself. The first thing I really learned in Al-Anon is that we don't have control over anything beyond the end of our noses—that includes other people, places, and things. When it comes to your dad's alcoholism, that's his business, his journey, his issue. Not mine, not ours."

*Well, this is radical,* Kyle thought. *And I always figured prayer was like a big one-armed bandit in the sky that pays off for the luckiest bastards, but with long-shot odds for the rest of us.* He held his breath as Ma went on.

"Compared to most in the group I go to, I've been in the program about five minutes, so I'm no expert—and no member should ever claim to be—but I know what's helped me. It's remembering this: I didn't *cause* your dad's alcoholism and I *can't cure it.* And I never was going to be able to, either. There's a step, the eleventh to be exact, that I try to follow in everything now; I'm just asking for knowledge of my Higher Power's will for me and the power to carry that out. Now I trust, just because some circumstance doesn't *look* fantastic at first glance, doesn't mean it isn't actually perfect. In the Universe's grand scheme of things."

*Does she feel way that about Dad going to jail? Will I someday about Maria breaking up with me—or Joe about Grandma dying?* In the shadows beside him, Ma had fallen so still, he turned his head.

"You awake still, Ma?"

"Yep."

That quiet little word struck him. He and Ma were sitting closer than they'd ever done, talking like he'd never imagined they would. He took a deep breath.

"So, you're cool with everything that happened with Dad—the accident and jail, and now him out in Utah while you're here, and Grandma dying tonight … and all?"

"Mostly, yes, I am. I'm very sad that Grandma's gone, especially for Joe's sake. And I'll miss her. But there's nothing to mourn around the life she led or the person she was. It was her time and now it's finished. And about your dad, yes, I'm okay with what's next."

She turned at the same time he did; he heard bare feet on the loft stairs, then Joe's hoarse voice.

"You're serene, Ma … like I expect Grandma is somewhere now."

"Thanks, Joe. And yes, I expect she is. How are you? Come join us."

*Serene … good word,* Kyle thought. Not one he'd heard much or would have used to describe Ma, but it fit. He remembered Joe making a comment at some point about Ma seeming less caustic. Somewhere along the line she *had* become more easygoing. But he hadn't really paid much attention.

At the sound of a footstep behind him, Kyle put his forearm up to keep Joe from walking into him on the floor and got a squeeze in return. The sharp sound of a ceramic clink followed.

"Ouch. What was that?"

"The bowls from our Not-Doughnut stew, ya big buffalo."

"Ruth's venison stew? That's what I need. I'm hungry."

"That's good, Joe. Let me—"

"Stay put, Ma. I'll get him some."

"Thanks, Kyle."

A shadow resembling Joe's hand appeared at eye level; Kyle grabbed it and hauled himself from the floor. Feeling the way, he made it past the hall coat rack and into the kitchen. He felt inclined to be quiet and go without lights as he heated Joe's stew, less for Vicky's sake—if she was even still sleeping—and more to preserve the mood in the living room. Despite the reason that had brought them all together, it felt like one of those rare times as kids—usually around Christmas before the drinking started—when all felt right with the world.

"Doughnut wouldn't come down with me." Joe's deep murmur came to him through the heavy gloom of the living room. "I think she's pillow drunk."

Kyle adjusted his return course toward the voice. "There's worse she could be," he said. Blind fingers poked him in the shin and he clamped them around the warm bowl.

"I don't know the story behind her disappearing, or need to," Ma said. "I'm just glad you got her back, Joe."

"Thanks, Ma … same. Perfect timing, eh? Good stew, too. Thanks Kyle."

From the sounds of it, Joe's talking and eating overlapped. Kyle sank back onto the floor, leaning against the couch with a grin.

"Timing … there's a good segue," Ma said. Kyle felt the cushion beneath his arm move as she shifted her position. "I need to tell you Joe, well, both of you … I called your dad to tell him about Grandma."

*I can guess what's coming, that careful tone gives you away.* Kyle looked through the grayness of the room to the lighter gray square of the porch window and caught a shooting star arc past. Ma would misunderstand his quick breath. Too late to show them, and anyway she had the floor.

"You know he flew back to Utah this morning? Well, given—"

"He's not coming for Grandma's funeral." Joe sounded as if he was commenting on there being no mail today.

"No, Joe. I'm sorry."

Kyle stared at the pale night, his mind blank.

"Too much for him," Joe said through a mouthful of stew.

"I think so. Yes."

Kyle turned back to Ma. "And he won't be coming back to Ludington, either." *I probably don't need to ask this, but hell, Maria suggested I try going for clarity.* "I mean later? Dad's not coming back."

"No. He'll stay out there with Tracy and her little boy." Ma laid her hand on Kyle's shoulder. "When I went out to visit, I told him I was letting him go. He was more relieved than sad and … I have to admit, so was I. So *am* I. It's high time I accept what is—who we both are, to stop pretending and move on. I'm sorry."

*Why? For not doing this years ago?* Kyle squeezed her hand and waited, listening for more. The refrigerator hummed behind the quiet sounds of Joe eating his stew then from the direction of the loft stairs, he heard a tiny chirrup and Doughnut's tail brushed his neck. *Making a beeline to Joe?*

"Oh, no you don't." Kyle snagged her as she passed, a silent shadow, cupping her between his hands and setting her on his shoulder. "My turn."

"Mip." Doughnut sat for a minute, considering her options, before settling against his neck to resume her raggedy chorus.

# Chapter Thirty-Four
## November 10th

"Jeez! It's cold."

Joe glanced behind him, where he hoped their tent might appear sometime soon.

"Whose idea was this, anyway?" Kyle added.

"Yours, mate." Joe grinned. "Like every other year." He crouched inches from their site's fire pit, staring at his pitiful, stubborn beginnings of a campfire. *How could it be so easy to start a fire at home and so crazy hard to get one going in a deserted campground? Still, setting up the tent was the real short-straw chore; the same tent they'd used as kids camping out back of the Gillians' farm. It had sucked then and it sucked now. Maybe I ought to drop hints for Christmas.*

"Where's the fire, man?"

Joe blinked up at Kyle, standing with one bare hand stuck in the armpit of the quilted jacket he wore; almost identical to the one Joe wore zipped up tight over a fleece vest. The other hand dug around in the jacket's deep pocket.

"The fire's where I should be," Joe replied, "in the cabin, in front of the couch where Vicky and Doughnut are probably curled together right now."

He'd barely heard Kyle bark, "Move!" when flames flared high in front of him. Joe fell back, landing hard on his butt, the odor of lighter fluid sharp in his nostrils.

Kyle turned back to the tent. "Only needed a squirt of Campers' Little Helper."

"Only need a new pair of eyebrows." Joe smirked as he got to his feet, feeling his eyebrows and knuckles for prickly evidence of singeing, just like every year. Minutes later, by the welcome light of the campfire, he watched Kyle unfurl two faded sleeping bags, like a matched pair of lizard tongues flicking into the tent's cramped mouth.

So what if they'd half freeze and barely sleep tonight? It always felt amazing to be out here, surrounded by November bare trees, the moon moving between their quiet branches.

Joe turned back to the fire and held his hands to the heat. He peered into the cloud of breath he produced with every exhale, and savored the soundlessness of the night. The tent zipping closed, as definitive as a 'clap-clap, all done!' announcement, snapped the silence. Kyle backed up to the fire and declared he'd kill for another brat and a beer.

"We just left that pub an hour ago." Part three of their annual script.

"Yeah, well … couldn't you go for another?" Kyle turned and held his hands to the flames, his face appearing to redden with the glow.

"Yeah," Joe replied. *This year I'm changing our lines.* "Or how about tomato soup in a mug?" He saw the flash of Kyle's crooked grin; they were on the same page, remembering the hours after Kyle crashed his Suzuki and Joe's makeshift attempts at feeding him.

"Ha! Sounds good." Kyle chuckled. "Got any stir sticks to drink it through?"

"Nope. All outta those; some pitiful, pawless creature used the last to suck up his mouthwash." Not getting a response, he looked over and found Kyle looking smitten with something deep in the flames. "That was a helluva night," Joe offered, squinting into the fire himself.

"Not my favorite." The little kick Kyle delivered to a pair of burning logs sent a shower of sparks above their heads. "But look what's happened since."

Joe sidestepped a flake of falling ash. "You're going to be an *artist.*"

Kyle raised an eyebrow and nodded, still looking smitten. "You're going to be a *dad.*"

*Oh yeah … Jesus!* Joe chewed his cheek. Vicky had only told him two Saturday's ago, diving onto him as he dozed on the porch couch, laughing and crying as she gushed the news. He actually still *forgot* it now and then. "And married for a month now; can you believe it?"

Kyle jammed his hands into his coat pockets. "Helluva summer."

*Was it only a summer?* Joe wondered. *Vicky, lost and found. Doughnut, lost and found. Dad, found … and lost. Grandma … lost. Ma? Kyle? Me? All found, it seemed, to some degree or another, with a lot of work ahead on all counts. Maria?* He glanced at Kyle. *The jury seemed to be out on that one.*

He shook his head in awe. "In a helluva life."

Kyle raised and dropped one shoulder. "Compared to lots, we got off easy. I guess."

Joe kicked stray embers back into the fire pit as he considered that. "Yeah, we did, really."

He stretched backwards with a loud yawn that grew and ballooned into a whoop. He punched the air as he did a tight little jig. He heard Kyle, outlined by the light of the fire, laughing at him.

"What do you call that—a Snoopy Dance?" Miniature campfires reflected in Kyle's eyes.

"Yeah, man. I've got to get it out."

"I'd join you, but you know … Hell, man, I'm *joining* you." Kyle whooped and howled and stomped beside him, then did a circuit of the fire, reversed direction, and headed back.

Joe punched the air again and gave Kyle an exuberant poke in the shoulder, ducking to avoid the vigorous return poke. "You're an idiot." *Crazy, in fact, and I love you.*

"Yeah, well." Kyle sported a goofy grin. "You're a little idiot."

Joe dropped his head back to look at the stars, a smile melting into his face, softening his jaw. He barely heard Kyle whisper, "Man."

A long minute, full of life, passed.

Kyle broke the silence, his voice quiet. "You took Grandma's dying a lot better than I thought you would."

Joe drew in a deep breath of cold air and blew it out, nodding. "Ma and Vicky both said the same." He wondered if he could explain this time. "I guess I'd known for ages she wasn't going to get better, but kept burying the thought. That made it tougher, digging my heels in, thinking I could do something. Watching her just get worse instead. Once she'd died though, well, that's it. It's not easier, just more … clear. Know what I mean? Out of my control."

Seeing Kyle's silent nod he went on. "I've always had this thing about stuff like that being like a moving sidewalk … taking us somewhere even if we do nothing and would rather stay put." He squatted to lay a thick piece of wood across the dwindling fire. "Pretty childish really … grandmothers age … people dying is … life. Time moves on and life moves forward—like it's supposed to. Anyway, in those first days after Grandma died, I dove into Al-Anon, and it really helped. Now it's a habit. But those letters Grandma had written to us and given to Ma to keep, that really helped a lot."

"Yeah, it was a great idea. Good she thought to do it while she had her marbles."

"Very cool. It felt like that *one final conversation* I'd been wanting, even though it was one-sided. Mine said stuff like she pictured Vicky and me growing old together and that she'd be watching out for our kids—their guardian angel." He stopped and swallowed hard. "We're talking about naming the baby after her if it's a girl."

Kyle's head snapped up. "Oh man, no! That's just wrong. Imagine the teasing the kid'll get being called 'Grandma.'"

Wiping tears of laughter on his sleeve, Joe unzipped his coat and shrugged it off. "Stay up if you want, you joker. I'm crawling in." He got Kyle's crooked grin for an answer and shot back his own.

*** 

Kyle listened to Joe unzip the tent door, toss his coat inside, and follow it in. *No way I could sleep just yet,* he thought. *That Snoopy dance didn't do the trick. I'm overflowing.*

The ground at his feet shone red, a fire-lit patch of parched earth and pine needles. He dragged over the cooler and sat on it, settling in to practice the meditation technique Maria had shown him.

He let his head fall back then forward and rolled his neck. Forearms against thighs, he focused on experiencing each sensation that arose, each breeze and touch of fabric against his skin, each scent, each quiet snap and pop of the campfire.

Remembering Maria's surprise when he accepted her offer to show him her favorite techniques, he smiled. She'd been saying her good-byes as she left the gathering following Grandma's funeral and had raised the idea out of the blue. He hadn't asked why, and of course he'd said "yes" with ulterior motives, but damn, the meditation seemed to be making a difference—and not just with handling his temper and impatience. He'd started feeling more open to finding ways to build on what he'd learned through the horses … upping his game overall. He pushed those thoughts away. Tonight he liked that his mind was filled with nothing—and with the world. Rich.

He stood when it felt right, not sure how long he'd been there, but the moon had climbed high and the fire had burnt down to embers that looked like miniature cities filled with tiny bright, high-rises.

As he pulled off his jacket, he felt the cold night air, a quick thief stealing every bit of warmth his coat had held inside. Taking his time, enjoying the chill, he put the fire out, tugged off his boots and ducked into the tent with his balled up coat in hand. The tarp he'd laid beneath the tent floor crackled as he moved, walking on his knees. He turned to zip the flap closed behind him, then stopped. Tying up the outer flap, he zipped the screen door into place instead and knelt at the door to savor the smell of pine smoke and lean close against the fabric screen for a view of the sky.

Months ago, he'd met a one-eyed cat called Doughnut who'd purred against his head while he stared up at crazy points of light. On that night, the stars had seemed to number in the trillions, all mocking his misery. Tonight, that cat was miles away—probably purring against an expectant mother's hair—and the stars he could see from where he knelt didn't mock, they inspired. White hot flickers through branches stripped of leaves—he could paint this … designer trees … black lace dripping crystals …

And gliding above it all, an enormous moon. Full in phase and full of intrigue, its beauty both icy and warm, it waited to be noticed by the oblivious millions living under its light. Maria had somehow gleaned his fascination with the moon and had once given him a notecard inscribed with a poem by a Zen poet. He'd kept the card, planning to depict the quote in a watercolor. It struck him now as the perfect summary of the past summer.

Imagining Maria could hear him, he whispered it aloud: "My storehouse having burnt down, nothing obstructs my view of the bright moon."

"Nice."

Kyle smiled at Joe's sleepy mumble. "Yeah."

He slotted himself into his musty sleeping bag; gripping its edge to stop it corkscrewing around his body as he turned onto his stomach, and dragged a couple wool blankets close to pile on later. The scent of their campfire had trailed into the tent, trapped on their clothing and in his nose. He bunched up his coat under his chest, and with his chin propped in his hands, looked over to find Joe waiting with a palm raised in the air.

"High five."

"Yeah." Kyle glanced at his own whole and healed hand, barely visible in the starlit interior, knowing the scars were fading and the fingertips were now stained with paint and ink. He reached over and slapped Joe's palm, "High five," then grinned at the sting. "Sweet dreams, man."

"Yeah, mate. Sweet dreams."

To You, Dear Reader,

Thank you for taking a chance on a new author! Unequivocally, this book was written for you. Writing it has been one of my top life experiences. Yet, more important to me by far, is the hope it will touch those who read it - and possibly even lead someone who is hurting to find healing. Stories so often do that for me, whether by the escape they offer or what I learn through reading them. If you feel the same, I'd deeply appreciate you sharing your reaction to *My View of the Bright Moon* by posting an Amazon review (maybe also via your social media?) in the hope it might inspire others to take a chance but especially that it may introduce Joe or Kyle or any of the others to someone they're meant to meet.

Would you like to read more about the lives of the characters you've met here? What happens after or came before this summer? If so, please let me know in your review! Because I'm in love with each one of them (though guardedly so with Keith). Given they live in my imagination now, I'd happily consider doing a prequel or sequel. There are other characters living there, too, though – like Catriona, Michael, Jenn, Jack, Geoff, Tracy, Grace, Benny, Jake, and Emily – all clamoring for air space and with quite different stories of their own but more or less near completion and ready to take over my waking hours, much of my nights, and all dinner conversations with my husband until they're in your hands.

Follow me on Facebook:
https://www.facebook.com/cathykernauthor

# Acknowledgements

First, my thanks and deepest admiration to: Lynn Thomas, co-founder of Eagala, for her inspiration and encouragement of my involvement with the organization right from the time we met; Amy Blossom, Eagala CEO, for guiding the work of an incredible team of practitioners across forty countries; and all of you practitioners who take your hearts and souls into the arena along with your clients and those magnificent, majestic or mini horses. Because of you, there is so much healing taking place around the world. Because of you, this novel exists.

A double thank you to my very generous friend, Kevin Moriarity, and to my beloved husband, Alistair, for all they did to ensure this book found its way to a wider audience; while Kevin expertly and, incredibly efficiently and patiently, managed or advised on the nitty gritty of publication, Alistair provided unflagging encouragement, practical support, and also, patience – my hero in so many aspects of my life.

While the above acknowledges those I credit with the start and finish of this, my first full-length novel, there were many in between who played a key role. Specifically, the members of the St. Charles Writers Group, in St. Charles, Illinois – then led by Richard Holinger – and later, those in his Night Writers' Group in Geneva, Illinois. Special thanks to Richard whose green ink revisions and comments grew increasingly encouraging and were always invaluable. There were too many members to list by name, but you know who you are, and I thank each of you for your critiques, insights, challenges, and for the praise that kept me afloat when I felt I just wasn't getting it right. (Julie, you always made my day and Don, you nearly always shook it – setting the bar high; thank you, both!) These groups yielded friendships which promise to be lifelong: my biggest hug of thanks to Kate Johnson for going above and beyond when this and subsequent books were underway but also for adding so much laughter to and beyond our writerly world! Warm gratitude, as well, to Elaine Cassell, Ed Heidrich, Wayne Jackson, and Doug Burman – keeping you all in my life despite the distance and time zones will always be worth the effort. I won't forget Jenny, Ellen, Treva, Stacy, Lucy, Julie, Hal, Kathy, William, Jamie, DJ, the Richards, Raj, Roger, Bruce, Judith *or the rest of you* – thanks for all your notes and comments as the book progressed; each of you played a part in this finished work. As did writing buddy Don (Donald) Hunt; congratulations on your two novels! We kept Smitty's, and the McDonald's and library café in Batavia afloat.

To dear friends Deb Brod, Karin Ruschke, and Lynn Fillmore, and the darling Natasha Dunn: thank you a hundred times over for your enthusiasm around reading early manuscripts; even your smallest comments helped bring something to life (e.g. the chill beneath a tree-lined driveway) and spurred me on. Joyful thanks to the team at Waterline Writers, what an honor and a kick it was to read an excerpt there! A very warm and humble thank you to both Katie Phillips for her early and thorough full-manuscript editing and (again) to Elaine Cassell for an equally incredible gift of the same many months and many changes later.

Numerous sources and non-fiction books informed my depiction of Grandma's Alzheimer's (e.g. *The 36-Hour Day: A Family Guide to Caring for People Who Have Alzheimer Disease and Other Dementias* – by Nancy L. Mace and Peter V. Rabins and *Dr Ruth's Guide for the Alzheimer's Caregiver: How to Care for Your Loved One without Getting Overwhelmed and without Doing It All Yourself* – by Dr Ruth Westheimer) and my portrayal of the Al Anon and AA experience. I hope to never take for granted today's mind-blowing accessibility to quality, in-depth information ranging from serious topics like these to when the Batmobile was on auction (now past, sorry) as well as to some of the best music ever recorded, (thanks Scott Shannon of True Oldies).

I remain beyond grateful to the Eagala training I received internationally (yay for SPUDS!) and to the countless individuals who contributed to the accuracy of this book simply through their kindness in answering my many questions and by sharing expertise that went beyond my questions. These include: the wonderful Marie Hancock, from Colorado Equine Specialists, for her belief in this book, for putting the right words into Joe's mouth so he could win Mel's trust over the 'how and why' of feeding horses, for offering thoughts on the scents Kyle would discover up close to Maria Horse, and for going above and beyond for EQs (big hugs to you!); Curt Nilsen, forever friend, for indulging this amateur enthusiast's car-related questions around their repair and detailing; Dr. Diane Ruschke for describing the initial and ongoing treatment of road rash; Doug McIntosh, the motorcycle buddy behind whom I spent a million happy hours in another life, for brainstorming with me what could have caused Kyle's crash; staff at The Oaks in Muskegon (thank you for the tour; I'd stay there!), and so many spokespeople ranging from the Michigan State Police, the corrections system in Utah (glitter!? who knew!), those numerous online authorities who spoke with me at length, the Art Institute in Chicago, the Ludington Library, the Ludington Area Center for the Arts, and all the friendly, anonymous Ludington locals who helped in my quest to ensure they and others in the area would recognize their charming town in these pages. You showed me the Mitten Bar, Barley & Rye, Blu Moon Bistro, P.M. Steamers (now Cork and Crown), the DQ, House of Flavors (resounding 'yum'!) and described the Curves, parking challenges, and summer bird life. To me, accuracy in writing extends to whether there are brown or black squirrels, what kind of trees are common, and when the adorable peepers are active. So, besides the thrill of hearing their interest in stocking this book, I was delighted when Bob and Carol of Ludington's Book Mark bookstore and café offered a fantastic bit of insider knowledge; their tip led to my husband and me experiencing 4th of July fireworks just like a local, while dug *into*, rather than on, the sand of Stearns beach! Thank you all!

The penultimate thank you: to the many crazy, sweet, wonderful friends – yes, including siblings and cousins and all of you from First Writes and Writers' Anonymous – who I've not mentioned but certainly *not* forgotten (nor will I ever) simply because I love you; and to Toi Toi the dainty, Yoda our 'supremely awesome gentlemen', and Dame Pistachio, our current nut, for providing endless joy and distractions as this book progressed through its many stages – in part with your inspiration.

And, though impossible to adequately express: all my love and gratitude to my parents. For instilling in us your work ethic, your integrity, your love of camping, nature, animals, and of books and reading through weekly trips to Elgin's Gail Bordon Public Library.

Though I have no experience of family holidays ruined by alcohol or arguments, far too many people do – and far worse. My heart goes out to those whose childhood or present life is marred by the effects of alcoholism, other addictions, and family dysfunction. My profound congratulations to everyone in the process of healing.

And the final and most heartfelt acknowledgement: to every reader who still carries this pain, at the time you are ready, may you find the healing that works best for the wounds you carry.

# About the Author

After an award-winning career as an advertising copywriter in the US and New Zealand, Cathy Kern retrained to focus on putting words to better use. She obtained her Masters in Applied Social Science Research then undertook roles in policy analysis, research, and evaluation, all typically centered on health and wellbeing or mental health.

First introduced to Eagala's* life-changing therapy in New Zealand when she was hired by Renée Keenan to evaluate her practice, Cathy subsequently met Lynn Thomas, the co-founder of Eagala, at a conference in Australia. Utterly smitten with everything about equine assisted therapy and eager to understand the model more deeply, she undertook Eagala training first in New Zealand then in the US. Her background and training underpin her commitment to accuracy in her work, reflecting best knowledge at the time of writing.

Cathy lives in New Zealand with her husband, Alistair, and a cat or two. She doesn't have a horse. Yet.

*Eagala-Equine Assisted Growth and Learning Association:
https://www.eagala.org/org

*Cathy (seated at the center of the photo) at Eagala training in Arizona (Picture credit: Marie Hancock)*